FEAR OF DIVERSITY

THE BIRTH OF POLITICAL SCIENCE IN ANCIENT GREEK THOUGHT

Arlene W. Saxonhouse

The University of Chicago Press / Chicago and London

Arlene W. Saxonhouse is chair of the department of political science at the University of Michigan.

The University of Chicago Press, Chicago 60637
The University of Chicago Press, Chicago and London
© 1992 by The University of Chicago
All rights reserved. Published 1992
Printed in the United States of America

01 00 99 98 97 96 95 94 93 92   5 4 3 2 1

ISBN: 0-226-73553-2 (cloth)

Library of Congress Cataloging-in-Publication Data
Saxonhouse, Arlene W.
    Fear of diversity : the birth of political science in ancient
    Greek thought / Arlene W. Saxonhouse
        p.   cm.
    Includes bibliographical references and index.
    1. Political science—Greece—History. 2. Greece—Intellectual
    life—To 146 B.C. 3. Sex role—Greece—History. I. Title.
    JC73.S34   1992
    320'.0938—dc20   92-5912
                                                                  CIP

∞ The paper used in this publication meets the
minimum requirements of the American National Standard
for Information Sciences—Permanence of Paper for
Printed Library Materials, ANSI Z39.48-1984.

This book is printed on acid-free paper.

For
Gary

Contents

Preface

In the field of comparative politics or comparative history, debates can rage about differences and similarities: is there something that makes the Dutch world of the sixteenth century distinctive, different from all those states around it, or should we look within it for what is similar to other states? Simon Schama (1988), whose grand study looks for those qualities that distinguish the Dutch from all others, uses the image of pigments: those pigments used in the Italian paintings and the Dutch paintings of the sixteenth century are the same, but the pictures themselves certainly are not. Should one focus on the pigments—the underlying unity—or on the differences that surface on the canvases? Or if we look at the economic systems of different countries we may ask, are there really peculiarities that account for the "Japanese miracle," or does the economy in Japan follow the same economic laws we discover in the American economy or the British economy? Is Japan different, or are claims of such differences merely hidden racism in sanitized dress? Should we be searching for the underlying unity, or do such searches lead to abstraction from variety, from subtlety, and often from the beauty of the many. Paradigms are desired in social science research, but does that desire lead to the assimilation of what cannot be assimilated?

In the world of ancient Greece, the world of the poets, the playwrights, the philosophers (and the historians with whom I do not deal in the text of this book), this conflict begins. On the one hand there is the fascination with variety—with exploring the vast diversity of human types. Thus, we hear of an Achilles, an Agamemnon, a Hector, a Priam in one epic, of a Calypso, a Circe, a Nausicaa, a Penelope in another. We also see what binds them together—what makes them one rather than many, united despite apparent differences. The most powerful scene in all of the *Iliad* is when ancient Priam, the king of Troy who has lost his son Hector, and the brilliant Achaean Achilles, who has killed that son, sit and weep together, acknowledging the common suffering of mankind. Or there is Herodotus, who takes us on wondrous travels to visit fabulous (in all the meanings of that word) societies, who nevertheless recognizes a common nature diversified by the tyrant custom, *nomos*.

This book is about the fear of diversity—a fear that differences bring on chaos and thus demands that the world be put into an orderly pattern. Part of that order is to see the unity underlying the apparent variety of the world we experience with our senses. It is the poetic art and philosophic reason that can go behind the observed, the physical differences, or the cultural dfferences between a Priam and an Achilles and make us recognize their common humanity. At the same time, though, the pursuit of unity can create a world that tries to eliminate that which is not easily accommodated into this underlying unity, a world that finds diversity so threatening that it collapses all into one, avoids the multiplicity of human experience, and leaves us immobile and sterile.

I do not intend in this book to suggest that the Greeks lead us to one or the other perspective. Rather, we see them grappling with the dangers of the extremes on either side. With the exception of the pre-Socratics, all the Greek authors with whom I deal warn of the danger of striving for too much unity; human beings are separate bodies, they emerge from particular families, they develop particularized relationships. The city will always be limited by that which it cannot fully assimilate into itself—for the Greeks, in particular, this was the female, sexuality, and the family. While the others warn us, however, it is only Aristotle who, accepting the centrality of sight for understanding, is able to overcome the fear and welcome the diverse.

I begin with Aristophanes' *Ecclesiazusae,* a comedy in which the women of Athens, taking over political power, try to destroy divisions within the city by conflating male and female, family and city, ugly and beautiful. The difficulties of doing this and the consequences of the attempt illustrate the dangers of trying to transcend differences, whether they be merely apparent to the eyes or by nature, and give to this comedy what I see as its tragic tone. It is, then, in the fragmentary writings of the pre-Socratics, of Thales, Anaximander, Heraclitus, and Parmenides, that we discover the early fear of diversity and how that fear leads them to dismiss what is seen in favor of what is unseen, which I deal with in part 1. They search for a unity in the natural world that can overcome the experience the senses have of a vast multiplicity. The playwrights bring this problem, in Cicero's language, down from the sky and into the heart of the city by posing for the audience the city's need for unity and yet its dependence on diversity. Creon here is presented as the prototype of the political leader who wishes to create through speech a unified political world untroubled by divisions that families and particularized individuals might introduce. In the end, he must learn that speech of the ruler manifested in the form of decrees cannot overcome what is observed. In a manner often described by the deconstructionists of today, the pre-Socratics and many of the tragic heroes of the ancient stage use reason and speech to create natural and political worlds that can exist only if the senses are ignored. It is the fear of diversity that leads beyond the senses, and the tragedians, through the portrayal of their heroes, show us the need for such an endeavor—and its tragic consequences.

In part 2 of this volume I turn to several of Plato's dialogues and find there a Plato who raises more questions about the necessity for political unity than has usually been acknowledged. While epistemologically Plato the "idealist" leads us beyond the senses and towards the forms abstracted from the particular, the translation of this epistemological model to the politics of the city raises many more questions and is far more qualified than has previously been recognized. Thus, I have titled part 2 "Plato and the Ambiguous Pursuit of Unity." In the final part I turn to Aristotle, who in the *Politics* rejects what he sees as earlier expressions of the fear of diversity and the drive to go beyond what the senses discover. He acknowledges the senses and uses them to explore a multiplicity of political regimes and the multiplicity of parts that comprise the regime—and thus he gives birth to political science. Epistemologically, Aristotle allows us—and encourages us—to see the many with our eyes and to build a polity out of differences rather than unity.

Debates about the "canon" have shaken academia over the last decade, and calls have often been heard urging us to acknowledge the diverse, to make "the other" part of our experience of ourselves. The texts considered in this volume all are part of the traditional canon, the product of dead, white, European males. Yet my goal is to demonstrate that, through a careful reading of these works, we have the opportunity to learn much about the capacity of the political community to incorporate the multiple and diverse and about the epistemological foundations behind such incorporation. Insofar as I turn to these dead, white males of ancient Greece, I find myself siding with the "unity" end of the continuum though they themselves teach of the importance of recognizing diversity. In their confrontation with questions of unity and diversity, one recognizes as well our own world, whether we look to comparative politics, comparative history, or the more policy-infused debates about multicultural societies and multicultural curricula. Despite 2,500 years and "apparent" difference, much remains the same about our fears and our expectations of the world of the mind and the world of the senses.

Acknowledgments

My debts are many and my thanks sincere. The National Endowment for Humanities helped to support early work on this book during the summer of 1983 and provided time off during the academic year of 1988–89. The Earhart Foundation funded work during the summer of 1990. The Horace H. Rackham Graduate School of the University of Michigan gave further support for research expenses. I am grateful for the generosity of these institutions. There are also many colleagues in political theory who have provided the intellectual context and, most important, the friendship that enables one to undertake a work of the sort offered here. Conversations with Peter Euben and Steve Salkever, always stimulating, always challenging, have reinforced a commitment to the study of the classical authors. Peter's extensive comments on the manuscript raised many questions, some of which I have tried to answer, most of which will set the agenda for future work. Jean Elshtain, Tim Fuller, Daniela Gobetti, Anne Harper, Don Herzog, Roger Masters, Mary Nichols, Jennifer Ring, Molly Shanley, Bernie Yack, and Catherine and Michael Zuckert, all in their individual and distinct ways, have helped me to frame the issues treated in this volume.

John Tryneski shepherded the manuscript through the University of Chicago Press and had the wisdom to seek the advice of Diskin Clay, whose careful reading of the manuscript has improved almost every page. Gary Shiffman was far more than a research assistant in the early stages of this work; Jennifer Clarke used her deep knowledge of Greek to help me with translations and transliterations; Eric DeWeese provided additional help with the preparation of the manuscript; and Mary Breijak survived, I think, a titanic battle with an antiquated word processing system to produce the final manuscript.

My children, Lilly, Noam, and Elena, continue to provide delight and distraction. As I have written, they have grown to become intellectual companions who now read, understand—and criticize—my work. To Gary this book is dedicated, a weak return for the years of love that he has given to me.

Early versions of sections of the following chapters have been previously published. Chapter 1: "Men, Women, War and Politics: Family and the Polis in Aristophanes and Euripides," *Political Theory* 8 (1980): 65–81; Chapter 3: "From Hierarchy to Tragedy and Back Again: Women in Greek Political Thought," *American Political Science Review* 82 (1986): 403–18, and "Reflections on the Theme of Autochthony in Euripides' *Ion*," in J. Peter Euben, *Greek Tragedy and Greek Political Theory* (Berkeley: University of California Press, 1986); Chapter 4: "The Philosophy of the Particular and the Universality of the City: Socrates' Education of Euthyphro," *Political Theory* 16 (1988): 281–99; Chapter 7: "The Net of Hephaestos: Aristophanes' Speech in Plato's *Symposium*," *Interpretation* 13 (1985): 15–32; Chapter 8: "Family, Polity, and Unity: Aristotle on Socrates' Community of Wives," *Polity* 15 (1982): 202–19.

1

A Tragicomic Prelude:
Aristophanes' *Ecclesiazusae*

... and the deed appears most hilarious.
Woman[a], *Ecclesiazusae*

It is before dawn on the comic stage in the Athens of
392 B.C. A woman waits, not for a clandestine meeting
with a lover, but for her female coconspirators. They are
to convene here before they set off, disguised as men, for
the assembly, the *ecclesia*. With their false beards, men's
cloaks and shoes, they are to fill up the assembly, propose
to those attending that political power in the city be en-
trusted to the women, and with a preponderance of votes
turn the proposal into a decree. Only on the comic stage
can we imagine such a conspiracy, and only on the comic
stage can we imagine it a success. Aristophanes wrote his
Ecclesiazusae to make the audience laugh and to win a
prize from the judges. Nevertheless, the comedy with all
its bawdy humor and absurd premises poses as well the
conundrums that any community faces as it deals with
differences in its midst—differences between the sexes,
between the old and the young, the traditional and the
novel, the city and the family, and especially between
the beautiful and the ugly or the good and the bad. The
women, by acquiring power in the city, obliterate one of
the critical differences between the sexes in Athens, and
having overcome that distinction, try to transcend many
other traditional divisions as well, only to discover that
in so doing they introduce chaos rather than a new order
to the city. New laws break down old barriers, but in
the drive for unity that the women politicians introduce
they may cause more harm to the city than the original dichotomies had done. The city of Athens depends
(as do all cities or political communities) on drawing its

boundaries, on defining its equalities as well as its differences; but how, where, and by whom those boundaries are to be drawn remains a problem that even the intelligent women of this comedy are unable to resolve.

Throughout this book we will be questioning the adequacy of the dichotomies that govern our political lives and asking whether bifurcations such as those between male and female, young and old, or public and private oversimplify differences and create false and destructive divisions within the city. Or are such boundaries, whether grounded in nature or created by the laws, necessary for political and epistemological order? Can we imagine a world in which boundaries disappear and a unified community emerges? The literature that remains from ancient Greece—whether it is the histories of Herodotus or Thucydides, the tragedies of Sophocles, the dialogues of Plato, or the comedies of Aristophanes—presents the political world as one of contending opposites.[1] Tearing at the core of the community, undermining the assumptions of simplicity and unity, these opposites threaten the assumed unity and comprehensiveness of the polis. Attic comedy and Attic tragedy (to which we will turn in chapter 3) lay bare these tensions, illustrating how they can undermine the stability, security, and identity of the city. The *Ecclesiazusae* as a comedy tries to smooth over those conflicts and erase the dichotomies so that the old divisions no longer undermine the health of the city. But such an obliteration of difference is possible only in comedy—if even there. It is tragedy that suggests the final impossibility of such resolutions on the level of human actions, and for this reason, we may consider the *Ecclesiazusae* Aristophanes' tragic comedy. Unlike the *Lysistrata*, where the men cease their battles, or the *Birds*, where the utopian Cloudcuckoobury is founded, the conclusion of the *Ecclesiazusae* leaves the audience dubious about the new regime and more aware of the problems raised by the rule of women than the joys of the envisioned fantasy.

In this chapter we will look in detail at the designs and consequences of this great new experiment in political rule and at the unnatural unity of opposites that it brings to a reformed, imaginary Athens. Once the women disguised as men have voted themselves into power, their leader, a certain Praxagora, becomes the leader of Athens as a whole. The women submit to her authority and Praxagora, with the unlikely power to declare on her own the laws for Athens, decrees that the differences between families will disappear as all private property is abolished and all is held in common. Exclusive relationships between men and women are forbidden; sexual

---

1. Lloyd (1966) builds half of his history of Greek logic on the prevalence of polar opposites in the writings of the ancient authors. See, as more recent examples, Vidal-Naquet (1986:xxi) and duBois (1982).

access is open for all. Dichotomies between male and female, public and private, old and young no longer control the relations of citizens and all (except, of course, slaves) become part of one unified family, eating, drinking, and sleeping together. The law that accomplishes this transformation of Athens into a unified family, where theft is impossible because there is no property and where adultery is impossible because there are no wives or husbands, undermines the differences that the earlier laws of Athens had concretized. In the *Ecclesiazusae*, we move from a society grounded on a series of differences to one where such differences almost disappear.

The issue that remains as we read or watch this comedy is whether these laws—both the old and the new ones—have any foundation in nature. Are the divisions that place men, but not women, in political power natural? Are those that separate families from each other and families from the polity grounded in nature? Or do regimes such as the one Praxagora institutes, which effaces all such distinctions, destroy artificial boundaries? I do not propose to answer such broad questions. Rather, this exploration of Greek thought is to draw out various ways of considering these problems, as well as the ramifications of one view or another. The comedy that Aristophanes presents in his *Ecclesiazusae* is not a happy one. While replete with gag lines and with language to make some of us blush, within the context of the play the unity that initially ignores all difference—and then tries to compensate for any differences that may exist—does not work; rather than bring the peace and security desired for the newly structured city, we are left with the uneasy feeling that the attempt to overcome opposites and oppositions within the city leads to new problems no less severe than the old ones, to yet greater impieties and injustices, and to the perverse strangling of natural human motivations. While the old ways of the city may be no more "natural" than the new ways in Praxagora's regime, the old Athens escaped some of the perversities that Aristophanes sees the new rule introducing into the city. As we study the specific events of the comedy, we will observe an elaborate minuet in which the new law dissolves old dichotomies and creates new ones while Aristophanes illustrates the inadequacies of any political world that tries to transcend all boundaries in order to be a complete, undivided whole. He recognizes the need for boundaries that differentiate men from women, the old from the young, the beautiful from the ugly, and the good from the bad. The political world would suffer were these differences abolished as the comedy illustrates, and rather than excite our fear of diversity, Aristophanes reminds us of the need to preserve rather than eliminate differences. His fear for Athens is that the citizens have ignored the necessary boundaries and thus lost the capacity to be citizens. He, like the playwrights we will consider in chapter 3, presents the dangers of yielding to the fear of diversity—only he does so by making us laugh.[2]

Women and Men

Immediately, the title of the comedy warns us that this is to be a play concerned with the outlandish juxtaposition of opposites. The women of Athens—at least those who were the daughters or wives of citizens— appear to have lived lives sheltered from the everyday world of political decisions and political conflicts. If they appeared in public at all, it was most likely at the religious festivals that often had more to do with menarche and fertility than with politics.[3] The Periclean phrase that assigns the

2. One worries that the following analysis may obscure the humor and fantasy of the comedy, or that the parallel may be made, as one anonymous critic of an earlier version of this chapter suggested, between this and Frederick Crews's *The Pooh Perplex,* but I plead here only that the brilliance of Aristophanes' comedies goes far beyond the ability to make us laugh. See, e.g., *Ecclesiazusae* 1155–57, where, through one of his characters, he speaks to the judges, asking that the wise judges note his wisdom and those who prefer to laugh note his humor. Whitman (1964:5–9) deals eloquently with this problem and surveys some of the debates. See also Strauss (1980:5–6). Aristophanes' comedies force us to think about the conventional views that we hold. The outrageous premises give us profoundly original persepectives from which we can question those convictions—usually in Aristophanes' case with the expectation that, despite recognizing the limitations of our traditions, we will ultimately, by the end of the comedy, return to the old rather than embrace the new values. There is little secondary literature on the *Ecclesiazusae* apart from discussions that try to analyze the direction of influence with regard to the city Socrates founds in the *Republic,* as if this were the central importance of the comedy. I will be concerned with this issue, but more from the theoretical perspective of political unity than from the perspective of women in politics or of communism. Substantive discussions do occur in Foley (1981), Strauss (1980:263–82), Bloom (1977:325–28), and Henderson (1975: 99–104); Whitman (1964:vii) explicitly excludes the *Ecclesiazusae* from his discussion because it "mark[s] a departure from Old Comedy proper."

3. Osborne (1985:157–74) provides considerable detail about women's participation in the religious festivals—and, specifically, about their isolation from the political activities of the city. While there has been a comparative boom in the current literature on Athenian women, the information about what their actual lives were like is still quite limited. The days of imagining that the women of Athens roamed the streets freely, attended the theater, and were companions to their husbands (Gomme 1937; Kitto 1951:219–36; Seltman 1956) seem to have faded, and we are left with more moderate statements such as that from Sinclair (1988:50), who comments, "In the political life of the city, Athenian women played no direct part, and their indirect influence, while not negligible, is very difficult to gauge." See also Harrison (1968:108–15), Pomeroy (1975:57–92), and Schaps (1979). Vidal-Naquet (1986:216), quoting Varro as quoted by St. Augustine, sets the exclusion of women from public life in mythical terms; originally women did have a voice in public affairs, but when there was the vote as to whether Athene or Poseidon would be the protector of Athens and Athene won, "The men took their revenge by deciding that 'from henceforth the women of Athens shall not vote; that children shall no longer be known by their mother's name; that the women shall not be called "women of Athens."'" Thus in the classical city there are no 'women of Athens'—only the wives and daughters of the 'men of Athens.'"

greatest respect to those women who "do not fall beneath [their] proper nature and for whom there is the least renown among men, whether for virtue or for blame" (Thucydides 2.45) may have been more of an injunction than a description, but it is certain that the political woman was not a concept gingerly tossed about in the parlance of the time. Thus, "women attendees at the ecclesia," as the title of the play would translate, is already more shocking than a title that refers to animals, abstract concepts such as peace or wealth, or even natural phenomena such as clouds. Indeed, this title suggests that the play will present that which, as the Athenians understood it, is unnatural: women in the *ecclesia*. The *ecclesia* was the key democratic institution in Athens, that which defined Athens as a democracy; it was here that the male citizens met to determine the city's policies. Women had always been denied any participation in this male realm. Men attended the assembly, all sorts of men, for all sorts of reasons, but only men.[4] Aristophanes' comedy, then, is to present the profoundly absurd vision of women active in the most democratic of Athenian political institutions. Unlike the women of Aristophanes' *Lysistrata*, who conspire to exploit their sexuality so that they may have an impact on the men's political decisions, the women *ecclesiasts* assimilate themselves to the men, breaking down the barriers between the sexes so that they may participate directly, like the men, in the principal institution by which politics functions in the city.

Praxagora's name underscores as well that this is a comedy that will join what has not before been joined. She, a woman, a wife of a citizen, acts (*prattein*) in the open forum (*agora*) of the city. Rather than remaining unseen in the women's quarters, where most women spent their time, or in the shadows of the predawn conspiracy, she bursts forth into the masculine realm of public activity to speak openly in the assembly, is adored by other women, and leads her husband to the marketplace as he shines in her reflected glory. The men have failed to reform Athens so that, in making speeches and passing decrees, she takes charge as if she were a man. Eager for the renown that comes to founders of cities like Theseus and great reformers like Solon and Cleisthenes, no woman "unspoken of" is she.

We first meet this remarkable woman before daybreak as she waits for the other women to arrive. In the lofty language of a Pindaric ode she addresses the clay lamp that she has used to find her way, raising by speech this humble household object to the level of the divine sun. Absurdly, she compares the high to the low and almost assimilates them. Absurdly, she

---

4. This is hardly to suggest that women were not important for the functioning of the city. See, e.g., Sinclair (1988:50): "In the maintenance of the oikos Athenian women made a crucial contribution, and not simply in terms of what was regarded as their primary role— child-bearing and child-rearing. In economic terms, women in well-to-do families supervised household affairs and the work of slaves."

will momentarily transform the female into the male, changing the humble creatures of the household's innards into the ones who express their sovereign rule by determining the fate of the whole city. It is certain that the meager light of the lowly lamp can never replace the brilliance of the godlike sun. It is also certain that in Aristophanes' vision women can never replace the mortal men who currently control the life of the city, even though the latter may be degenerate fops who care little about the welfare of the city.

While the lamp can become a sun in Praxagora's speech, speech alone will not transform her women into men. The transformation can only be accomplished by fooling the senses of the men in the assembly, making them see as one, as undifferentiated, what is diverse, according to the city's principles of categorization. On the simplest level of convention, the women have agreed to steal their husbands' clothing, their tunics, their shoes, and their walking sticks. But the clothes are not enough. One glance at those red-figured vases of the sixth and fifth centuries that show women with their white faces suggests how important the difference in complexion was for defining the differences between male and female.[5] The women (i.e., Aristophanes) know that this difference is not grounded in nature, but rather that it is the result of women staying indoors where the sun cannot weather or tan their skin. Since the convention of keeping the women indoors ensures the pallid complexion of the women, the differences can be easily overcome: the women conspirators oil their bodies and their faces and spend time in the sun.[6]

Likewise, Athenian women, to make themselves sexually more alluring, shaved under their arms and plucked their pubic hair. Women who are to appear as men must stop transforming their bodies in this way and allow their hair to grow. As one woman reports: "First, I have the armpits with hair thicker than a forest, just as it was agreed upon. And then, when my man went into the *agora*, I oiled my whole body and stood for the whole day darkening it" (60–64). The next woman reports that she has tossed out her razor so that her whole body might become hairy. The clothes, the razor foresworn, the sunshine on the oiled bodies all blur the visual lines

5. Irwin (1974:111) discusses the use of the word *leukos* (white) for women and *melas* (dark) for men in Greek poetry: "We assume, then, that the dark and light contrast in Greek poetry reflects a contrast between men and women with regard to their social status and functions. Men worked outdoors, women in the house; men were tough and hardy, women soft and vulnerable." She concludes later (129), "The Greeks thought that a dark complexion signified manliness. . . . A fair complexion . . . signified effeminacy in men." See also duBois (1982:111).

6. Nevertheless, those seeing the women in the assembly assume that they must have been shoemakers (i.e., men who spend their lives sitting in the shade) because of the whiteness of their complexions (385).

that distinguish in ancient Athens the male and the female. There are actions as well. Praxagora admonishes the women not to swear by Aphrodite (190); they must swear by Zeus. They must leave their wool working at home and they must remember that when they vote they are to raise their arms and not their legs.

There is, however, much of themselves that these women cannot transform by tossing out the razor and by darkening their bodies. Certain physical characteristics of the female body do not come only from conventions and do differentiate female from male. These are the parts of themselves that they must hide in order to assimilate themselves into the male form. Here enter the false beards (68) and the exhortations to take care that nothing of their bodies shows as they climb over the seats in the assembly (95–101). No amount of tanning, no unused razor can change the natural differences between male and female. Despite all the costuming, they cannot escape that they are still women. And so they must suffer the discomfort of their false, itchy beards, and they must use the men's cloaks to cover themselves completely.

The challenge for Praxagora is far more complex than simply fooling the senses so that women appear to be men in the assembly. On the one hand, she must obscure physical differences as she sends her women to the assembly, but on the other hand, in the speech arguing that the city must entrust itself to the women, she must draw out the differences between the sexes in order to explain why it is that the women would be better suited to rule over the city than the men have been. She must play both sides of the argument. In her practice speech before the assembled women she proclaims that the city suffers from a steady stream of bad rulers (176–77). Perhaps one time out of ten they act for the sake of the city, but mostly they pursue individual gain. Why, then, should we believe that women would be any better at ruling than the men have been?

To show that they will be better, Praxagora argues that they are different. Women, as mothers, would be less likely to embroil the city in wars. Like the nineteenth century suffragettes who argued that the vote for women would transform politics into a gentler endeavor, Praxagora claims that women "being mothers will be eager to protect those who are soldiers." She asks rhetorically, "Who more than she who bore them would send grain off to those in the army?" (233–35). The greatest emphasis, at least in the practice speech, is, however, on the woman's attachment to the old patterns of behavior, the old laws or *nomoi*. While the men, unthinkingly enamored of whatever is new, enact all sorts of novel policies, accomplishing little, if anything, the women continue to follow all the old ways as they carry on the variety of activities in the household. They dye their wool "according to the ancient custom, not changing according to personal whim; they roast barley, just as before; they carry goods upon their heads, just as before; . . . they annoy their husbands, just as before." The phrase *hōsper kai pro tou* resounds at the end of a series of sentences (221–28). Arguing for the most radical proposal ever presented to the assembly of the Athenians, Praxagora appeals to the old. However, once power has been transferred to the women, she will completely dismiss the old in order to create a completely new regime—one that so fundamentally changes the whole structure of Athenian society that the women attendees at the assembly seem almost modest next to it. Even Praxagora quakes to present her revolutionary plan before those who for so long have acted according to the traditional ways (583–85).

At the foundation of Athenian society was a sharp, clear demarcation between male and female. Unlike the ambiguity of other divisions such as public and private, citizen and noncitizen, even slave and freeman,[7] there was no ambiguity about the differences between male and female, between those who fought the city's battles, debated the city's policies, and voted in its assemblies and those who bore the child, wove the cloth, and stayed within. Yet, in the *Ecclesiazusae*, Aristophanes has questioned, albeit for the sake of comedy, the certainty of such demarcations. Some differences are merely a matter of conventions; some that exist by nature can be hidden by an appropriately draped cloak or false beard. Such questioning allows a critical boundary to be crossed, and women become participants in the world that had previously been the exclusive realm of male action. Aristophanes does not turn his women into men, however; he simply shows that the certainties that separated them, which placed one group in the public sphere, the other in the private sphere, are no longer certainties. Having questioned the most basic of social divisions in Athenian society, all other social divisions likewise become subject to question—in particular, the separation of the private world of the household from the public world of the city.[8]

In order to acquire power, Praxagora made analogies between rule in the household and rule in the polity; she gave assurances that women's success in running the household could be transferred to their rule in the city. Once in power, analogies are no longer necessary. Rather, there is the identification of the city and the family. Congruent with the removal of assumed divisions between the sexes, Praxagora destroys the traditional divisions between public and private that marked Athenian life. By bringing the female into the public world, by making her ap-

7. As Aristotle will show us (*Politics* 1.5), but cf. Finley (1981:249).
8. We can note as well that, were Praxagora to carry through this dissolution of social boundaries, she would destroy the city of Athens that distinguishes between Athenians and foreigners. Citizenship would disappear and a universal regime would be necessary.

pear the same as the male, Praxagora also brings together polis and family and melds them into one.

Public and Private

In what must be one of the most grotesque scenes in all comedy, Praxagora's husband moans and groans onstage as he sits upon his chamber pot suffering from a severe case of constipation. Finally, getting his symbols all confused, he prays to the goddess of childbirth to relieve him of his torment—and she does. Old comedy, in part, gets its laughs by making public what had traditionally been kept private. The comic stage ignores the traditional boundaries of decency as both sexual and gastronomical drives appear openly before the audiences. Men strut on stage with red leather phalloi, and those men portraying women wear costumes with symbolic female genitalia;[9] frequent asides concerning where and when one can relieve oneself are part of the comic prattle. Under Praxagora's guidance, the same disregard of traditional barriers that kept some activities private marks her new regime. The distinct realms of public and private with distinct activities and distinct aims disappear as family and city are melded into one and all that had been hidden is brought into the open.[10]

Before we consider how Praxagora achieves this and the implications of this melding, we must look at the meaning of the Greek words most frequently translated by public and private.[11] *To idion*, the private, entails that which is distinctive, that which separates one individual, one family, one city from another. The emphasis here is on distinctiveness and separation. Thus, while it can refer to an individual concerned with his or her own welfare, it also can be used to say, for instance, that *phronēsis*, reason, is *idion* to human beings because other species of animals do not reason.

9. Henderson (1975:111). In general, Henderson is helpful in clarifying the use of obscene language in the comedies and, by implication, obscene actions as well. "By 'obscenity,'" he explains, "we mean verbal references to areas of human activity or parts of the human body that are protected by certain taboos agreed upon by prevailing social custom and subject to emotional aversion or inhibition. These are in fact the sexual and excremental areas" (2).

10. Humphreys (1983:1) expresses well the distinctions: "The contrast between public and private life in classical Athens was sharp. Public life was egalitarian, competitive, impersonal. Its typical locus was the open arena. . . . Monumental architecture clearly differentiated public buildings, religious and secular, from private houses. Oath-taking was extensively used to mark the transition from private status to public role."

11. I have dealt extensively with the relationship between public and private elsewhere. See especially Saxonhouse (1983a), but also Saxonhouse (1980). See also Humphreys (1983: chaps. 1–2). Foley (1981) argues for a continuum on an economic level between *oikos* and *polis*, rather than the demarcation that Humphreys and I, for example, stress. Of course that continuum exists, but the breaks are, I find, more powerful.

To koinon, in contrast, emphasizes sharing, what it is that individuals or families or citizens have in common. As Aristotle says at the beginning of Book 2 of his *Politics,* a polis must be a *koinōnia,* since it must share something, at the very least the land on which it is founded. A family is also a *koinōnia,* sharing the goods of the household, the gods, and so forth. With regard to the city, though, the family is *idion,* distinct with its own property and gods. The public, as we are to understand it in the Greek sense, is the process of sharing. Praxagora's husband, Blepyros, unfortunately shares with us his particular gastrointestinal difficulties. The stage becomes an arena in comedy in which the distinctive and the peculiar are opened up to and shared with all.

In making her original speech in favor of giving power to women, Praxagora had condemned the men of the city for being concerned only with their private affairs, *ta idia,* and indeed, we see this in the speech of Euaion, who, according to the report of Chremes, appeared naked in the assembly, and claimed that the city would be saved if only men like he could demand clothing from clothmakers and blankets from furriers (408–21). According to Praxagora's argument, women in the household will save the city because they care little about what is private. Indeed, look at how women share secrets (443–44) and how they share property: "They exchange among themselves their cloaks, gold and silver jewelry, drinking cups even when they are alone with just one other woman, and not in front of witnesses and they return everything and do not steal" (446–49). The private realm inhabited by the women, as presented here, is far from the litigation and conflicts of the public world.[12] The rule of women brings this community, this sharing, this *koinōnia* into the realm of the city.

When Praxagora returns home in the midmorning, pretending ignorance of the events in the assembly, her husband announces, "They say that they handed the city over to you." Praxagora asks, "For what? To weave?" "No, by Zeus," responds her husband, "to rule" (555–56). At this Praxagora rejoices and rattles off the benefits that the city can expect: no robberies, no jealousy, no poverty, no reproaching others, no debts. The world will change when women come to power. The attempt to fool the senses was one thing; now in possession of power, they become distinct, offering the city a new vision in which *to idion* is immersed within *to koinon* so that sharing takes precedence over, indeed removes, the boundaries between people.

12. See above, note 10, and Humphreys's comment that oathtaking was characteristic of the public world. The women Praxagora describes have no need of oaths. Foley (1981) suggests that, because women could not use property for individual advantage, they could be symbolic of the community that was absent in the public sphere.

Praxagora institutes her radically new regime, opposing all that is old (583–85) by changing the relationship between public and private. Significantly, she does not envision the possibility of men taking over responsibilities within the household. In her model, taking women out of the house leaves no one to care for those actions that go on within the household, the *oikos,* such as feeding, clothing, and reproducing. These activities must all now become the responsibility of the polity.[13] Thus, she transforms the city into a household where women still feel comfortable ruling (although on a far grander scale) and where the men simply enjoy the consequences of the female's rule. What was once the city is now obliterated by the family. All that traditionally had engaged the attention of those involved in political life disappears. No judging will take place since there will be no crimes committed, no conflicts to be adjudicated within the household,[14] no foreign policy to worry about since the women will not engage in wars, and no taxes to impose since there is no private wealth. As the family expands, the city recedes to nothingness.

This expansion of the family means the expansion of the *koinon,* the sharing that goes on within the family. Praxagora begins, "I say it is necessary that all, partaking of all things, share (*koinōnein*) everything . . . and it is necessary that there be neither rich nor poor . . . but I will make the means of life one common (*koinon*) thing and the very same for all" (590–94). Her husband wonders, "How will it be common (*koinon*) for all?" (595), and Praxagora explains: "First of all I will make the land common (*koinon*) for all and silver and whatever else belongs [now] to each individual one. And we women managing and taking heed of the affairs of the city will nourish you from all this common (*koinōn*) wealth [597–600] . . . and now life will be from that which is common (*ek koinou*)" (610). As Blepyros continues his questioning, imagining all sorts of situations that relate back to the old ways, such as debts, trials, wives, Praxagoras must continually remind him that the old ways have been left behind now that "all wealth is held in common (*en toi koinoi*)" (661). Even if something such as a cloak is taken away (an unlikely occurrence to begin with), Blepyros would go to the central store and bring back a better one "out of what is common (*ek tou koinou*)" (671). After all this, Blepyros still cannot quite fathom what the mode of life will be that his wife as

13. Strauss's (1980:270) analysis of this section of the play is unfortunately marred by what I, at least, see as old stereotypes: "They [the women] can not impose on the men the duties formerly fulfilled by the women without having to fear instant revolt; there is no way but to transform the city into a single household."

14. Praxagora does seem to forget some startling examples from the panoply of Greek tragedy of intrafamilial conflicts that did require adjudication, most notably the story told in the *Oresteia.*

leader plans to create, and Praxagora explains once again: "One common (*koinēn*) to all. The city I say I will make one household breaking down all the households of the city into one" (673–74).[15] The harbors will become wine cellars and the courtrooms will become dining halls for the city turned household. Assignments to a particular dining hall will recall how jurors in the past—when there were trials—were assigned by lot to their court rooms. The destruction of boundaries between individual, private families is complete, and Praxagora sings a song of celebration enumerating the many sensual pleasures that will delight the citizens, both male and female, of the new Athens.

Praxagora has blended home and city. There is no realm of privacy, of "idiocy" left. With the walls between houses broken down, no distinction remains between mine and thine. There is only "ours." Moreover, not only property is communalized. Parents are common as well. All older men are fathers; all older women are mothers. Disrespect for the elderly will disappear as each younger person as son or daughter will show filial respect for his or her elders (641–43).

The new world Praxagora creates with her decrees that transform public into private and private into public promises a life of unending pleasures rather than one of unending conflicts over mine and thine, ours and theirs.[16] It is appealing, and the characters enjoy imagining its delights. It is all lots of fun, that is, until the barriers to and consequences of this blurring of the boundaries between private and public, between mine and thine and ours, become obvious. In particular, we are confronted in the final scenes of the comedy with the problems of law-abidingness, incest, and the equalization of the beautiful and the ugly, the good and the bad.

Once Praxagora has articulated her vision of the new Athens and by her authority has decreed it into existence, Praxagora leaves the stage and the implementation of her plan begins. The citizens must break down the walls between houses (whether figuratively or actually remains unclear) and pool their resources; the sieve and the chamber pot that once were private possessions must now belong to all. Not all citizens, though, are equally willing to obliterate the distinction between what is their own private possession and what is common to all. Indeed, one man, Man B as he is referred to in the texts, appears to think that such willingness would make him an unfortunate soul, a *kakodaimōn*, possessing neither sense nor

15. Ussher (1973:170) on the phrase, *surrexas' eis hen apanta* at 674, offers the following comment: "Plato writes in terms of 'houses.' But Praxagora seems to think of alterations that will make a single dwelling for the people (thirty thousand)."

16. As Foley (1982:16) envisions it, Praxagora's new Athens, as a "welfare state," enables men to enjoy all that they would enjoy in the home as the gift of the city, namely, sex, food, and clothing.

property. Asked whether he plans to bring his goods to the *agora*, he answers, "Never, by Poseidon, but first I will test these things frequently and observe how it goes" (748–49). He marvels at the foolishness of the man, Man A, who neatly prepares to have his things added to that which is to be shared. The latter explains why he is willing to yield all his goods: "By Zeus, but I intend to carry these things away to the city into the *agora* according to the laws that have been decreed" (759). "Is it not necessary for me to obey the laws . . . those that have been decreed?" (762–63). To his cynical companion he replies, "What a madman you are!" (764). But he cannot convince the doubter to participate and to follow the law. The miser, the one who cannot simply move from living in a world with boundaries to one without them, will preserve and guard what he has until he sees what the many are willing to do (769–70). Anyone with any sense does as the gods do with their outstretched hands, he proclaims, preferring to receive goods rather than to give them (778–80).

The society Praxagora creates depends on lawfulness, that is, the priority of the law over the self. The man about to yield his goods must set a priority on obedience to the law over a concern with his own private interests. His opponent sees no need to accept the law and, claiming the gods as his model, will not obey until he sees how the law can serve his own advantage. The two men debating whether to turn over their property to the city represent the two types of citizenship: the miser is similar to the male citizens who had been running the city before the women took over. They are the ones about whom Praxagora complained in her speech. The law-abiding man is in fact like the women who accept the law and the interests of *to koinon* over their individual concerns, who set a priority on sharing over the individual. In a reversal of the usual images, women have practiced sharing within the family, while in the polis men have emphasized the private. The sharing male citizen, Man A, can become a member of Praxagora's city while the male who keeps all to himself, Man B, cannot. Praxagora requires that her citizens, like the women in the family, accept the priority of what is common, what denies distinctions or boundaries between individuals, over what is particular. Her communism demands that boundaries be obscured. The "idiot" will not obey her laws. Just as she obscured the boundaries between male and female with the men's cloaks and the foresworn razor, so her city depends on the ability of men as well as women to live without boundaries. Praxagora's laws deny that which separates one man or one woman from another.

At the same time that Praxagora's reforms by law compel the men to overcome the boundaries between them, the underlying impiety of such a transcendence reveals itself in the laws added to complement the immersion of the city into the family. Having rejected the traditional marital bonds between husband and wife characteristic of the old family structure, Praxagora had proudly proclaimed, by Apollo, her "demotic plan," one that mocks the elegant and the well-to-do: foolish and worthless men (*phauloteroi*) will have prior rights to sleep with beautiful young women, and ugly, old women will have the same privileges with handsome young men (626–30). The innocent and stupid Blepyros asks a not-so-stupid question: "How, when we live like this, shall each individual be able to recognize his children?" As if this were a meaningless question from a dense man, Praxagora asks in return, "Why is it necessary?" (635–36).

In this world of sharing all things, where *to koinon* dominates the conversations to the exclusion of *to idion*, Blepyros cares about the loss of his own child—his individualized immortality—more than he does about the loss of the household items he will soon have to contribute to the common storehouse. Such self-identification is for Praxagora relevant neither now nor later. She, who had argued that mothers care more for their sons than fathers do, and thus that mothers would be more generous and less militaristic, is willing to give up her child, should there be one, under the compulsion of a system that obliterates all differences, be it between one child and all others, or between one mother, father, aunt, uncle, and another. Specificity of relationships disappears in a world where boundaries fade. Thus, all children are sons and daughters and all older men and women are mothers and fathers. No walls distinguish households, no boundaries (except age) distinguish fathers from other men. All is, remember, common.

However, this community, this expanded household unifying the city at its most basic level, must breed in its midst incestuous relationships. If *by law* an old man must have intercourse with a young woman before a young man sleeps with that young woman, and likewise for old women and young men, and if *by law* the old are the parents and the young are the children, then *by law* incest must be commited with greatest frequency. In the final scene, a young maiden tries to rescue her lover from an old hag. The hag quotes the law that requires the youth to have intercourse with her, but the maiden, resisting, declares: "If you establish such a law, you will fill the entire land with Oedipuses" (1041–42). At such a thought, the first old hag runs away in dismay, only to be replaced by two older and uglier women who care not at all that the child sleeps with his mother, that no boundaries are maintained between one's father or mother by nature and all others. The final expression of the destruction of boundaries between public and private goes far beyond Blepyros groaning on the stage and praying for relief. For as *to idion* fades, incest becomes the order of the day and the underlying theme and outcome of Praxagora's reforms.

As with the distinction between male and female, the distinction between public and private provided a paradigm that controlled much of Greek thought. The city of the woman who by her sex and her name incorporates a set of oppositions takes these two realms and obscures the differences between them. The consequence is incest, and it is here, in the sexual reforms that arise as a result of the transformation of the city into a household, that we begin to feel the unease and in a sense move from an exuberant comedy to a more troubling tragedy.[17]

The Ugly and the Beautiful

The ugliest part of the comedy, even uglier than Blepyros and his chamber pot, is the final third of the play. A beautiful young girl waits for her beautiful young man, but the meeting between the two is forestalled by the appearance of one, two, then three vile old women who demand obedience to the law and insist that the young man enjoy the "pleasures" they may offer before he is allowed to visit his young mistress. This scene acts out the consequences of the most disturbing of Praxagora's decrees. While she successfully fooled the men's senses and made them think that female was identical to male, and while she had decreed the obliteration of the differences between the public and the private worlds, she next professes to enforce an identity between the old and the young, the beautiful and the ugly, not simply to break down barriers between them. She acknowledges that the identity does not exist by nature, that men and women do not desire equally the beautiful and the ugly. They prefer the beautiful. Laws will be necessary to force men and women to desire and make love to the ugly, just as laws will be necessary to have the possessors of property yield their goods to the common storehouse in the city.

The communalization of households has destroyed the notion of husbands and wives. No privacy and no individual, private partners remain. Sex is open to all. But Blepyros worries: as an old and ugly man, he will be left out of this sexual paradise of multiple partners. The beautiful and the young women will not want to bother with him. To satisfy the desires of the old and the ugly, to make them supporters, indeed defenders of the new regime, Praxagora passes her laws on sexual relations. She provides for the distribution of sexual pleasure, not in any fashion according to worth, but so that differences between the young and the old, the beautiful and the ugly, are to disappear and are made irrelevant in the satisfactions of sexual desires. Thus, she proposes, "The lowly and snub-nosed

---

17. One need only think about the power of Sophocles' *Oedipus* to realize how important the problem of incest was for the Athenian audience of both tragedy and comedy. On the significance of the incest theme in that play and why it was so threatening, see, among many others, Segal (1981 : chap. 7) and Saxonhouse (1988a).

man will lie beside the noble and the esteemed women, and if you desire the latter, first you will bang the ugly one" (616–17). By nature the
lowly and the noble are not equally desirable; Praxagora's laws remedy this
inequality. In the past, sex had been distributed to the young and the
beautiful and denied to the old and the ugly, a situation that acknowledges
differences and thus a situation that cannot be sanctioned, indeed must be
prevented, in this world where all is one, where all is common.

While Blepyros may thrill at the passage of a decree that provides sexual
access to the young and beautiful, access he would not otherwise have had,
he also in his own silly way acknowledges how opposed this decree is to
the natural longings of human beings. "They [the young and beautiful
girls] will flee the shameful and lowly men and head towards the beautiful
ones" (625). Praxagora has provided against this with her law that works
for men as it had for women: "The more worthless men must guard the
more handsome men after dinner and prevent them, in accordance with
the rules of the city, for it is not allowed for those who are beautiful to
pass the night with women before they have serviced the shameful (*aischros*) and the small" (626–29).

The violence that this law does to nature is expressed most vividly in
those final scenes where the ugly hags try to drag the young man to their
huts. As each of the hags explains, "It is the law (*psēphisma*). . . it seemed
best to the women if a young man desires a young girl, let him not pound
her before first he bang an old woman" (1012–17). Should the young
man not come willingly, the old women can drag him off (1020). And
then they warn him, "Our laws must be obeyed" (1022). Their reasons
are similar to those of Man A as he explained why he would yield his own
goods to the common storehouse, in contrast to Man B, who would wait
to see if anyone else obeyed the law. In the previous scene, there was
sympathy for the law-abiding Man A following the laws of the women
and obliterating the distinction between the self and the whole; the scenes
with the old hags demanding obedience to a law that equalizes the ugly
and the beautiful, however, raise questions about the virtue of obeying
such laws. From sympathy with the man who obeys the law in the scene
about property, where we may be torn between a desire to share and a
desire to have one's own, we move to sympathy with the man who wants
to disobey the law. Here, as the beautiful youth is forced to make love to
the old woman, there is no ambiguity about distinguishing between the
appealing and the repulsive, and it is here that Praxagora's city begins to
crumble.

Though the youth tries various excuses, such as exemption because of
merchant status, in the end he is ready to accept the law and sleep with
the old hag. The intercourse that he envisions, however, leads to death

rather than birth. He advises the hag to prepare her bed as if it were a funeral pyre. The law, by equating the ugly and the beautiful, engenders sterility rather than life. It is the young woman, eager to keep her young man to herself, who conjures up the issue of incest and the image of Oedipus and frightens the first old hag, thereby preventing this particular perversion of natural desires. But the girl saves her lover only to have him become the object of yet another hag's pursuit. This second hag again appeals to the law: "It is not I, but the law that drags you" (1055–56; 1077). Finally, with a third old woman pulling at him, he obeys the law and leaves the stage with the old woman rather than the young girl. Before he does so, he sings a funeral song. Three times unlucky is he to have to spend the whole night and the next day fornicating with a stale woman, and he will find another such one waiting for him the next day. He predicts that he will not survive such misfortune and requests burial at the mouth of the harbor, with the old hag as a memorial stone on his grave (1098–1111).

Praxagora can never make the ugly and the vile beautiful and appealing to the eyes and longings of the human being. The senses draw both the young and the old men to the beautiful girls and the senses repel the men from the old and the ugly. Praxagora, though, can pass laws that try to obviate distinctions between the beautiful and the ugly and thereby turn what is ugly into what appeals. She must attempt to accomplish this through legislation precisely because nature has not done so. Praxagora's model community had worked to break down all distinctions between individuals and groups of individuals such as families. The walls between houses could be destroyed, and difficult as it may have been to implement, Praxagora could envision a house for a family of thirty thousand.[18] The differences between men and women could escape the eye through a quick change of clothes, a false beard, and tanned skin. But the grand proposals begin to falter and look particularly ugly when the obliteration of distinctions moves to issues of the beautiful and the ugly, *kalos* and *aischros*.[19] At this point the comedy turns ugly and is tinged with morbidity rather than life. While we recognize the young girl as beautiful—far more beautiful than the old hags—we are not to treat her as such. We are to distribute to the shameful equally what is due to the noble.

No doubt, as others have suggested before, the target of Aristophanes'

18. See above note 15.
19. One needs throughout this section to remember the equation in Greek thought between the beautiful, *kalos*, and the good, and the ugly, *aischros*, and the bad. Plato, of course, in his portrait of Socrates, especially in Alcibiades' speech in the *Symposium*, questions the equation of *external* beauty with the good, but this is part of his attack on the traditional values of Greek society.

sardonic wit here is Athenian democracy that, according to its critics, refused to acknowledge the differences between the noble and the shameful,
which made equal those who were not and thus instituted a regime of the
incompetent.[20] Indeed, Praxagora refers to her plan, especially the laws
about sexual relations, as *dēmotikē* (631). Her laws will appeal to the
masses precisely because they obliterate the distinction between the beautiful and the vile. In Aristophanes' presentation, however, such an obliteration, or such a pretense that the ugly can be made desirable, leads to
death and dirges. The equation of the ugly and the beautiful is the final
expression of the boundaries overcome during the previous action of the
play. Its connection with the motivating principles of Athenian democracy
makes the play a political critique of Athens, but the comedy has raised
questions that go beyond a critique of the democratic regime. It poses for
us a world in which all dichotomies are subject to question—the dichotomy between male and female, between public and private, and now
between ugly and beautiful. The earlier scenes of the comedy had playfully
explored the inadequacies of such dichotomies and had helped us envision
a world that ignores such boundaries between individuals and between
groups of individuals. The final scene, however, forces us to question
whether we can live in such a boundary-free world, whether we do not
make divisions, see differences, and require those differences for the basis
of our lives in the community and as individuals able to make choices. The
final scene reinforces the drive to discriminate that which had been happily
tossed aside earlier. Incest may have been at first lightly ignored as the
impious consequence of the earlier drive to unify the public and the private. But the abandonment of all natural delight in the beautiful (and
therewith the good) is the more weighty consequence of this law attempting to obscure distinction between the attractive and the repulsive.

The movement of the play finds us at the high point near the beginning
where articulate and able Praxagora boldly acts against the conventions of
the society, against what has been accepted as natural by her own community. She shows her competence to enter the public realm, crosses
boundaries, and acquires political power for herself and for women. We
see the women of this play emerge from the predawn darkness to declare
and then to lead a new Athens. We then observe a decline as the comedy
moves us away from these articulate women to the vile old hags scram-
bling about, calling upon obedience to the law, as they force an unwilling
youth to have sex with them. From the public action of the beginning, the

20. Strauss (1980:276) sees Praxagora's regime (and thereby Athenian democracy) as a
law privileging the naturally inferior at the expense of the naturally superior; see also Vidal-
Naquet (1986:218); Bloom (1977:325–26); Henderson (1975:100).

play descends into the private world of sexuality with which women were traditionally associated. Thus, we are witness to the deterioration of the women's wonderful dream of transcending differences and overcoming boundaries. We see the undermining of each of those laws that had tried to obscure difference, laws that left Athens a land populated by Oedipuses and Jocastas, awaiting some ugly moment of final self-realization.

The inability of Praxagora's proposals to break down completely the differences between public and private, and especially between the beautiful and the ugly, and thus her failure to create the totally unified city leaves the audience still laughing at the absurdities and obscenities on stage, but uncertain about the political life of any city that might try to efface the differences between male and female, city and family. The world as we see it is a realm of multiplicity, with men and women, old and young, families and cities. We categorize that world according to one criterion or another—for example, sex, age, beauty—but we often find those categories inadequate. Clearly, the categorization that precludes capable individuals such as Praxagora from exercising political power and sends fools like her husband to the assembly is inadequate. But where do we turn? The new decrees of Praxagora obliterate old dichotomies, based on inadequate divisions. Nevertheless, the goal of unity within this new regime is no less contrary to nature than the divisions that existed in the old Athens before the conspiracy of women. More than in any other play by Aristophanes, the tragic undercurrents of the primary themes keep us from celebrating at the end as the drunken maiden appears to lead off the citizens to the banquet.

The political community Praxagora had tried to institute offered an expanded vision of political unity that inspired much of the thinking and writing about the Greek polis. The desire to make one what appeared multiple, to look for unifying principles rather than for divisions, is emblematic of Greek thought. While Aristophanes could turn this into comedy with the absurd vision of political women, this pursuit of unity could also be expressed as the darker fear of diversity. Leaving comedy behind for the moment, it is to this fear that we turn next.

Part One
The Fear of Diversity

"On account of wonder (*to thaumazein*) humans both now and at first began to philosophize." So writes Aristotle near the beginning of his *Metaphysics* (982b12). *To thaumazein*, as with our English word "wonder," contains within it also the notion of awe. Philosophy begins not only with wonder, but also with a certain fear, a fear of an external world so vast and so varied that it can swallow up the human being. Philosophy comes into being as a tool with which we can control that universe and subject it to our own reason, make orderly what appears to be chaotic, although, of course, it goes well beyond that role in its maturity. It is the diversity of our world that evokes both our wonder and our fear.

In this part I will go back first to that period in time when "humans first began to philosophize," the time of the pre-Socratics, and then to the Attic playwrights, the tragedians, of the fifth century B.C. The pre-Socratics make occasional allusions to the political organizations of humans: for example, according to Heraclitus the *nomoi* or laws are walls of the city, and his emphasis on an underlying unity or "one" may translate into the rule of one or a monarch in the city. More often, however, we will find the pre-Socratics using analogically the language of political community to describe a cosmos ordered according to justice and equality.[1] The political language is to help us understand nature; it is not designed to tell us

1. Vlastos' classic article (1947) provides the full account of the usage and significance of this language in the Presocratic authors.

about our politics. The pre-Socratics present the problem of the one and the many; they make us aware of the tensions between the mind and the senses, but they write of an epistemological realm that remains distant from the activities of men and women living in cities. The tragedians then show us the political consequences of the epistemological fear of diversity articulated by the pre-Socratics. By bringing the fear of diversity into the city, the tragedians present in dramatic and highly problematic terms civil ideologies, captured in the words and actions of tragic heroes, that create a unified polity by denying the "other" and what appears to be dangerously diverse. We will see first in chapter 2 how the fear of diversity gives rise to philosophy as an epistemological search for a unity beyond what the senses perceive, and then in chapter 3 how that same fear brings tragedy to the heroic leaders of cities, those who, like the philosopher Parmenides, sought wholeness rather than diversity.[2]

2. I use the word "diversity" rather than the word "plurality," which appears often as a translation of *ta polla* (the many) and which appears in much of the literature on the pre-Socratics, because I want to emphasize that I am discussing not only many *similar* units that can be put together or separated like billiard balls, but also differences, e.g., differences between male and female rather than simply between many men. These differences will be important when I return to the relationship of the family to the polity in the later chapters.

The Pre-Socratic Challenge

2

Ultimately, most physicists hope to find a unified theory that
will explain all four forces as different aspects of a single force.
Indeed, many would say that this is the prime goal of physics
today.

Stephen W. Hawking, *A Brief History of Time*

In the beginning, Hesiod tells us, Chaos came into being
and thereafter broad-breasted Gaia. The sequence is fast:
Tartaros and Eros follow, then from Chaos came black
Night, and from Night, Aether and Day. Earth gives
birth to the Heavens, equal in size to herself, and she
brings forth the mountains, the seas, and deep Okeanos
(*Theogony,* 116–33). Out of one, be Chaos an undifferentiated whole or a vast empty space, emerges the vast
natural array we see around us. Hesiod in myth and
poetry captures the relationship between the one that
existed at some long distant point in time and the multifarious world we currently experience. As Hesiod elaborates the successive emergence of the many divine and
natural forces, he gives us no answers to the whys and
wherefores of their coming-into-being—except perhaps
for the universal passion of *erōs,* which allows many of
the divinities and natural phenomena the possibility of
sexual generation. The whys of the process do not form
the center of his narrative. Rather, it is in the shift to the
so-called nature philosophers or the pre-Socratics, those
to whom we generally assign the origins of philosophy,
that we begin to recognize a confrontation with, rather
than a mere acceptance of, the vast diversity of the world
around us. It is a confrontation that raises the question
that Hesiod did not ask: is there anything that can unite,
draw together, and, particularly, make comprehensible
to the human mind the vast world we see around us? Or

do we see the universe simply as the unfolding of one divine force after another?[1]

Hesiod understands the variety of our world as a genetic problem: where do the night, the day, the female, our troubles, and our sufferings come from? How do we find origins? For many of the early Greek philosophers, the problem continues to be genetic. Though the language may lose some of the anthropomorphic images as we move from Hesiod in the seventh century B.C. to the sixth and fifth century authors, the effort is similar. We observe a multifarious world in which many gods frolic and in which many objects exist. Where does this world come from? As we move to the end of the sixth century B.C., the question does not remain exclusively genetic. Though the language of epistemology as such was foreign to these thinkers, they saw in the vast diversity of the world the danger that the human mind could never comprehend such vastness. The task before them was to overcome that multiplicity and subdue the world to human understanding by simplifying and organizing the world we experience. The answer to both the genetic and the epistemological problem lay now in a uniform element out of which all emerged and which, for some, continued to serve as the unifier of the world around us.[2] The search for that one element, that from which all things emerge and into which all perish, could be understood as the drive for epistemological power over nature. By reducing the natural world to a "one," we can comprehend it. In its vastness, the natural world would elude our intellects.

Thales and Anaximander

> Nature loves to hide herself (*Phusis kruptesthai philei*).
>
> Heraclitus

Let the Milesian Thales be our first example of a pre-Socratic philosopher here; as the "first philosopher," according to tradition, he sits on the cusp between Hesiod and the more explicitly abstract thinkers who follow. Thales was an "activist philosopher": he predicted eclipses and engineered

1. The literature, e.g., Kirk, Raven, and Schofield (1983:73), describes this movement with the wonderful simplicity of the move from *muthos* to *logos*, from poetry to reason, but unfortunately such a formulation ignores the *logos* of Hesiod and the *muthos* of the pre-Socratics. Lloyd (1966:3–6) gives a nice history of the scholarly use of the notion of a " 'pre-logical' mentality" in the literature on ancient Greek thought.

2. Stokes (1971:38), citing a correspondence that he had with Vlastos, suggests the conjunction of the genetic and the material: the pre-Socratics, it is suggested, go from " 'all the X's *come from* Y and Z' to 'all the X's *are* Y and Z.' The Milesian thinkers would have slipped almost by accident . . . into the 'beginning' as the stuff of which things were made."

the rechanneling of rivers (DK 11A6);[3] he could read the stars and help the sailors navigate their ships (DK 11A3a); and he cornered the market on olive presses, made his fortune (DK 11A10), and then fell into the well because, as he gazed at the stars, he looked at the heavens rather than at his feet (DK 11A9). The stories of his activities became part of the folk legends about philosophers,[4] but concerning his actual thought and writings, if there were any, we know very little. Here we must rely primarily on Aristotle's distorting lens. All ancient references to Thales' thought (though not to his deeds) appear to depend on Aristotle's language and interpretation (Kirk, Raven, and Schofield 1983:93–94).

In Aristotle's version, Thales did speak of an *archē* and a *stoicheion*, a fundamental principle or material out of which all things are composed.[5] However, Aristotle's history of the philosophy that preceded his own is subject to question, especially since, according to a tradition at least as old as Thucydides, one's own greatness is confirmed by the inadequacy of one's predecessors. In particular, "those before us who have studied being (*ton onton*) and philosophized about truth" (*Metaphysics* 983b1–3) made the fatal mistake of considering *only* the material cause, the stuff (*hulē*) out of which all things come and into which all things are dissolved when they perish. "The size and the shape of such an *archē* all [the early philosophers] do not say is the same thing but Thales the leader (*archēgos*) of this sort of philosophy[6] says that it is water. Wherefore he also said that the earth is upon water, taking perhaps (*isōs*) this conjecture from observing that the nourishment of all things is moist" (*Metaphysics* 983b19–25; also *de Caelo* B13, 294a28).

We will never know whether Thales used the words Aristotle attributed to him and, if he did use them, whether he meant "matter" as a substrate out of which all that we now experience is made or whether it was rather

3. I have used Diels-Kranz, sixth edition, for the fragments. See Bibliography for complete reference. The first number refers to the chapter in Diels-Kranz; "A" indicates that the passage comes from the section of the chapter including the testimonia about the philosophers; "B" indicates that the passage comes from the section of the chapter that includes actual fragments of their supposed writings; and the number following the "A" or "B" refers to the the number of the fragment in that section. For a very different translation of the fragment in the epigraph, DK 22B123, see Heidegger (1984:113–16).

4. He receives somewhat better press in Herodotus's *Histories*, where he is depicted as giving good advice to the Ionians faced with subjection to the Persians (1.170); predicting an eclipse (1.74); and, according to a story of the Greeks that Herodotus does not accept, redirecting a river's flow so that the army of Croesus could cross (1.75).

5. Kahn (1960:120) explains the metaphorical origins of *stoicheia*, whose primary meaning is letters of the alphabet. "Only with Aristotle does *stoicheia* appear as an abstract expression whose metaphorical value has been largely forgotten."

6. If the story of his eclipse prediction is true, Thales probably flourished around the beginning of the sixth century B.C. Kirk, Raven, and Schofield (1983:76, 86).

the original substance out of which all else arose.[7] If it is the former, we will not know how this works; if the latter, we will not know why, where there was water, suddenly land, people, rocks all emerged. Nevertheless, in the hints that do remain for us, Thales tried to offer a means for going beyond what we see to discover the unique element out of which our world arose in the past or is currently made in our present. The variety of our universe, in a sense, becomes comprehensible because it all collapses into one element of which the multiplicity we observe is just an expression.

Implicit in Aristotle's reconstruction of Thales' thought—as of the thought of the other Ionian philosophers as well—is the inadequacy of our senses. With our eyes we can see only change, diversity, and multiplicity. We see sticks, stone, fire, trees, babies, sail boats, a massive array of objects too varied to set into any order in and of themselves. We must go beyond the senses to discover what order there may be. If Thales said that all things are water, he could not have said it because he relied on his eyes, or any of his senses. The eyes do not see the tree as transformed water; they see the tree as bark, leaves, twigs, and so forth. Our senses do not give us the mechanisms by which we can order the world or transform the world of constant motion and change into one that stands still long enough for us to comprehend it. Our eyes are unreliable. A man standing close to us appears taller than the distant pine tree. When he stands next to the pine tree he appears shorter. Which is he? Taller or shorter? To know this, we must move beyond our senses.[8] Thales set the stage for other philosophers' adventures in this direction, particularly his supposed "relative, student, and successor," Anaximander (DK 12A2).

While we in the modern world may find absurd or quaint Thales' possible suggestion that the *archē* of all things is water, an extreme example of a search for a unifying force that transforms our sensuous experience into an ordered unity, Anaximander makes proposals much more familiar to those of us who live in a world that has seen the development of systems of thought embracing intangible and unifying forces, Christian or Hegelian. Grappling with the problem of diversity as Thales appears to have done, Anaximander also looks for the underlying *archē*. Indeed, he may be the first of the philosophers actually to use this term in this context.[9] Reject-

7. See further Mansfeld (1985:119) on this question.

8. Certainly, the unseen is present in the Homeric poems: wars result from the conflicts between unseen divinities; Zeus nods and events are accomplished; Athene grabs hold of Achilles' hair. But the unseen here are divinities consciously interfering in human affairs. Among the pre-Socratics, Xenophanes seems to hold a unique place as the empiricist in the group, the only one who encourages his readers to understand through their senses. Fraenkel (1975).

9. See especially Kahn (1960:29–32); but cf. Kirk, Raven, and Schofield (1983:108). Seligman (1962:26) argues that *archē* here could only be temporal, suggesting "beginning and origin, and not . . . 'principle of a material kind.'"

ing the water of his supposed mentor, he proposes the "boundless," the *apeiron* (*tina phusin apeiron*), "out of which come to be the heavens and the kosmos within them" (DK 12A9–11). Diogenes Laertius tells us that Anaximander was the first to draw a *perimetron*, a map, of the earth and the sea—a claim repeated by others. That is, the world we experience is bounded, has its limits; we can encompass this world by drawing lines on maps to express those boundaries. But behind this world is that without boundaries, which in its turn gives the order, stability, and boundaries to the world we do perceive.

Anaximander, in what may be the only authentic fragment of this period of Milesian thought, preserved in a text from Simplicius,[10] moves beyond the observable water and anything else that we might call an element (DK 12A9). Unlike water that may be visible in some places, invisible in others, Anaximander's *apeiron* is never visible; "it resembled no one kind of matter in the developed world . . . the lack of positive identification was conspicuously implied" (Kirk, Raven, and Schofield 1983:110). Or, as Aetius complains, "This one [Anaximander] errs not saying what the *apeiron* is, whether it is air or water or earth or any other body" (DK 12A14).[11] It is, though, always enfolding and always steering that which we do observe, according to certain principles of order. In particular, Anaximander's *apeiron* establishes laws that govern the movement of the elements we do see.

Appealing to principles that derive from our political and social relations, the *apeiron* is the source or genesis for those things that are and their destruction as well, "according to necessity (*kata to chreōn*)" (DK 12A9). Further, Anaximander tells us, the elements must pay a penalty and retribution to one another for their injustices. The cosmic portrait offered is of elements in motion, constantly impinging on each other or taking away from one another, and crossing boundaries: it is the movement we see every day with our eyes. Behind that movement is an invisible force that controls the elements, keeps them, as Vlastos says, in a dynamic equilibrium (1947:172), just as the gods enforce justice among men. Anaximander appears to have gone well beyond Thales, whose water was at most a unifying element. The *apeiron* also provides an order and stability to moving objects so that we can comprehend not only the unity of the objects we see, but the structure of their motion.[12] Though Anaximander may not have dealt with how the multiple actually emerges from the *apeiron* (Kahn

10. Kahn (1960:166); but cf. Kirk, Raven, and Schofield (1983:106, 118).

11. Vlastos (1947:169) points out that Anaximander "was going against the general trend" by denying infinity to any of the opposites, i.e., the material, observable stuff.

12. Vlastos (1947:173) emphasizes the importance of Anaximander's contribution to classical thought: that nature is "a self-regulative equilibrium, whose order was strictly immanent."

1960:195), the important point for our purposes is that the *apeiron* is there—invisible and ordering, being itself without boundaries but maintaining boundaries. In the possibly Christianized reading of this fragment by Hippolytus (DK 12A11B2), the *apeiron* becomes everlasting and ageless (*aidion* and *agero*), in contrast to the world of flux where punishment and retribution abound and must be enforced.[13] The *apeiron* thus provides the order behind the movements we observe with our senses.

I turn in the rest of this chapter to two of the giants among the pre-Socratics: Heraclitus and Parmenides.[14] Flourishing around the end of the sixth and the beginning of the fifth centuries B.C., both writers followed the tradition of Thales and Anaximander and questioned the adequacy of our senses to comprehend the world around us. Rather than just searching for a unifying element or principle, they also brought in the question of motion. For Heraclitus, it is by understanding motion and transformation that we can go beyond our senses and understand the underlying unity of a world that appears diverse to the eyes and to the ears. For Parmenides, in his turn, denying motion denied the reality of a diverse world; such a world for him appeared to the inadequate senses, but did not have about it any truth. Both philosophers are in many ways outrageous, presenting the world to their audiences from radically new perspectives clearly intended to shock. Their outlandish claims startle their readers out of a complacent acceptance of what they perceive with their senses and what they have learned from the poets. Both thinkers posed for the Greeks of the next several generations the task of explaining how it is that we can know and how, from a world that is diverse, multiple, and differentiated, we can find and comprehend an orderly unity—cosmological or political.

Heraclitus: The Philosopher Who Laughed

> "My good Adso," my master said, "during our whole
> journey I have been teaching you to recognize the evidence
> through which the world speaks to us like a great book. . .
> the endless array of symbols with which God, through His
> creatures, speaks to us of the eternal life."
>
> Umberto Eco, *The Name of the Rose*

13. Kahn (1960:167) emphasizes that "there is no place either in the wording of the fragment [Simplicius' version] or in the immediate context, for any penalty or wrongdoing which could involve the Boundless. . . . Merely on grammatical grounds, there is no term in the fragment, which could refer to the *apeiron*."

14. As will be the case throughout the rest of this book, the selection of authors and works considered is always subject to question; my aim is not to offer a history of the whole of Greek thought. There are others far better qualified than myself to do this. Rather, I am looking to the works and the authors that best serve to aid us in our reflections on the concepts of unity and diversity and their impact on the ways that we think about politics.

According to the hardly reliable report of Diogenes Laertius in his *Lives of the Ancient Philosophers,* Heraclitus, having finally become an out-and-out misanthrope, withdrew to the mountains where he survived on grasses and herbs. Such a diet had the expected digestive consequences, and Heraclitus returned to town to seek a doctor who could make "from rain a drought." The riddle understandably confused the doctors, who thus could not cure him. So Heraclitus found a cow stall where, he hoped, the heat of the manure would draw off the excess moisture in his body. Instead, he died.[15]

The story Diogenes tells is no doubt apocryphal; nevertheless, it captures key features of Heraclitus's writings. Like the riddle he presents to the doctors, the fragments rely on oxymorons and ambiguities. "The ruler at Delphi neither speaks nor hides, but gives signs," writes Heraclitus of Apollo (DK 22B93). He could have written here of himself as well. He does not speak to us openly, for we can comprehend him and the secrets of nature only through ambiguous signs.[16] In Diogenes Laertius's biography of Socrates, we hear Socrates react to a treatise by Heraclitus (supposedly given to him by Euripides): "What I understand is noble; I think this also about what I do not understand. Except that it has need of a certain Delian diver" (II.22). Diogenes also calls him a "crowd-reviler,"[17] chiding the mass of men, *hoi polloi,* for their unwillingness to comprehend and their failure to see the unity underlying all things. Finally, in his desire to transform heavy rain into a drought, we see the concern with the balance of opposites and the unity of the elements that we often ignorantly suppose to be opposites. It is with this latter point that I am most concerned, but it cannot be separated from the other two aspects of his thought, namely, the obscurity of his writing and his apparent misanthropy.

We know little about Heraclitus's actual works, how they were structured, whether they were simply presented as Nietzschean aphorisms, or whether they were parts of a more sustained prose document. Our unreliable Diogenes Laertius (IX.6) claims that there was a work by Heraclitus called (as were indeed most of the other works by the pre-Socratics) *Peri Phuseos.* This work was supposedly divided into three parts: the first dealt with an unspecified "everything (*panton*)," the second and third with perhaps somewhat more manageable "politics" and "theology." According to Diogenes, Heraclitus deposited his book, written very unclearly (*asaphesteron*), in the temple of Artemis. The obscurity was to ensure that only the able (*dunamenoi*) should come near it and that the com-

---

15. Diogenes Laertius, *Lives of the Ancient Philosophers* IX.3.

16. See Heidegger's wonderful essay on *alethea,* concealment and nonconcealment (1984:102–23).

17. *Ochloloidros* is the word used by Diogenes, IX.6.

mon people should not scorn it. By the time of Aristotle's *Metaphysics*, Heraclitus's name had been transformed into a verb, most likely meaning to speak obscurely (1010a11). Despite (or perhaps because of) its obscurity, the work achieved such reknown that a school of followers appeared called "Heracliteans" (Diogenes Laertius IX.6). Our journey to these obscure fragments—made even more obscure by their divorce from Heraclitus's context and their incorporation into the arguments of others—can never approach a full statement of Heraclitus's purposes and claims. Rather, we shall read them as signs offering insights into the vision of a world order that Heraclitus left for us. We shall not scorn as he feared the masses would do, but instead try to be among the able who can begin to understand the power of seeing the world as he did.[18]

The editors of Heraclitus's fragments seem to agree only about which fragment must have been the one introducing his work. Immediately, Heraclitus describes humans as ignorant (*axunetoi*) for they do not know what is everlasting. From his other fragments we know that this ignorance is of the unifying, though unseen, *logos*. While he may scornfully describe the many, *hoi polloi*, as simply accepting the opinions of others without thought (DK 22B17), his hatred of men has not so much to do with their weakness of moral character and their incapacity to make just decisions or to perform heroic acts of courage. It is for their failure to know rather than their failure to act that he condemns them (DK 22B73). In other words, he reviles the many because they fail to see the truth as he sees it and, indeed, to listen to him as he opens the truth to them in his writings. When he speaks to them, most men are uncomprehending (*axunetoi*), not listening; they are like deaf men who "as the saying goes, are present while absent" (DK 22B34).

Humans are deaf because, while they ignore Heraclitus, they listen to the words of the poets. "Homer," Heraclitus asserts with unabashed force, "deserves to be thrown out of the contest and flogged along with Archilo-

---

18. Kahn (1979:2) insists that we read Heraclitus as a great prose poem carefully crafted to capture nuances of meaning and echoes of previous authors. Osborne (1987) rejects Kahn's proposals and insists in her turn that we cannot separate the fragments that we have from any pre-Socratic author from the philosophic or political intent of the author whose writings yield the fragment. My role is not to judge between these two extremes, but to use the fragments as possible ways of confronting the problems that motivate my general investigation. While I have great sympathy for Osborne's claims about the dangers of taking fragments out of context, I do not think that this invalidates the fragments. Osborne, though, alerts us to the importance of care so as to avoid ascribing to the fragments meanings that they could not have had at the times at which they were written. Heidegger (1984:102–03, 105) takes a middle ground and concludes that we along with the ancients are justified in calling this thinker "the Obscure."

chus" (DK 22B42). Even Plato, who more than a century later will wage his own battles with the poets, will never condemn so openly the premiere literary and ethical work of ancient Greece. There is no explanation of why Homer deserves such a curt dismissal, but another fragment from Hippolytus suggests that Homer, though "wiser than all the Greeks," nevertheless, like other men, was "deceived before the knowledge (*gnōsin*) of that which is apparent" (DK 22B56). Hesiod is dismissed as well. He "is the teacher of most; they understand that this one knew the most who," Heraclitus scornfully notes, "did not know Day and Night, that they are one" (DK 22B57).[19] Or, if the many choose not to listen to the unknowing poets, then they use the mob as a teacher, not knowing that the "many are evil (*kakoi*) and the few are good (*agathoi*)" (DK 22B104).

The attack on the poets and on the many as teachers may account for fragments that suggest the greater reliability of the eyes as witnesses than the ears (DK 22B101a),[20] but elsewhere both senses are scorned as "witnesses" for humans who have "barbarian souls" (DK 22B107), souls that speak a foreign language. Heraclitus speaks here not of a Greek ethnocentrism, but of the souls that cannot communicate because they do not speak the common language that Heraclitus tries to teach them. This is a language that reveals the bonds of community among all things, and perhaps among all humans. "Speaking with mind (*xun nooi*) it is necessary to hold fast to what is common (*xunoi*) to all, just as a polis to its law and by far more strongly" (DK 22B114). The word play of *xun nooi* and *xunoi* is obvious, but especially worthy of note in the context of this discussion. The community that Heraclitus tries to create among all men depends on the use of one's mind, the *noos*, not on one's senses nor even on a common language such as Greek.[21]

Throughout the fragments, Heraclitus denigrates any reliance on the senses or even wide experiences: they teach nothing (DK 22B40). The attack on senses, though, is not simply because they are unreliable, but because they separate men from one another as the mind does not. The senses lead to what we in our own language might call subjective percep-

19. See also DK 22B106, where Heraclitus describes Hesiod as one who made some days good and some days bad, but did not know that "the nature of every day is one."

20. Kahn (1979:106) comments: "It expresses not so much an epistemic ranking of the senses as the reliance upon direct experience rather than upon hearsay."

21. The fragment continues with the note that the human law is nourished by the divine law, giving to Heraclitus the natural law theories of the Stoics and the early Christian writers. I am uncomfortable with this attribution to Heraclitus of themes that emerge much later in intellectual history, though it would further clarify the unifying force of the *logos*. However, it is not necessary in any sense for our understanding of Heraclitus. See further Kahn (1979:102).

tions. The eyes and ears of human beings allow for private, individualized experiences; the senses take the world and appropriate it for each individual separately. Thus, the many who rely on their senses do not speak to one another, do not communicate in a common language, do not acknowledge their unified existence. "Though the *logos* is shared, the many (*hoi polloi*) live as though they have private thinking (*idian . . . phronēsin*)" (DK 22B2). The knowing soul, the one capable of a common, not a "barbarous," language, perceives the unseen and thus that which is common (*xunon*) rather than particular (*idion*). "To think (*phronein*) is common (*xunon*) to all" (DK 22B113), but "they do not understand what they experience; the many seem to themselves" (DK 22B17). They live according to their senses, which means they live distinct, isolated lives, ignorant of what unites all and makes all one. "For the ones who are awake, the cosmos is one and common (*koinon*),[22] but each individual (*hekaston*) of the sleeping is turned away towards the particular (*idion*)" (DK 22B89).[23] Knowledge is thus unified in the *logos* and the *logos* in its turn unifies humans. This unity, though, can come only from the soul and not from the senses. "One could not find the limits of the soul, so deep is the *logos*" (DK 22B45).

The uncertainty about Thales' first principle, whether it was genetic or the current matter out of which all is currently comprised, does not plague us in our consideration of Heraclitus. The unity Heraclitus presents is clearly not genetic; it characterizes the world in which we currently live, if only we would use our common minds and not our private senses to discover it. The soul that is awake, that listens "not to me, but to the *logos*," agrees that "all is one (*hen panta einai*)" (DK 22B50). That soul acknowledges the fundamental unity of all things, becoming like the gods and unlike the many, for it sees beyond opposites to an underlying, hidden harmony. Heraclitus's language became famous not only for its obscurity, but also for its paradoxes, its claims that X and not-X were the same. It is the deaf men, the unknowing men, who create oppositions and divisions where the gods see only unity: "For the divine all (*panta*) is beautiful and good and just, while humans have taken some things as just and others as unjust" (DK 22B102). Humans, with their souls perceiving the particular, separate what the gods unite; they impose distinctions, calling some things

22. Kahn (1979:104) notes that this must be Plutarch's word, for Heraclitus always used *xunos*.

23. Nussbaum (1972) interprets these fragments in terms of the individual; if individuals have psyches that cannot make the connections from one thing to the next they are *axunetoi* and like deaf people. She sees the *xunon* and the commonalities as intrapsychic, whereas I am suggesting that the community is interpsychic. The unity of all humans rather than only the unity of the individual soul seems to me to be the intention of Heraclitus here.

good and some bad, while the gods and the knowing souls recognize the unity of all things and that this unity is good.

In a typically paradoxical claim by Heraclitus, he indicates how by dividing, distinguishing, and discriminating we destroy the primary unity of all things. "Sea water," he says, "is most pure and most polluted; for fish it is potable and a savior, but for humans it is not potable and destructive" (DK 22B61). This could be interpreted as bordering on Sophistic subjectivity and an early expression of the Protagorean "Man is the measure of all things."[24] But we must be careful here. It is precisely the subjectivity that Heraclitus is criticizing, not praising. Both fish and humans perceive the ocean from their individualized perspectives, what is particular to them and what is not common to all. Each sees only the parts rather than the unified whole. Likewise, there is the famous "The road up and the road down are one and the same" (DK 22B60). When standing on the top of the mountain, the road appears to descend, but from the bottom it appears to ascend. This seems to be precisely Heraclitus's point, and it works even with language: "The name of the bow is life; its work is death" (DK 22B48). Those who look at the road (or the sea) from their personal, particular, and private (*idion*) perspective see only the part rather than the totality, and thus they become mired in a land of contradictions and paradoxes.[25] The mind that speaks the language that is common to all and takes no particularized stance sees no contradiction, no paradoxes, no divisions. It discovers the harmony that is not visible: "The hidden (*aphanēs*) harmony is stronger [better] than the open [harmony]" (DK 22B54).

Heraclitus is perhaps most vivid in his insistence on the harmony of all things when he presents the constructive tension that seems to set opposites apart. The bow and the lyre present the examples of harmony arising out of conflict. In both the bow and the lyre, there must be forces that are opposed to one another for each instrument to function—to send the arrow into the air or to emit the note. He calls this a back-stretching or a back-turning, depending on whether one reads *palintonos* or *palintropos*. In either case, it is only those who understand (*xuniasin*) who can see that in the very process of drawing apart it agrees with itself (DK 22B51). Those

---

24. In Osborne's (1987:169) analysis of Hippolytus's use of this passage, this is precisely the implication that it has: it is "Heraclitus' denial of distinctions of dignity and moral value in his epistemological statements concerning the visible and the invisible."

25. Many commentators, e.g., Stokes (1971), Kahn (1979), Furley (1987:32–33), seem to take statements that equate opposites, up and down, day and night, as statements of change. For instance, Stokes (1971:92) on DK 22B126: "The cold is warm, the warm is cold," suggests that the cold changes into hot. But there is no need to suggest such a transformation. The cold is hot, the hot is cold. To talk of hot and cold as distinct is the response of a private individual who does not know the unity of all things.

who see only the pulling of the string and not the countervailing force of the bow fail to see the "harmony" that emerges from this tension, or the unity that arises from the apparent opposition.

In Heraclitus's world view, apparent opposites must work in tension with one another. Without such opposites, there is no coming-into-being. Against Hesiod, for example, who tells us that the powers of *erōs* drive together various divinities who then give birth to new divinities, Heraclitus posits war and conflict as the father of all things. "The counterthrust brings together and from drawing apart comes the most beautiful harmony and all things (*panta*) come into being according to conflict (*erin*)" (DK 22B8; also DK 22B80). Elsewhere, instead of conflict, *eris*, he talks of war, *polemos*. In the Homeric version of the human universe, war leads to death and destruction. Heraclitus supposedly scorned the poets who said, "O that conflict among men and gods might be destroyed." For they did not understand that "there would be no harmony unless there were high and low notes, nor would there be living creatures were there not male and female, both being opposites" (DK 22A22). In the perverse view of Heraclitus, war leads to birth, but we only understand this when we see the unity of apparent opposites, those things that appear to be opposites to those who do not know. The intellects of those who do not know cannot grasp the harmony of life and death, both of which arise from war and conflict. "All things come into being according to conflict (*kat' erin*) and necessity" (DK 22B80).

While Heraclitus reviles his less enlightened neighbors, his insistence upon the unity of all things despite (or perhaps because of) conflict allows a curious note of equality to pervade his thought. Though most do not listen to Heraclitus or their reason, still "it belongs to all humans to know themselves and have sound thinking" (DK 22B116). Claiming that war is the father and king of all things, Heraclitus adds, "Some he has shown as gods, some as mortals, some he makes slaves, some free" (DK 22B53). It is war, it seems, that defines who is to be god and who is to be human, who is slave and who is free. There are no intrinsic qualities of worth. "As the same thing there exist living men and the dead man, the one who is awake and the one who sleeps, young and the old. These things having changed are those and those having changed back are these again" (DK 22B82). Again, in DK 22B62: "Immortals are mortals; mortals are deathless." The oppositions fade before the ultimate unity and equality of all things recognized by the mind. The differences that we posit between men and gods, slaves and free men, arise from the inadequacy of our *logos* to recognize the unity of all things. To talk of gods in opposition to men is to rely on the foolish myths that fill the works of the poets. To see differences between the young and the old is to rely on the unreliable senses.

With no inherent differences there is no natural hierarchy, no natural slavery for, as the wise know, all is one. Heraclitus tells us that *hubris,* the pretension of superiority to another, must be quenched "more than fire" (DK 22B43). In perhaps his most outrageous and offensive fragment, Heraclitus claims: "Corpses should be thrown out more quickly than dung" (DK 22B96). No burial rites are to be performed for the dead body. No ceremonies wishing the soul well on its journey to Hades. Rather, we find a view of the human body as no better than dung, to be discarded as distasteful garbage. In a world where all is one, there can be no justification for offering greater ceremonial treatment to one object rather than another.[26] The distinctions of value that we attribute to one object over and against another derive from our conventions and are not founded in the natural unity of all things. The inequality of wisdom that allows Heraclitus to scorn *hoi polloi* must be blamed on the inadequacy of their education and, in particular, the deceptions that the poets have perpetrated. The many do not know because they do not listen to and try to understand Heraclitus. It is not because they are unable to comprehend, were they to listen carefully and work their way through his ambiguous speech. Yet, he must speak obscurely because the reality he posits cannot be apprehended by obvious and discrete categories. Our senses make us see the world as immediate and obvious. Heraclitus is to teach us to use our reason by learning to accept and to go beyond the paradoxes he presents to their inherent unity. What inequality exists in our world is there because the many are wedded to their senses and the stories of the poets.

When Parmenides in his writings proclaims the unity of all things and denies all distinctions, his vision of a unified reality entails the denial of all motion and change. Heraclitus, in contrast, despite his own insistence on the underlying unity, continues to allow us a world in which there is motion, a world in which unity can be consistent with change. The world that does change is not chaotic or disorderly. Rather, we find a flux that is consistent with stability.[27] Those who set up an opposition between change and stability create false dichotomies, ones that appear only to those who do not know the true *logos* that all is one. They do not see beyond the apparent opposition to the fundamental harmony that incorporates both motion and stability. "Changing it rests (*metaballon anapauetai*)" (DK 22B84a), is perhaps the starkest fragment of Heraclitus's vision, but the river fragment is probably the most famous. "For those stepping into the same river, other and other waters flow" (DK 22B12). In Plu-

---

26. Nussbaum (1972:158) reads this passage as a denial of individual identity in the corpse itself and criticizes others who fail to acknowledge the radical nature of the fragment.
27. Kirk (1954) offers perhaps the strongest statement of this view of Heraclitus's work.

tarch's formulation of Heraclitus's statement, it appears: "It is not possible to step two times into the same river" (DK 22B91).[28] This is close to how the fragment appears in Plato's *Cratylus* (402a) and in Aristotle's *Metaphysics* (1010a12). We should note, however, the difference between these two fragments. In Plutarch's version, Heraclitus is the theorist of constant change, of the world of flux in which there is no stability, in which our universe moves instantaneously from one state into the next. Plutarch's fragment continues with the claim that one cannot touch two times any mortal thing, but that it changes and comes back together, that it comes near and goes away. The fragment suggests an uncertain, variable world beyond human comprehension and control, one that is always flowing.[29] The former fragment, by contrast, suggests the constancy of our world despite the appearance of change. The river is the same despite its motion, though the waters always change and flow by us. With our eyes we see and with our bare toes we feel the waters rushing past, but with our mind we understand the unity of the river and thus the constancy and harmony that lies behind all motion and all conflict.

Few are the fragments in Heraclitus that deal directly with the political life of the Greek city. We do read that the *demos* must fight on behalf of the law (*nomos*), just as they fight for the walls of the city (DK 22B44), and we can read into this prescription the preference for the unseen unity that binds the city together rather than for the visible structures of the walls that enclose a city. For one who insists on the unseen unity of the cosmos, the plea on behalf of the unseen *nomoi* appears an obvious analogy. Or we read in DK 22B33: "It is the custom (*nomos*) to obey the advice of one (*henos*)." We may choose to read into *henos* "one man," or we may read "the one." If we choose the former, Heraclitus would be the defender of monarchy in preference to any sort of democratic rule, but such a reading and such an analysis would hide in its turn the broader theoretical issues that Heraclitus's works raise.[30]

Struggling with the same problems that the earlier pre-Socratics had

28. There is also DK 22B49a: "We step into and do not step into the same rivers, we are and we are not," which Diels-Kranz accepts as genuine but Kahn (1979:288) does not. Debate among scholars rages about the authenticity of all the river fragments. Kirk (1954:373) sees only DK 22B12 as genuine; Vlastos (1955:343) claims that B12 is the least likely to be genuine.

29. Note that this is the view most often associated with Heraclitus; see also Furley (1987:34), with whom I would agree when he says that the skepticism implied here is inconsistent with the other fragments.

30. Vlastos (1947:166) points out that the scorn for the crowds expressed by Heraclitus is not peculiar to Heraclitus and that, in fact, he seems to show more interest in what is "common" than most of the other pre-Socratic philosophers.

grappled with, Heraclitus sees a world of multiplicity and constant change. With his desire to go behind the observed world, he discovers a basic unity of all things and a constancy despite apparent change. In the consideration of any political community, there is thus the need to find such a unity despite apparent diversity and opposition, as well as the need to discover constancy over time. Aristotle, in the very beginning of Book 3 of the *Politics,* will take Heraclitus's problem and place it directly into his consideration of what in the world is this thing called the polis. He will have to discover the unity of citizens in the constancy of the *politeia* (political regime), despite the succession of generations. Heraclitus's writings—the bits and pieces that are left to us—show how the cosmic problems became patterns for the political order. His solution that we must find order and unity in the unseen *logos* that we discover with our minds allows for the diversity we perceive with our senses. Because of this unseen unity, apparent conflict (even war) between opposites gives birth to beauty and life rather than leading to death and destruction. Heraclitus is not afraid of diversity; it is only those, the many, who do not know and who do not listen, who are threatened by the conflict that arises from differences. Those who do know, like Heraclitus and whoever can comprehend his ambiguous speech, recognize that unity encompasses differences, that the lyre and bow must be stretched in opposite directions to create harmony, that men and women are necessary for there to be the birth of the next generation.

Montaigne, in his essay "On Democritus and Heraclitus," quotes the Roman poet Juvenal, who compared the two philosophers: "One always, when o'er his threshold stepped, laughed at the world; the other always wept." Democritus could laugh, Montaigne tells us, because of "finding the condition of man vain and ridiculous . . . whereas Heraclitus having pity and compassion on this same condition of ours, wore a face perpetually sad, and eyes filled with tears" (1965 : 220). I beg here to differ with both Juvenal and Montaigne. Heraclitus does not grieve because all is flux; rather, he delights in the knowledge that, despite the change and diversity around us, all is one and the same. Tension is a source of creativity that we need not fear. "Conflict is justice," or "Justice is conflict and all things come into being according to conflict and necessity"(DK 22B80). We live in a world in which corpses are no better than dung, where wisdom, not physical prowess nor ancestry, defines the only level of inequality—and where wisdom is a matter of listening, of which all humans are capable, not a matter of privilege. A cosmic order unites the apparent lowest and highest, mortals and gods, into a satisfying and complete who' Parmeni-des whose ideas we turn to next is not so sanguine.

The Truth According to Parmenides

> Yesterday, passing the open door leading into the private
> garden, I saw Fenwick with his mallet raised. The steam from
> the tea-urn rose in the middle of the lawn. There were banks of
> blue flowers. Then suddenly descended upon me the obscure,
> the mystic sense of adoration, of completeness that triumphed
> over chaos. Nobody saw my poised and intent figure as I
> stood at the open door. Nobody guessed the need I had to
> offer my being to one god; and perish and disappear. His
> mallet descended; the vision broke.
>
> Virginia Woolf, *The Waves*

Heraclitus celebrates the underlying unity of opposites and opposition it-self. Thus, male and female are necessary for birth, and Homer erred when he prayed for an end to the conflict that characterizes human life. Parmenides denies opposites and opposition, leaving no room for conflict in his world system. When writing of male and female, he refers to "hateful childbirth and intercourse" that send male to mingle with female and the opposite, female to mingle with male (DK 28B12.4–6). In the Parmenidean world such "mingling" belongs to the defective way of human opinion, far from the unmoving truth, revealed by a Goddess, of "what is." This is a truth that has nothing to do with coming-into-being and indeed denies that coming-into-being is even possible. Parmenides, as he too urges humans onto a way of knowledge that is abstracted from their senses, eliminates the differences that underlie the unity of Heraclitus's world.

With his obscure and ambiguous aphorisms, Heraclitus consciously eschewed the poetic form of those earlier teachers of men, who taught falsehoods such as day and night were distinct from one another and some days were good and others bad, rather than all is one. Although Parmenides is no less radical in his conclusions and the message he wishes to convey, he in contrast models his writings on the epic form.[31] He writes of a young man, the *kouros*, presumably himself, guided by the Maidens of the Sun, who have left their house of Night and who take him into the light at the gates of Day and Night (DK 28B1.9–11). Within those gates the narrator learns what is true, what is false, and what are the opinions of men. The truth is told to him by an unnamed Goddess, and he reports this truth back to those who listen to Parmenides' poem. While we may have difficulty interpreting certain passages in this poem, these difficulties

---

31. Mourelatos (1970:chap. 1) is especially helpful on the epic qualities of Parmenides' poem; see also Coxon (1986:9–11). Fraenkel (1975:1) argues for the literary allusions to Pindar's 6th Olympian.

arise from our own distance from the language and images that Parmenides uses and from its fragmentary nature. Parmenides aims to present an argument so clear, so persuasive, so straightforward that we cannot fail to acknowledge its power. No phrases that turn life into death or hot into cold cloud his writing. He writes for all, not only the able, and dismisses all ambiguity with the simplicity of the truth that he intends to convey: "what is" is and "what is not" is not and cannot be (DK 28B2.3,5). This truth takes us beyond differences, beyond conflict, incompletion, motion, generation. We need not deal with opposites and dichotomies for the simple reason that in Parmenides' world of truth they do not (and need not) exist. His poem is divided into three main parts: first, a poem where motion and the senses prepare for the lessons of both the second part, the Way of Being or "what is," and the third part, the (non)Way of Seeming, of "what is not."

The prologue to Parmenides' poem describes in vivid detail the journey taken by the *kouros* to the Goddess from whose speech he is to learn all that one must know, both "the unmoving heart of persuasive[32] truth," and the opinion (*doxa*) of mortals in which there is no trust (DK28B1.29– 30). We sense the speed of the chariot that carries the young man forward as we read of horses "full of thought" who draw the chariot with its axles glowing, sending forth a whistling sound (DK 28B1.4–8). The Maidens of the Sun themselves "hasten" the chariot forward. Near the end of the journey they are all stopped at the gates with the huge, stone fitted doors guarded by "much avenging" Justice. The Maidens appease her with soft words, and the gates open. The youth is brought before the Goddess who, taking his right hand in hers, says, "It is necessary that you learn all things" (DK 28B1.28).

Throughout this journey and the lesson itself, the young narrator is passive. He is carried and he listens. He has the *thumos,* the desire or enthusiasm (DK 28B1.1), to go on the journey, but he accomplishes nothing by himself.[33] He must be brought to the Goddess in a chariot drawn by horses (mares, we might note) and guided by the Maidens. "They [the horses] carried me," he says (DK28B1.4).[34] When they all arrive at the

32. Much ink has been spilled over whether this word is *eupeithes* or *eukukles,* well rounded. Either reading of the manuscripts is consistent with my understanding of Parmenides. *Eupeithos* has the unfortunate connection with the world of seeming, while *eukuklos* binds the truth to the spherical image of being presented in fragment 8.43; it may be difficult to imagine a "well-rounded" truth, while one can imagine easily a persuasive truth.

33. I disagree with Coxon (1986:157), who admits that "P. regards himself as still drawn by the mares," but then goes on to transform the mares into "his own impulse to philosophize."

34. Cf. the reference in the Goddess's speech below where she mentions the horses "which carry you" (DK 28B1.25).

shining gates guarded by Justice, it is the Maidens, not the youth, who with soft words (DK 28B1.15) persuade Justice to open the gates so that they, the Maidens, may drive the chariot bearing the youth to the Goddess. Even then the youth says nothing: "The Goddess received me enthusiastically and took my right hand in hers" (DK 28B1.22–23). Throughout this whole section of the poem, the young man is led and controlled by women.[35] The only act in which he finally engages is the report of what has been revealed to him.

Many have been the suggestions as to who or what the Maidens of the Sun symbolize as they lead the youth to the Goddess: Parmenides' own driving passions for enlightenment (Fraenkel 1975:2–4); allegorical representations of the senses that can open the doors guarded by Dike;[36] and intelligence (Coxon 1986:157) all have been proposed. Whatever allegorical role, if any, the Maidens may play, the description of the journey itself is startling when considered with regard to the truth that the youth is to learn. These early passages of the poem (a sizable portion of the remaining fragments) build upon images that work against the truth revealed by the Goddess. They function within the world of opinion that Parmenides appears so eager to reject. From the very first line we hear that the horses will carry the young man as far as (*hoson*) "my *thumos* reaches." The "as far as" suggests a boundlessness, an ill-defined space that cannot characterize the completely bounded world of "what is." The eyes are indeed necessary to see the burning axles and the ears must hear the whistling of the chariot wheels as they turn. Nonetheless, both the eyes and the ears of men are mocked in Fragment 6, where we learn that the human race, relying on its senses, is both blind and deaf. The route to the Goddess with its many sights and sounds is one filled with appeals to the banished senses, senses that are left behind once one learns the lesson that the Goddess teaches.

In his extensive analysis of the language and literary references of the poem, Mourelatos (1970:132 n. 44) alerts us to the frequent use of compounds of *polu-* in the description of the route that the narrator takes to the goddess: *poluphēmon* (1.2), *poluphrastoi* (1.4), *polupoinon*(1.14), and *poluchalkous* (1.18). *Polu-*, as a prefix meaning "many," should characterize the way of seeming, not of truth. "What is," as it is revealed to the youth by the Goddess, cannot be described by adjectives that suggest any sort of multiplicity since "what is" is one, never many. The discovery of "what is" is to alleviate the confusion brought on by the "many" that the senses may

35. Coxon (1986:159) notes that it is unusual to have female charioteers.

36. Freeman (1953:142): "[W]hen he arrives he turns his back on these deceptive organs, yet there is no doubt that he came thus far by means of them. Therefore does he himself not admit that something is due to them."

perceive. Before his instruction by the Goddess, the youth is alert to multiplicity, to time, and to unlimited space. After the encounter, he needs only to talk in this language to those who have not been initiated, who have not had the truth revealed to them. The prologue thus reports a hurried escape from the world of multiplicity into a satisfying whole, where the mind need not be disturbed by senses that seem to perceive axles burning and wheels whistling.

Adding to the texture of the prologue may be the sexual overtones of the young man eagerly being escorted to the guarded chambers of a Goddess who reveals "truth" to him. As mentioned above, in Fragment 12 the Goddess, describing the opinions of mortals, talks of the "hateful" mingling of male and female. Sexuality must characterize the prelude to this poem (the world before the truth has been revealed) and the consummation of the youth's initiation into the truth. It is perhaps a mingling that is not hateful since the product will be the transcendence of sexuality and of the differences between male and female that sexuality implies.

To learn from the Goddess, the young man must shed his deceptive senses that perceive what is many, that see the world as divisible into male and female, night and day, light and darkness. The unity of the world appears only as a sort of revelation. If we interpret the journey as an allegory of the way to the truth, then the experiences that we have of the many may allows us to approach the threshold of the Goddess, but we still need divine guidance to learn the truth. We cannot discover it on our own. Within the chamber of the Goddess the actual communication of the truth is a private experience, neither shared with nor dependent on other mortals. The individual journeys to knowledge, not to the community of knowledge that Heraclitus envisioned. Indeed, the journey takes us "past cities" (DK 28B1.3)[37], away from men and towards mythical and divine beings. The Goddess herself describes the road that the youth has travelled as "outside the trodden path away from human beings" (DK 28B1.27). The narrator has left his fellow mortals far behind to learn for himself the unmoving heart of truth. For Heraclitus, mortals discover the *logos* by acknowledging their community with one another, but *xunos* and *zun nooi* have no place in Parmenides' journey. This is a point to which we shall return later. Let us here turn instead to what it is that the Goddess teaches

---

37. This accepts the reading of *astē* in the manuscript at this point. See Nussbaum (1979b:68 n. 18), who accepts this reading, as opposed to Coxon (1968:69 and, more recently, 1986:158), who emphasizes that *astē* is not in the manuscript. Manuscript N of Sextus has *astē;* manuscript L has *atē*. See also Austin (1986:156 n. 2). Mourelatos (1970:22) reads *kata pant' astē* as "to all towns" which suggests that knowledge must come after the full experiences of the world. Mourelatos's attachment to the Homeric model for Parmenides' poem would make this reading especially attractive to him.

the youth who has been carried to her chamber far from the paths of others and what it is that he, "hearing the tale," is to preserve and carry away from this encounter (DK 28B2.1).

"It is necessary that you learn all things," the Goddess has said to the youth (DK 28B1.28). The "all" that he must learn includes the truth of "what is" and the unreliable opinions of mortals. To teach him "what is," the Goddess centers her lesson on the absence of differentiation, on the complete identity of all reality. The opposites that enchanted Heraclitus in their underlying unity and that enabled the youth to ascend to the Goddess's chamber simply do not exist in the unmoving truth of Parmenides' Goddess. There is no "many out of one" nor "one out of many" in her world. The *phusis* of the earlier cosmologists retained the root notion of *phuo,* to grow, to come into being. There can be no nature as growth in the Goddess's world. Growth implies change, which in its turn implies differences, and differences mean the presence of "what is not." This is impossible for Parmenides, who presents not a cosmogony, but only an unchanging, immobile, uniform cosmos.[38] In this cosmos there is only "what is." The "many" populate a false world that we imagine with our senses, but precisely because it is multiple we cannot know it. The unity of the truth can never dissolve into different parts, except in the beliefs of men led astray by their senses.

To understand "what is," the Goddess provides us with what she calls "signposts" (*sēmata*) of which, we might say, there are "very many" (*polla mal'*) (DK 28B8.2–3). "What is" is unborn (*agenēton*), not to be destroyed (*anōlethron*), unmoving (*atremes*), and complete (*teleion*) (DK 28B8.3–4). Birth and destruction belong to the belief of mortals; completion can find no home where there is constant change. The various traits of "what is" are all interconnected: as unborn and indestructible, "what is" cannot partake of "what is not." To be born implies that there was a time when one was not and, since "what is not" cannot be, birth becomes impossible—as does destruction. Destruction implies that "what is" will become "what is not" some time in the future. But once again, "what is not" cannot be. Thus, nothing of "what is" can be destroyed. With the denial of birth and destruction, temporality disappears, or as one scholar phrases it, Parmenides "has managed to detense the verb" (Owen 1974:273). There is no past, no future, only now.

It is the same with the attributes of completion (*teleion*) and indivisibility. We understand that "what is" is immobile insofar as we recog-

---

38. Mourelatos (1970:104) comments: "By the late sixth century the nascent language of mathematics must have offered a clear and consistent model of the use of the tenseless 'is.'"

nize that it is whole, without beginning, without cessation, far from birth and destruction, unified in itself (DK 28B8.26–28). "It lies by itself," the Goddess claims (DK 28B8.29). In its wholeness and completion, it is isolated, needing nothing other than itself.[39] Thus, it does not need to move either to incorporate anything else to itself or to discard any aspect of itself. "And thus it remains firmly (forever) there" (DK 28B8.30). Incorporating perfection in its own completion and wholeness, to move would mean to depart from that perfection—something "what is" cannot do. "Strong necessity (*Anagke*) holds what is in bonds of a boundary" (DK 28B8.30–31).

The demand for the completion and wholeness, for the immobility and indestructability of "what is" blends in with Parmenides' epistemological perspectives. We cannot assign causality here and say that the epistemology determined his description of "what is," nor that his understanding of "what is" leads to his epistemology. The two, though, are clearly interdependent. Perhaps it is in Parmenides' epistemology that we see most vividly the demand noted earlier in this chapter, that the world be subdued to human comprehension. As Parmenides understands the nature of knowledge, we can only know "what is," what is unified, what is whole, what is complete. A world of many things that is in constant motion as objects come into being and then die or are destroyed cannot be comprehended by the human mind; such a world lies outside of human knowledge, subject only to untrustworthy opinions and incapable of being spoken.[40] Only that which is bounded, limited, and unmoving can, in contrast, be known. To know is to know "what is." There can be no knowledge of "what is not," for "what is not" does not, according to the pronouncement of the Goddess, exist. Parmenides' Goddess seems to go so far as to identify thinking and "what is." The passage reads, "It is the same thing both to think and to be" (DK 28B3). The Goddess explicitly tells the youth, "You cannot know that which is not for it is not to be accomplished," to which she adds, "Nor would you speak it" (DK 28B2.7–8).

This unmoving, unborn, complete whole that Parmenides' Goddess describes has no room for duality, much less differences or oppositions. "It is not divisible since all is alike (*homoion*)" (DK 28B8.22). Indivisible

---

39. Cf. Mourelatos (1970:119). We will return to this aspect of "what is" with regard to Diotima's speech in the *Symposium,* and the gods of Book II and the Callipolis of Book V in the *Republic.*

40. Once again, we can note a serious problem since it is obvious that the Goddess does, in the second half of the poem, speak of the many beliefs of mortals, and the narrator in the first part speaks of the many sights and sounds that lead him to his Goddess. It is unclear where such speech belongs if one were to accept the Goddess's claim that only "what is" can be spoken.

unity binds "what is" from all sides.[41] "You will not cut off 'what is' from clinging to 'what is'" (DK 28B4.2). The indivisibility of "what is" is in part captured by the suggestion that we must think of the whole as a sphere in which there is no beginning, no end, no discrete part. "It is completed (*tetelesmenon*), from all sides like the bulk of a well rounded sphere . . . equal on all sides" (DK 28B8.42–49). The mind of mortals, not the Goddess, divides "what is"; men try to "scatter" it (DK 28B4.3). Human error enters as soon as mortals established two forms (DK 28B8.53) rather than one. In particular, "They distinguished (*ekrinato*) opposites in the body and put on signs apart from one another," and they separated the brilliance of the light from the darkness of the night. (DK 28B8.55–59). Throughout the poem, the false way of mortal opinion leads to duality, multiplicity, and diversity, the very opposites of true being. As soon as we allow difference to enter, there is birth, destruction, movement, and most especially, incompletion.

In particular, by the very process of naming the objects we perceive, we divide up the world. Parmenides has his Goddess comment, "So all things are named however many names mortals have established, thinking that they are true, coming into being and being destroyed, being and not being, changing places and changing bright color" (DK 28B8.38–42). The process of naming allows mortals to separate what is whole into parts. But there is only one thing of which mortals can speak and which they can name, and that is "what is."[42]

Among the differences that mortals introduce with their naming of discrete objects are those that appear to separate the sexes and that lead to the "hateful mingling" of opposites mentioned above. In the world of "what is," there can be no mingling because there are no opposites, and nor is there the "hateful birth" that results from the hateful mingling of the sexes. There is no generation at all. By transforming sexual intercourse (here we cannot forget Aphrodite) and childbirth into what is hateful, Parmenides underscores the radical nature of his poem. Rather than attack war, death, and disease, he attacks the traditional pleasures (and the results) of sexuality. No Helen waits for her Paris to be lifted from the bloodshed of war and brought back to her chambers. The pleasures of sex entail hated opposites rather than the unified whole of "what is." Such pleasures seduce men's senses, make them delight in opposites, when in fact they should dismiss opposites as false divisions of a beautiful whole.

Where there is creation, sexual or otherwise, possibilities are opened

41. Nussbaum (1979b: 71) goes so far as to suggest, "The *genesis* argument thus becomes subordinate to and part of the larger argument rejecting differentiation."

42. Nussbaum (1979b) develops this point extensively to illustrate Parmenides' attack on all conventionality as a process of naming.

up; there are no limits and thus no ends, no wholeness, no *telos*. Love and desire and the sexual satisfaction that goes along with them become detestable because they mark a world divided against itself (Austin 1986:7). In a fragment that could be easily misinterpreted as yet another sign of the Greeks' misogyny, the Goddess remarks that mortals believe "Boys are on the right and girls are on the left" (DK 28B17). This most likely refers to the side of the womb on which the fetus is nourished. Rather than reading this as a comment on the sinister character of the female, as would be the current tendency, this passage shows how mortal opinion, far removed from truth, divides the world into opposites, right and left, male and female. Perhaps in the differences between the two sexes we find the most powerful example of where mortals have established oppositions that cannot exist, since "what is not" is not. In the context of the entire poem, these differences are the result of faulty mortal beliefs, worthy of scorn by the men who "are to outstrip you in intelligence" (DK 28B8.61).

As with the description of "what is," the lessons on what mortals believe bring in the epistemological problem of how one can know "what is not." The Goddess intends to show that one cannot know "what is not," and thus that the way of opinion is a route that wanders aimlessly. In contrast to the speeding chariot hastening the narrator to the chamber of the Goddess, opinion has no direction since it only pursues "what is not," and "what is not" can only lead nowhere. Since the way of opinion is characterized by its multidimensionality, the Goddess restrains her student from this road of inquiry, a road that "two-headed mortals travel wandering and knowing nothing" (DK28B6.4–5). These mortals are two-headed because they distinguish, they posit differences, and they divide the world by names. They appear to themselves to comprehend multiplicity, when in fact it cannot be comprehended. Thus, these two-headed mortals, in their helplessness with their wandering minds, are carried along, deaf and blind, lacking in judgment, thinking that to be and not to be are the same thing. For such mortals the journey that they take must always lead back on itself again, offering no end, no cessation to their inquiries (DK 28B6.9).

The Goddess announces that she will keep the youth from this aimless route of inquiry, and she enjoins him, "Do not let habit force you on the route of many experiences" (DK 28B7.3). We learn not from the experiences that depend on our faulty senses but from the revelation received from the Goddess, transmitted by Parmenides, and confirmed by our own reason. The eyes are "unseeing" and the ears echo so that they cannot hear (DK 28B7.4). "Judge (*krinai*) the much contested refutation," the Goddess says (DK 28B7.5). As in the philosophy of the other of pre-Socratics, Parmenides insists that it is to our reason that we must turn, not our senses. The deceptive senses hide the real world from us. Parmenides' poem proposes one vision of a world discovered by reason.

The philosophy of Parmenides openly and emphatically denies the multiplicity that we perceive with our senses. All, for him, is unified in a complete unchanging whole; to talk of differences is to divide what cannot be divided and to introduce "what is not" into a world where "what is not" cannot be. It is also a philosophy that, unlike Heraclitus's, does not allow for any sort of community. With its emphasis on the identity of the isolated whole, the uniform sphere, it cannot incorporate into itself the great variety we find in the sensible world. In Parmenides' thought, the fear of diversity becomes paralyzing. His own congress with the Goddess gives birth to a philosophy that denies birth. In Heraclitus's thought, the creative power of conflict and difference is celebrated; while castigating the senses, he nevertheless understood the unity of the world as derivative of its opposites. For Heraclitus, community could emerge from diversity, revel in and rise above it, rather than completely destroy it. Parmenides sees only the isolated knower of an undifferentiated wholeness, abstracted from a body that would cause him to follow aimlessly his senses in an undefined multiplicity of directions.

Parmenides' attack on the senses and their perception of motion, remains for us only in the scattered lines of the surviving fragments of his poem. It is in the vivid arguments of Zeno, though, that Parmenides' very abstract language acquires a concrete flavor, bringing home the absurdity of motion, space, and divisible bodies.[43] Zeno's fragments give us a series of famous paradoxes intended to show the impossibility of motion in space and time. There is the case of Achilles trying to overtake the slowest runner who has set out on the race course before him. The swift Achilles can never catch up. He must first traverse one-half of the distance to the other runner but before that, half of the half. Since space is infinitely divisible, the fastest man can never reach the slowest (DK 29A25, DK 29A26; see also Aristotle, *Physics* 239b14–28). Along the same lines, there is the example of the arrow that cannot reach its target and the runner in the stadium who cannot reach the finish line. The arrow must be at one place at one point in time and thus it can never move, while the athlete must run half the distance in an infinite regress. In no way do I intend to propose solutions to Zeno's puzzles. Philosophers from Plato and Aristotle on through the twentieth century have been engaged in this task. I rather wish to indicate how the puzzles themselves give expression to the princi-

43. Some read Zeno as opposed to motion (Aristotle in particular) or as against plurality (Plato's *Parmenides*) as does Owen (1975:145); these need not be understood as distinct aims.

pal themes of Parmenides' work: first, the impossibility of motion and thereby of difference and, second, the inadequacy of the senses.[44] With his puzzles, Zeno applies the *sēmata* of Parmenides to show how the physical world in which we live denies what we claim to see with our eyes. Though we see Achilles run swiftly past the slowest runner, though we see the arrow hit the target, though we see the athlete reach the finish line, we know that all these sights are impossible in a world that is not divisible. Therefore, we need to turn to the mind that knows that only "what is" can be and that it is whole, indivisible, unborn, and immobile.

Conclusion

Early Greek philosophy does not stop with Parmenides, Heraclitus, or even with Zeno's inventive puzzles. The elaborations are many, but my aim here is to set forth the challenges posed by the pre-Socratics rather than go through each philosopher's response. The problem was, for them, simply put: is the diverse world we perceive with our senses the "real world," or is there something other than what our senses perceive that gives meaning to this diversity. For the pre-Socratics, these problems are expressed largely in epistemological and physical terms. The Athenians of the fifth and fourth centuries bring these questions down from the clouds and situate them in the world of the polis. The search for the underlying unity of nature that goes beyond the senses that we find in the pre-Socratic authors reappears in the dramatists of the fifth century B.C. and the philosophers of the fourth as they search for the unity of the polis. As Victor Ehrenberg phrases it in *The Greek State:* "The state is and must be one, whereas society is a plurality. . . . This clash of opposing forces was experienced all the more violently in the Polis . . . because in the unity of the Polis they could not see that distinction between state and society" (1964:89). For Jean-Pierre Vernant, "This problem of the one and the many, implicit in social practice and expressed in some religious contexts, would be rigorously formulated only at the level of philosophical thought."[45] Yet, in Vernant's own analysis, the military formation of the phalanx becomes the first practical mechanism whereby the "whole" emerges from the parts. The earlier individual warrior who had been

---

44. Kirk, Raven, and Schofield (1983:277) question whether Zeno is appropriately called a Parmenidean since his puzzles assume the infinite divisibility of space and time to illustrate the impossibility of motion. The debate on this issue is irrelevant for my purposes, since Zeno's puzzles call into question both the sense and the possibility of a motion that depends on divisibility.

45. Vernant (1982:45 n. 10). See also Mourelatos (1965:357) who, in trying to help explain the pre-Socratic understanding of the relation between the seen and the unseen, looks in his turn to the model of the polis.

driven by his *thumos* and motivated by a pursuit of individualized renown
is transformed into a member of a unity and must learn to restrain his
individuality so as to demonstrate "a complete mastery of self, a constant
striving to submit oneself to a common discipline." Vernant sees in the
phalanx the origins of the democratic polity comprised of equals with "the
city made of the citizen, an interchangeable unit" (1982:63).

The unity of the phalanx and then the democratic polis is accomplished
by establishing the identity of apparently diverse individuals. No man is
braver or more skilled than his neighbor. Their sameness makes them interchangeable on the battlefield, in the assembly, and on the juries. The
vision of the citizens as parts of an undifferentiated, unified city comes
into conflict with the institution of the family, which is not based on the
identity of the parts but on their differences. The tragedians and the philosophers of the fifth and fourth centuries B.C. will confront the very different models of unity—one from the idea of identity that seems to find
its early home in the thought of a philosopher like Parmenides, and one
from differences among the members that is exemplified by the family.
They will warn their audiences about the dangers of striving for too much
unity.

To resolve their sense of the conflict between unity and diversity, Heraclitus and Parmenides had to turn to the *logos* as superior to the senses.
Trying to organize their world, the philosophers had often to deny their
senses; thus, while Parmenides saw motion, his mind told him objects
could not move since all motion entails "what is not." Heraclitus felt both
hot and cold, but his mind told him that they were one, and while Zeno
saw Achilles win the race, his mind told him that this could never happen.
In the conflict between the mind and the senses, the mind was declared
the winner; what was unseen and what was unified claimed victory over
diversity and the observed. It is on the Attic stage that we observe the
tragic consequences that arise when this victory, which took place on the
theoretical level in the writings of Heraclitus and Parmenides and Zeno, is
translated to the lives of men and women as political creatures. The tragedians take the epistemological victory of the mind that was articulated
by the pre-Socratics and show its consequences for the city. By setting
these views of reality into the context of the lives of men and women
inhabiting the political world, they uncover for us the inadequacy of a
devotion to an unseen unity, dependent on the *logos,* that denies the diversity that the senses perceive. The playwrights make us aware of the alternative claims of the senses that particularize rather than universalize. We
cannot claim in any sense that the Greek playwrights spent their spare time
poring over the fragments of the pre-Socratics as we have just done—as
much as we might like to imagine such a scene. Rather, the problems

posed by the pre-Socratics were the same ones that the playwrights confronted as they viewed men and women in the city, facing the problem of what defined the unity of the polis and how and whether it could incorporate differences. Heraclitus and Parmenides had unified epistemologically the external world by subordinating it to the mind. The playwrights in their turn show us the dangers of that subordination that unifies through the reason while discarding the differences that the senses perceive. It is then to the ancient tragedians that we turn in the next chapter.

3 Women and the Tragic Denial of Difference: Three Versions

Though a funeral oration, Pericles' speech at the end of the first year of the Peloponnesian war, as recorded by Thucydides, talks mostly of the city, little of the dead men, and not at all of their bodies (Loraux 1986:3). Rather than graves for their corpses, those who perished will live on in the undying memories and hearts of men throughout the world (Thucydides 2.43.2–3). At the end of his speech, Pericles addresses the families of the deceased warriors, urging the sons and younger brothers to emulate those who died for the city and urging the mothers to bear more children for the army of the city. He then offers his notorious advice to the women of Athens, telling them that she who is least spoken of, whether for praise or for blame, is she who has least fallen below her nature (Thucydides 2.45.2). Stay out of public life, out of public consciousness, he says to the women grieving for their lost sons and lost husbands. Indeed, Thucydides does banish women from his *History* as we read on of men's words and men's actions, but not of women. Pericles' injunction (via Thucydides) that the Athenian women disappear from male consciousness was not followed, however, by the playwrights whose productions (with only *Philoctetes* as an exception among extant plays) all place representations of the female powerfully before their audiences. Whether for praise or for blame, the female is spoken of often on the theatrical stage.[1]

1. This chapter relies heavily on earlier essays. See, in particular, Saxonhouse (1986a; 1986b).

The actual life of citizen women in Athens of the fifth century B.C. was a sheltered one, little resembling the flamboyant picture Aristophanes offered us in his *Ecclesiazusae*. Yet, the portrayal of women and the concept of the female in the works of the Athenian playwrights and philosophers is far more complex and sophisticated than the facts of women's daily lives or the words of Pericles might lead us to believe.[2] The city of adult males saw on stage the powerful portrayal of women—women whose existence, as the playwrights reflected on the human condition, could not be denied as curtly as Pericles had chosen to do in his funeral oration. Reflecting critically on the world in which they lived, the Athenian playwrights questioned for their audiences the structure of the Athenian polis: the focus on power and its pursuit, the centrality of rationality and its efficacy, and the drive towards uniformity rather than multiplicity, all of which tried to move the city towards an unrealizable unity. Parmenides subjected the world to an undifferentiated unity accessible only to the human mind but not to our senses. The political leaders who are portrayed on the ancient stage similarly attempt to ensure unity through the denial of difference.

Appeals within the language of the plays to ancient stories of a city's founding often helped to give expression to the unified vision of the city. The focus back to a particular point in time when all was a unified whole could undermine the threat of current observed multiplicity. In particular, in two of the plays that I shall discuss in this chapter, autochthony, birth from the earth, provided the mythical grounding for unity and the exclusion of that which is other—especially women. Autochthony myths are central to the founding of both the Thebes of Laius, Oedipus, Creon, Eteocles, and Polyneices, Antigone and Ismene, and to the Athens that was home to the audience watching these plays. According to the Theban tale, Cadmus kills the dragon of Ares, and upon the advice of Athene, sows the dragon's teeth in the land that is to become Thebes, thus acting to appropriate that land for the city. From these teeth grow a crop of helmeted, armed warriors, who immediately set upon one another in fratricidal battle. The five survivors of this conflict, the Spartoi ("those who have been sown"), become the ancestors of Thebes' noble houses. Claims to nobility and to Theban land found their origin in their autochthonous birth. Athens likewise had a series of autochthonous characters inhabiting the myths of its origins. The exact relationship between them all is not now entirely clear, if it ever was, but the early kings Cecrops, Erichthonius, and Erechtheus (which may be just another name for Erichthonius) all either have the shape of snakes for the lower part of their bodies or are associated with snakes, indications that they arose from the earth. A fuller discussion

2. Many scholars have marveled in one fashion or another at this disjunction: Gomme (1937); Shaw (1975); Pomeroy (1975: chap. 6); Foley (1981: 133).

of the theoretical significance of autochthony will introduce chapter 5,[3] but here we might note that the myth of autochthony unites the city. The myth may create a false unity, but it never the less distinguishes or separates out one city from the varied external world of chaos. Unifying and ordering, autochthony establishes origins in time and place.[4] However, as a founding myth, autochthony also demands the exclusion of the human female from the origins of the city. The city and its public space is the realm of male warriors or male rulers who have sprung from the earth. These men are not to be divided by their bonds to separate mothers or to separate wives, and they are not to be returned to a private realm that may raise questions about the universality of polis and its goals. The city in its idealized and mythologized origins is peopled from a single source—the earth—and is not dependent on the diversity entailed in heterosexual creation.

The tragedians, looking at the variety of human actions and human passions in the city and not at a Parmenidean world of "what is," saw that the denial of difference through myths of autochthony or through speech, as we will see in our discussion of *Antigone,* entailed violence and, in particular, engendered sterility. The tragic heroes aim at a political simplification that parallels the epistemological simplification pursued by the pre-Socratics. The action on the Attic stage, however, makes evident the impossibility of a polity as unified and complete as the Parmenidean One. Tragic endings occur as the tragic heroes, in their search for the perfection of a unified, ordered whole, are themselves never complete. Mired in a world of multiplicity and opposites, the heroes aim for an unattainable rational and social simplicity.

To raise these questions about order, unity, power, and rationality, the playwrights often turned to the female, for in her difference from the male she revealed a diversity in nature that threatened the physical order and rational control at which the polis aimed.[5] When confronted with the

---

3. All discussions of autochthony must, of course, go back to Lévi-Strauss's original analysis of the Oedipus myth as providing "a kind of logical tool which relates the original problem—born from one or born from two?—to the derivative problem: born from different or born from same?" (1967:212). My aim is to draw out the political implications of this myth, and here Loraux's work (1979) has been invaluable. For a study of Lévi-Strauss's analysis in relation to the Erichthonius myth, see Peradotto (1977).

4. Loraux (1979:4) points out "l'éfficacité unifrante" of the autochthony myth as opposed to the story of Theseus's *Synoikism.*

5. Foley (1981) has a fine review of the work done up until the publication of her book on women in ancient tragedy. She includes as well an interesting discussion of the methodological issues that must be considered in the study of women in ancient tragedy. Though I approach the topic from quite a different perspective, I have great sympathy for the view expressed by Lefkowitz (1986:39–40): "I would suggest that they [Greek men] be regarded as pioneers in recognising and describing with sympathy both the life and the central importance to their society of women . . . male poets did not hesitate to allow them to make

female, the leaders must face the problem of difference and complexity for she, by introducing human reproduction, underscores the male's dependence upon that which is other. The female is not simply another word for "the city" as *chthōn* or *gē* (the land or the earth) often are. In their distinctiveness, women are not so easily assimilated into the wholeness of the city. The poets introduce the female as a constantfjreminder ofthe diversity out of which the world was made and as a constant warning against the attempt to see the world as a uniform whole and, therefore, subject to simple answers and rational control.[6] The female revealed the inability of human courage and human intelligence—often expressed through political action—to dominate the natural world through the denial of variability. He who tried to dominate may have gained stature as the hero, but he was the tragic hero since such attempts at power and at the imposition of simplicity brought only disaster. The female shows the male leader that there is something other than the abstract city created at some autochthonous moment and kept alive by the mind and by speech.

In this chapter I will look at three plays from the corpus of ancient tragedy. Though the selection of which plays to study is not entirely random, I do think that the themes I find in these plays emerge as well in many of the other tragedies. Aeschylus's *Seven against Thebes,* Sophocles' *Antigone,* and Euripides' *Ion* form the basis of the following analysis.[7] All three plays portray men who wish to deny their dependence on women and who wish to build a political order where women are not only, as Pericles desired, closeted away from view, but missing and unnecessary

---

articulate and poignant observations about the futility of all that their men had prized so highly. They assume an important role in drama because they are . . . natural victims, and thus are able to represent the human condition, man's true powerlessness before the gods." Much of the criticism of women as portrayed in ancient tragedy has focused on women as the destroyers of civilization, or at least as threats to civilization. This is true especially with regard to discussions of the *Oresteia*. For the most powerful and effective statement of this view, see Zeitlin (1978); also Pomeroy (1975:99). I address these interpretations in Saxonhouse (1984a). The issue, though, is why women have this role and, while claims of misogyny may appeal to our feminist sensibilities, they may not be constructive intellectually. Rather, by understanding the playwrights' sympathy for the incorporation of diversity, we get, I believe, a richer sense of their concern with the limits of unity.

6. Gellrich (1988) writes a thoroughly provocative study of the attempt by literary critics over the ages to impose on Greek drama and on the Aristotelian analysis of tragedy theories that emphasize the resolution of conflict. As she notes in her introduction (8), "The approach of literary theoreticians to such enigmas in tragedy, to indeterminacies that resist assumptions of unity, order, and coherence, is broadly speaking the subject of this book." See, e.g., p. 69.

7. Aeschylus's *Suppliants,* Sophocles' *Oedipus at Colonus,* and Euripides' *Bacchae* are other tragedies that could have formed the basis of the analysis of this chapter—and will provide the bases for future analyses along these lines.

because of the threat that they pose as that which is other. The play-wrights, though, rather than approving of this dismissal, show us the in-adequacies of these attempts to oversimplify the political world. I do not read the plays as justifications of the particular political arrangements that may have existed in Athens of the fifth century B.C., nor as warnings about the threats that women pose to the male order. The plays do offer analyses of the structure of the city and reveal the tension-laden relations between its parts. As poet, the playwright serves as the city's teacher—not its speechwriter.[8]

Aeschylus's Seven against Thebes

Seven against Thebes is the conclusion to Aeschylus's version of the Oedi-pus trilogy.[9] The preceding two plays do not survive. We do know, how-ever, that the action of the earlier plays included Oedipus's curse on his two sons, Eteocles and Polyneices. The precise nature of the curse and the reasons for it as presented by Aeschylus remain unclear for us reading but one part of the three-play sequence.The action of the play is straightfor-ward. A hostile force from Argos besieges Thebes. Polyneices has joined the Argives and is the moving force behind their attack from without, while Eteocles leads the Thebans in their defence of the city. Eteocles presents himself as the calm leader of the besieged city while a chorus of terrified townswomen sing of their panic, thereby earning the reproaches of a manly and brave Eteocles. He fears that the disordered ravings of the women will instill fear among the soldiers. The central section of the play presents the report of the Theban spy who tells of the warriors (and their shields), those men who have been assigned to lead the attack at each of Thebes' seven gates. To each gate Eteocles then assigns the Theban war-rior most suited to defend against the particular attacker. At the seventh gate stands Polyneices, and it is to this gate that Eteocles assigns himself—certain that he will there fulfill the curse his father had called down upon his sons. The messenger returns to report the mutual fratricide. The play concludes as Antigone and her sister Ismene mourn the death of their brothers and react to the decree announced by the city council that Eteocles is to be given full burial rites, while Polyneices' body is to be cast unburied outside the city.[10]

8. For further development of this point, see Euben (1986:21–31). Gellrich (1988:68) emphasizes a similar role with somewhat different language: "[T]ragedy explores the forces that fragment identity and make moral decidability problematic; its orientation toward the social context is interrogative and even adversarial, for it holds us in the grip of conflicts that various mechanisms of culture aim to neutralize and dissipate."

9. The ideas in this section owe much to various articles and books on Aeschylus's *Seven*. Among those consulted that significantly influenced my thinking are Bacon (1964); Benar-dete (1967); Orwin (1980); and Winnington-Ingram (1983).

10. Much debate centers around the authenticity of this final section. I treat it as authen-

As with all Greek tragedies, *Seven against Thebes* is embedded in a series of myths that lie behind the action, but which surface in the poetic rendering of that action and help to draw out the central themes of the action. In particular, it is the myth of autochthony, as noted above, that gives meaning to the action of this play. It is the earth as mother that the Thebans defend from the Argive host, not the human females who live within the walls of the city.[11] In the very first word of the play, Eteocles recalls his earthborn ancestor, Cadmus. *Kadmou politai*, he addresses those standing on stage,[12] and shortly thereafter speaks of the city of "Cadmeians" (9).[13] Eteocles looks towards the origins of his city that exclude the female, thereby denying human motherhood.[14] In denying his own origins, Eteocles envisions the perfection of a city without women, but it is a perfection that both nature and the playwright deny him.

After reminding the audience of the autochthonous ancestry of the city, Eteocles portrays himself as a captain of a ship "guiding the tiller" (2–3). He is, as Vernant has called him, "the *homo politicus*, as conceived by the Greeks of the fifth century," embodying "all the virtues of moderation, reflection, and self-control that go to make up the statesman" (1988b: 35–36). As such, he urges the defence of the city and the gods of the land,

---

tic, convinced by the thematic connections with the earlier parts of the play and by such arguments as those put forward by Orwin (1980).

11. As Thalmann (1978:46–47) notes with regard to the mother of Eteocles and Polyneices, "Aeschylus seems to have kept her anonymous deliberately to maintain the ambiguity between the physical mother of both Oedipus and his sons and the earth mother." Zeitlin (1982:29–36) develops the significance of the autochthony theme in this play and its relation to the incest that characterizes Oedipus's family.

12. Who are these citizens? Considering his later expressions of misogyny, it is unlikely that Eteocles is speaking to a female chorus on stage. Vidal-Naquet (1988:278–79) raises the possibility that the "citizens" are Athenians and that Thebes is simply "a mask" for Athens, but he rejects this in favor of the proposal that there must be extras on the stage. See also Hecht and Bacon (1973:21); Hutchinson (1985:41).

13. Hecht and Bacon (1973:72) note that any mention of Thebes is absent from the play. Rather, the city is described by reference to this autochthonous founder. They explain the absence of "Thebes" by Aeschylus's intention to keep the action in the distant past. Hutchinson (1985:42) finds nothing "significant nor remarkable" in the use of Cadmeians than Thebans. Orwin (1980) sees in the use of Cadmeians Aeschylus's undermi autochthony theme because Cadmus calls to mind his marriage to Harmon erosexual generation, rather than birth from a single mother for the cit

14. This denial in psychoanalytic interpretations of the play m incestuous marriage of Jocasta and Oedipus. See Caldwell (1 should, however, remain aware of the problematic nature tions of ancient plays. For valuable warnings abor Ingram (1983:27) who, without eschewing the reminds us that "words may be more important (1988:277), who insists that Eteocles "is not 'a huma. He is a figure in Greek tragedy."

equating the city with the earth, the beloved mother who nourishes her offspring, so that defence of one is the defence of the other.

> So the honor of this mothering land may not be
> extinguished
> either for her children whom she brought forth and
> cherished,
> or for herself, their parent and devoted nurse.
> For when you were infants on all fours,
> dandled upon her nourishing hills and valleys,
> she welcomed the familiar burdens of child-rearing,
> tended you, brought you up, so that
> you would be filial keepers of her house,
> bearers of shields, and fit
> for such need a moment as this.
>
> (16–20)[15]

As Nussbaum has phrased it, Eteocles extends "to the entire population a legend told of a few of the earliest occupants" (1986:39). He does not see the women who will make up the chorus as the mothers who themselves need to be defended. Defence of the city is not for the sake of the women within the walls, but for the land. Using words for land or earth (*chthōn* and *gē*) throughout his speeches, Eteocles thus replaces the human female as he conceptualizes a city without families. Eteocles' focus on the preservation of the city causes him to abstract from the variety of human relations that comprise the city. He understands only the citizens' (and here we need to emphasize only the male citizens') relationship to the city, not the complex set of relationships to others, such as those who may be members of one's own family.[16]

Into Eteocles' vision of male exclusiveness, male courage, and male calm intrude the Theban women of the chorus: "I shriek great fearful pains" (78). Panicked, they sing of the frightening noises of an approaching army:

> Slamming, clashing of steel, hoof-stomping and clubbing
> increase, possess and deafen our land.
> They rumble and thunder
> like a swollen, rock-dashed, hillside torrent.
>
> (83–86)

15. I have used here the translation by Hecht and Bacon (1973:22) but have retained the ne numbers of Hutchinson's edition of Aeschylus (1985). Subsequent extended quotations l be from this translation. Brief translations will be my own.

One needs to contrast here Book 6 of the *Iliad* and the encounter between Hector e female members of his family, especially his mother and his wife. Arthur's essay uggests the basis of this changed response by noting the change in the political

The women beseech the gods to prevent the violence raging outside the city's walls from entering the city and bringing with it slavery for themselves. The women's screams and their disorderly movements call forth from Eteocles one of the most famous misogynist speeches from ancient tragedy. He had just presented himself as the calm captain with a firm hand upon the tiller who had urged his male citizens not to give into panic (34–35). *Thremmata,* he calls the women, vile things (181). They endanger the city with their disordered screams.[17] As the women had complained about the noises of the approaching army, Eteocles now uses vivid verbs to describe the wailings of the female chorus, howling like dogs, hateful to those who practice moderation (186). Then he implores, "Neither in evil times nor in dear prosperity, may I be co-living in the same house with (*xunoikos*) the race of women" (187–88).[18] Women filled with terror, as are the ones before him, cause evil to the household and to the city (191). Eteocles does not acknowledge that without this "evil" there would be neither household nor city. The age of earthborn men is past, despite his invocations and his dreams. If the city is to survive, if the household is to survive, then he must live with the race of women. But Eteocles sees the female only as a danger, because she alerts men to what is other than the city or the earth out of which he claims the city grows.

Eteocles' reaction to the women is to deny them a place in the city, to deny that there is anything other than the city. The city is the whole of Eteocles' existence.[19] It would be better if only the city could do without women, if creativity could again come from the earth to which Eteocles is willing to devote himself. "O Zeus, what a race of woman have you bestowed" (256). The women respond: "A wretched race, just like men whose city is captured" (257). Unlike Eteocles, who wishes to exclude women, these women recognize that, despite the differences between the male and the female, they are united with the men by a common concern for the city. Eteocles' vision is of a city that is one, rather than divided between male and female.[20] The one time Eteocles does ask the women to

structure from Homeric times to the fifth-century polis, in particular the increasing centrality of the polis in a man's consciousness of who he is.

17. Bacon (1964) develops the theme that the women create a danger within the city walls, parallel to the danger posed by the invading army outside the walls.

18. Zeitlin (1982:19) offers a generous reading of these lines: "Yet by this act of negation, Eteocles would also seem to counter Laios' original violation of the injunction against begetting progeny."

19. With regard to Eteocles' attention to the city, Winnington-Ingram (1983:50 n. 89) comments, "Without attaching undue significance to such statistics . . . [I] note that . . . [this is] . . . a play in which *polis, polites* and other words of this same root, occur on the average of every 15 or 16 lines."

20. Vidal-Naquet (1988:280–81) comments, "It is the males, the issue of mother earth—and the males alone—who defend the mother earth." See also Bacon (1964:30).

participate in the defence of the city, he asks them to offer a sacred *ololugmos*, a well-minded paean to give courage to their *philoi*, their loved ones or their family, thereby loosening the fear of battle (268–70). The *ololugmos* he asks them to make, however, is specifically a male war cry, one not normally offered by women.[21] In other words, the only way that the female will be useful to the city is through this transformation into men or by taking on the roles of men. Insofar as they are women, Eteocles can only acknowledge them to exclude them.

Much of the first third of the play involves the confrontation between the fearful females and Eteocles' masculine rejection of their fears.[22] Often this attempt to exclude the female entails the insistence on silence, that is, disappearance. As with Pericles' women, the women of Thebes are not to enter the realm of public discourse either for praise or for blame. They are not to speak, for when they do speak, when they do use *logos*, they talk of what is other than the city and its land; they talk of lives as women with bodies that can be violated by the deeds of foreign invaders. In contrast to the silence Eteocles demands of the women, he himself asserts, in the first line of the play, "It is necessary to speak. (*Chrē legein*)." But he, as one who controls the affairs of the ship of state, speaks only for the men. At the end of his own speech asserting that he will keep the Cadmean land safe against slavery, Eteocles states, "I hope to speak of what is the common concern (*xuna*)" (76). This precedes by one line the entrance of the women—those whom he excludes from speech and from a common interest in the city. Threatening destruction by public stoning for anyone, "male or female or whatever is in between" (197) who does not listen to his authority, he warns that those things "without"(*taxōthen*) are of concern to men: "Let women not participate in public deliberations (*mē gunē bouleuetō*)" (200). He continues: "Being within (*endon ousa*) do not cause any harm: Do you hear or not—or do I speak to one who is deaf?" (201–02). Despite such warnings, the women continue to express their fear and Eteocles continues to insist "Is it not a concern of mine to deliberate about these things? . . . will you not be silent?" (248–52), until finally he bursts out, "O wretched one, silence, do not frighten your loved ones" (262). The women at last respond: "I am silent: With the others I shall obey the doom that awaits us" (263). These words that affirm their

21. Vidal-Naquet (1988:281); Hutchinson (1985:87): "By stressing this correspondence, Eteocles separates the cry from the women's wild ululation."

22. Obviously, I have little sympathy with interpretations such as that of Hutchinson concerning lines 182–286 (1985:73): "This scene might seem at first to treat with disproportionate fullness a narrow subject unimportant to the story . . . the situation, the submission of the chorus, and the structure of the sections of dialogue ensure that we should feel Eteocles to be essentially in the right."

silence, Eteocles tells them, he prefers to their earlier words (264). Eteocles, the man with his hand upon the tiller, has and uses *logos* while the
women, whose shrill wailings, far from the rational *logos* of the male
leader, spread fear throughout the city, must learn silence.[23] Eteocles as
leader speaks using his language to create order by dismissing the feminine
passions.

There is nothing unusual in Eteocles' insistence that the women be removed from public debate about public affairs. We see this in Pericles'
speech, and we see it in the laughter that can be evoked by the transgression of such a norm.[24] Aeschylus does not allow a complacent acceptance
of this norm, however, and the exclusion perpetrated by Eteocles comes
to take on a darker meaning in the play. The female chorus cannot sustain
the male war cry with which they begin their song after Eteocles' departure. Rather, they evoke the pain that the women will suffer when the
enemy invade not just the land that is mother to the male warriors of
Eteocles, but the actual homes where the women who are also mothers
and daughters of those warriors live.

> [T]he pale, unfamilied girl becomes the whore
> and trophy of her captor, forced to spread
> for the sweating soldier, triumphant, hate-inflamed.
> Perhaps a dark deliverance may occur
> > in that foul bridal, the untamed
> violence of that battle-grounded bed.
> > > And there may come to her
> > > a species of relief,
> an end of tidal groans, weeping, and grief.

> (363–68)

Eteocles had sought to exclude from his execution of the war any sensibilities about the women's suffering. The chorus reminds us here that
more is being defended than the abstract city and the land over which
Eteocles rules.

During the central part of the play, the spy sent off to the Argive camp
returns and describes for Eteocles each one of the Argive warriors who
have been assigned to the seven gates of Thebes. Eteocles, continuing to
captain the ship of state (652), in turn sends a Theban hero to defend each
gate, on occasion recalling his earthborn origins or his bonds to his
mother earth. The first warrior sent to meet the arrogant, violent Tydeus

23. One can contrast here effectively the central scene of the play where the spy, a male member of the city and its forces of defence, repeatedly uses forms of *legō* in response to Eteocles'
requests that he speak, beginning with *legoimi* at 375; also 451, 458, 526, 568, 632, etc.
24. See further Vidal-Naquet (1988:280).

is Melanippos. He "is a thorough son of this land / a shoot sent up from the seed of the dragon's teeth / sown by Cadmus and by Ares spared, / therefore genuinely of our soil (*egchōrios*)" (412–13).[25] He is one who can hold off the hostile spear from "the mother who bore him (*tekousei mētri*)" (416). Eteocles literally means here the mother earth. Megareus, sent to face the Argive Eteoclos, is the "seed of Creon, of the race of the Spartoi" (474). If he dies, he will pay back the nourishment of the earth (*tropheia chthoni*) (477). The messenger evokes the same images. Quoting the Argive priest, Amphiaraos, who foresees the tragedy awaiting all the participants in this conflict, asks of Polyneices, "What kind of Justice quenches the spring of the mother and the land of your father by your eager sword?" (584–85). Meanwhile, they all ignore the women who nourished the young, who live in the city, and who comprise the chorus.

Upon learning that Polyneices stands at the seventh gate of Thebes, Eteocles resolves to meet him, setting the stage for their mutual destruction. With the earth as the mother, Eteocles can avoid the complexity of the multiple ties of relationships that exist apart from the city-bonds. Polyneices attacks the land, the mother-city. He thus stands at the seventh gate as a ruler of hateful foreigners, as an enemy and, Eteocles notes almost incidentally in this litany of negative phrases, as a brother: "Is anything else more just / ruler against ruler, brother against brother, hated one against hated one?" (673–75).[26] Nurture in a common womb is ignored despite the impious implications of such negation in Greek thought. The chorus of women reacts strongly to this prospective killing of brother by brother. Exalting the ties of kinship in response to Eteocles' call for his armor, they address him as "Son of Oedipus" (677) and warn, "This death, self-killing (*autoktonos*) in this way, for the two men of common blood (*androin homaimoin*), there is no old age (*geras*) for such pollution" (681–82). The language is suggestive: there is no old age, that is, the pollution is always present; there is no growth, no generation, for this pollution is the denial of generation. The chorus reaffirms the focus on kinship ties, ties that may be in opposition to those created by the city. The denial of women earlier in the play was part of Eteocles' exclusive focus on the bonds of the city, where all come autochthonously from the earth as mother and all are governed by his calm reasoning. The chorus suggests how the claims of autochthony can lead in Eteocles' case to the impieties of "*autoktony*," self-killing, in the slaying of his brother.

25. Zeitlin (1982:62) discusses the particular appropriateness of sending an autochthonous hero against Tydeus, whose shield carries the image of the heavens.

26. Nussbaum (1986:38), commenting on these lines, phrases it well: "[T]he category of brother does not seem to work the way the other two do, towards justifying Eteocles' decision."

Aware of the impiety, of the killing that is not allowed (*ou themiston*) (694), the women speak to him as if he were a son, *teknon* (686),[27] urging him to eschew the madness that he previously had condemned in them. As Vidal-Naquet and others have noted, a change does occur after Eteocles realizes that the curse of his father shall be fulfilled.[28] Previously, he had been able to abstract without ambiguity or tension from the issues of family; thus, he had been able to ban the women from public discourse. The powerful curse of Oedipus and its fulfillment forcefully recall to Eteocles his human origins from a human female and a human male. He is not, and cannot be, a child of the city. Connections with other human beings are not simply defined in terms of who is a citizen of which city or, as it shall be neatly phrased when Polemarchus engages in discourse with Socrates, who is friend and who is foe. Those connections are defined also in terms of who is one's father and who is one's mother. This realization brings on the madness of Eteocles, the transformation from the *logos* of the political man to the passions previously associated with the female and the family. It is the women who now urge him to cast off the rule of "evil desire" (*kakou . . . erōtos*) (687–88). It is the women who urge calm and who ask to be obeyed (*peithou gunaixi*) (712). The earlier commands for silence and for female withdrawal are replaced as Eteocles allows the women to speak, albeit briefly (*oude chrē makran*) (713). They enjoin him: "Do not go to the Seventh Gate," and they repeat the warning about shedding the blood of his brother (714). But the words, now allowed to women, have lost all efficacy. "You with speech (*logoi*) do not blunt the edge of the sharpened spear," he tells them (715). Recognizing the evils (*kaka*) given by the gods, he nevertheless refuses to flee (719).[29]

Thus the chorus sing again of the self-killing (*autoktonos*) death that will occur when the brothers meet (734), and the messenger who returns to report the deaths repeats this theme of self-killing (805). The chorus sees the bond between the brothers, but Eteocles, as leader of his city, cannot allow such ties to muddy the clear distinctions between friend and

27. Hutchinson (1985:155) notes that in the *parados* the women had described themselves as *parthenoi* (110, 171), young maidens. The transformation in Eteocles evokes a matched transformation in the chorus.

28. Zeitlin (1982:28) sees neither a change in Eteocles nor a tragic ending. The conflict and the mutual killing in her analysis are the necessary solution to and conclusion of the curse: "[T]he city can now be saved again only by the reciprocal destruction of the brothers, the last of the line of Laios, in order to expel from Thebes the subversive principle of 'no difference.'" See also, however, p. 189.

29. Winnington-Ingram (1983:52) sees Eteocles as caught between two worlds—the "new" polis that requires the selfless devotion of its citizens and the *genos*, "an archaic relic." "He dies as a member of a doomed and disastrous family, despairing of his race."

foe. The simplicity of the definitions of the city cannot, for him, be undermined by the diversity of natural ties. The anguish of the play arises as Eteocles realizes, with the acknowledgment of the completion of his father's curse, the evils in which he must now participate and the inadequacies of an earlier understanding of the nature of the city that could pretend completion without females and without family. The gods, the curse, the women, all remind him that this vision of political unity brings about its own destruction, just as the excessive unity in the family of Laius destroyed that family.[30]

The city has been saved, the messenger reports. The women (the children nourished by the mother, who he calls *paides mēterōn tethrammenai*) (792) need fear no longer the slavery they had envisioned in the first choral ode. The chorus, not knowing whether to rejoice at the salvation of their city or lament the death of the two brothers cursed by their father, acknowledge in their song the multiple relationships that Eteocles and Polyneices had tried to keep at a distance. The appearance of Antigone and Ismene remind the audience that the elimination of the family for the sake of the survival of the city is not possible. The sisters enter to mourn the deaths of their brothers; they describe the common sufferings of the family of Oedipus, this closest of all families. The unity that Antigone and Ismene affirm in their mournful song, however, is torn asunder at the final appearance of the messenger, who now reports the decree that will impose distinctions between the brothers. He says, "It is necessary for me to proceed to announce what has seemed best and was approved by the council of this city of Cadmus" (1005–06). This is the formal language of the assembly. They have met and they have spoken. "It was decreed," the messenger reports, "to bury Eteocles for his loyalty to the land (*chthōn*) with the beloved tomb of earth (*gēs*)" (1008). The city also passed a decree concerning the corpse of Polyneices: it is to be thrown outside the city's walls, where, unburied, it will be fodder for the birds and dogs. This is the punishment for he who warred against the Cadmeian land (*chthōn*). Through their speech in the assembly (1020, 1025), the men of the Cadmean city have separated the brothers.

Antigone rejects this artificial distinction and announces (*legō*)(1026) that if no one else is willing to bury Polyneices, she herself will bury him, accepting whatever risk may come from her burying her own brother (1026–29). She is not ashamed to disregard the speech of the city, for she is concerned with the community, the wondrous and dreadful community (*deinon to koinon*) (1031) that exists between herself and her brother, who had grown in the self-same womb, child of the same suffering mother and

---

30. For a study of the family as too close, too unified, in the story of Oedipus, see, e.g., Vernant (1988c: 136–37) and Segal (1981: 217–24).

ill-starred father. "My soul willingly shares unwillingly in these evils" (1033). In defiance of the city's sense of its own potency, she says, "Let it be decreed by no one (*mē dokēsatō tini*)that hollow-bellied wolves will eat his corpse" (1035–36). Against those man-made decrees she stands as a woman: "I, although I am a woman, shall devise this" (1038). When the messenger warns that the city will be forced in these things, Antigone ignores, even mocks, his threats, and in her turn orders that he limit his speech (*mē makrēgorei*) (1053). It is speech on which the city is based. She acts on the basis of bonds of kinship, not the bonds created by the words of assemblies.

The chorus of Theban women watching the interchange between Antigone and the messenger is torn in two directions, capturing the tensions inherent in the preceding action of the play. Half the chorus denies the decree and sides with Antigone. They acknowledge the inadequacy of the justice decreed by men. It has no consistency over time. "The justice that the city praises is sometimes one thing, sometimes another" (1070–71). Dependent on the speech of men that Eteocles so praised, the justice of the city yields, for half the chorus, to the universal anguish felt by those grieving for their dead. The other half of the chorus bends to the city's decree, accepting the unity between justice and the speech of the city, acknowledging the distinction between brothers that the city can create, and thereby honoring the man who most of all kept the city from capsizing amidst the stormy waves that assaulted it.

The play leaves us with no resolution.[31] Although Thebes still stands, the brothers are dead and the women are divided. Eteocles, fulfilling the curse of Oedipus, pollutes the city by shedding his brother's blood. Eteocles' misogyny, based on his rejection of what is other, of what turns attention away from the orderly unity of the city, had been necessary for him to face his brother in battle and to act in the interests of the city, though not in the interests of piety. After his death, the city, now dependent on its own reason in its assembly, continues to deny the diversity within the city. The city defines friend and enemy and, like Eteocles, it ignores the "wondrous and dreadful community" of the family within that makes complex a world that it wishes to be simple. The tragedy thus continues.

Sophocles' Antigone

The women in *Seven against Thebes* feared slavery, they feared for the city threatened with destruction, and they feared for the young girl raped by a foreign soldier. They see the world around them as multifarious, and in

31. Zeitlin (1982: 19), rejecting the authenticity of the final scene, does see the resolution in the "perfect coincidence of oracle and curse" as the end recalls the beginning and Thebes remains.

their wailings they express concern for the safety of both the city and the family. In Sophocles' *Antigone,* we meet a woman who will yield nothing to the city,[32] who, like her male antagonist, prefers to see the world as uniform, lacking in complexity.[33] Those willing to accept a world marked by complexity, by the tensions inherent in any action, are summarily dismissed as disloyal by both main characters. This unifocal perspective gives both Creon and Antigone a strength and a clear sense of direction; they remain unconcerned with, and mostly scornful of, what is other, of what makes the world multiple rather than one.[34] For Antigone there is the family that has died; for Creon there is only the polis that has survived. In both instances, this power-giving firmness of a uniform vision leads to death; for Antigone, it leads to her own death, and for Creon, it leads to the death of his son and his wife. It is in the "minor" characters in this tragedy that we find those who do not accept a world that is uniform and simple, who deny that our social and political and religious lives can be comprehended by an all-encompassing worldview that prescribes good and proscribes bad. The minor characters do not demonstrate the force of character we so often associate with heroic stature,[35] but they do underscore the inadequacy of those who may seem to be secure in their ability to encompass the variety of human experience into precise rules.

The story of *Antigone* is so familiar that I need not repeat it here, except to note that Sophocles' play begins where *Seven against Thebes* leaves off and that, in Sophocles' version, it is not the Council of Elders that decrees that the corpse of Polyneices shall remain unburied. It is Creon, brother to Jocasta and uncle to Oedipus's children, who prohibits the burial. Thus, the decision to leave the corpse to the elements and to the wild animals is that of one man, just as the attempt to bury the corpse and give it the appropriate funeral rites is the choice of one woman. Aeschylus's chorus

32. Lane and Lane (1986), rejecting most of the writing about Antigone as "the literary equivalent of the political practice of blaming the victim" (163), conclude that Antigone is the "epitome of responsible citizenship" (182). It may be that in her actions she illustrates what the city should have done to save itself, but it is unclear that Antigone is acting from motives even remotely political.

33. Amidst the huge bibliography on Sophocles' *Antigone,* I have found most helpful Knox (1964); Benardete (1974–1975); Nussbaum (1986:51–82); and Gellrich (1988: 44–71). Note that references to Benardete's article will be according to the system of paragraph numbers that he employs throughout his three articles.

34. Benardete (1974–1975:8.6 n. 18), commenting on the originality of Sophocles' version of the Antigone story, makes the point that "Sophocles' invention consists in unsexing Antigone and giving her attributes of Aeschylus' Eteocles."

35. Consider Gellrich's (1988:255–65) cogent presentation of the inadequacies of contemporary interpretations of the tragic hero in ancient tragedy as more indebted to Kantian philosophy than true to the fifth-century dramatists' presentation of "an irreducible ambivalence, or more accurately, multivalence" (263).

of women had been divided in its response to the decree prohibiting burial. Sophocles' chorus of townsmen wavers uncertainly, usually persuaded by the last speaker they have heard.

Near the beginning of *Antigone,* there is the justly famous choral ode in which the townsmen of Thebes sing about the "wonders" (as it is usually translated) of man (or the less mellifluous "human being," since the Greek here is *anthropos*) (332–33). The translation "wonders" (*deina*) does not, however, capture the ambiguity of the term *deinos,* a word that entails more terror than wonder. The guard afraid to report the burial he and his companions were to prevent explains his long introductory discourse: "*Ta deina* create much delay" (243). He hardly means *ta deina* in a positive way. Antigone, condemned to isolation in a cave outside the city, says later in the tragedy, "I seemed to Creon to err (*hamartanein*) and to dare *ta deina*" (914–15). We can hardly say that Creon admired Antigone's deeds, daring or otherwise. The uses of this word throughout the tragedy remind us that the term generally suggests trepidation rather than admiration,[36] but it is precisely this ambiguity that captures the tragedy of this play.

At the beginning of the play, the chorus can sing joyously of these wonders; by the end, they resign themselves to a world controlled by the gods to whom men must learn to submit themselves. In the final lines of the play, they intone, "To have wisdom (*to phronein*) is by far the most important part of happiness, and it is necessary not to befoul the things that concern the gods" (1348–50). In the early optimistic phase of the play, the wonders of man include all the actions of man's intellect whereby he has been able to conquer the natural world around him.

> Many the wondrous things [*deina*], but none walks the earth
>   more wondrous [*deinoteron*] than man [*anthropou*].
> This thing crosses the sea in the winter's storm,
>   making his path through the roaring waves.
>
> And she, the greatest of gods, the earth—
> ageless she is, and unwearied—he wears her away
> as the ploughs go up and down from year to year
> and his mules turn up the soil.
>
> Gay nations of birds he snares and leads,
> wild beast tribes and the salty brood of the sea,
>
> . . . .

36. E.g., 243; 323; 408; 690; 1091; 1097. Nussbaum (1986:52) suggests the French "formidable" as a more appropriate translation than "wonders." See also Segal (1964:53) and the references in his footnote 13.

He controls with craft [*mēchanais*] the beasts of the open air,
walkers on hills

. . . .

Language [*phthegma*] and windlike
thought and the feelings which are part of rule in the town
he has taught to himself.

(332–56)[37]

The portrait is of man the creator against nature, controlling the seas,
wearing down the earth, capturing the birds of the air and the animals of
the sea. "Hades alone he has not devised a way to escape" (361–62).
Unspoken here is the life that man cannot create by human craft against
nature. More than the finality of death, which throughout the play appears
less than final, it is the incapacity of the main characters to create life that
marks the tragedy of this play. That creation entails a mutuality, an *erōs*,
an acceptance of another that neither Creon nor Antigone allows.[38] Were
there an English word that captured all the nuances of *ta deina*, it would
replace the word "fear" in the title of this work, for the term "fear" there
suggests both awe and wonder at the multiplicity of the world we see
around us as well as the trepidation that the multiplicity will overwhelm
us. The chorus, while wondering at all the achievements of human craft,
learns also to fear the destructive force of those crafts.

The optimistic chorus sing their ode on the "wonders" of man after
they learn from the guard that there had been an attempt to bury the body
of Polyneices. The attempt illustrates the daring of man, but curiously
there is something of a mismatch. The daring performer of the burial rites,
whom they assume to be human, acted not against the nature that man in
his wondrous actions controls, but against a decree articulated by the
leader of their city and announced to the city as a whole. The daring entailed the opposition to art, the political craft of Creon. Indeed, as the play
progresses, Antigone tries to bind herself to an unchanging nature that
resists the arts of men as the animals resist capture and the earth resists
plowing. It is Creon, not Antigone, who dares to act against nature. It is
he who exemplifies the man wondrous in his daring, creative in his attempts to control the natural world. While in the first lines of his speech
to his citizens he attributes to the gods responsibility for whether the state
"shakes" or "stands upright" (162–63), he nevertheless holds all power
and acts, as he says, for the welfare of the city. Action in Creon's political
world means speech. "For me whoever guiding straight the entire city
does not take hold of the best plans, but from some fear holds back, con-

37. Apart from the first and last sentences, the translation is that of Elizabeth Wyckoff in
Sophocles (1960).
38. I will discuss the *erōs* ode below, pp. 71–73.

fining his tongue, he seems now and has always seemed to be the worst" (178–81). The ruler of the city must speak: "I would not stay silent" (185). In speaking, in using his *logos*, Creon pronounces decrees that will preserve the city against the threatened destruction of natural forces of greed and self-interest.

Law, which is *astunomos*, is a human creation; according to the ode, it is one of the acts against nature that man "has taught to himself" (355). The city does not come into being by itself. It is created by man's "passions of town rule," just as man builds houses to shelter himself from the rain. As Benardete has noted, the loyalty to the city that Creon praises and demands of his citizens derives from reason, not biology or nature. "Love of country . . . begins in calculation. One has to figure out the need for it" (1975:12.6). Creon must persuade the townspeople to make just this calculation. No one survives when the ship of the city does not sail safely (189–90). To ensure its safety, the ruler speaks and his speech is law or, more specifically, the pronouncement (*kērugma*) becomes law by the mere fact that it issues from the voice of the ruler. The play begins with the proclamation (*kērugma*) of the general (*stratēgos*). Antigone then asks Ismene in the opening lines of the play, "And now what do you say about this *kērugma* that the *stratēgos* has just now set before all the people of the city?" (7–8).[39] Creon's *kērugma* is announced openly and clearly to the city as a whole. Ismene, who acknowledges, as Antigone does not, the power of the polis and of men, fears for her sister, who plans to act though the decree forbidding such an action has been spoken to the city (*aporreton polei*) (44), and "when Creon has spoken against it" (47). Creon in his turn talks of himself as the creator of the *nomoi*, the laws of the city: "With such *nomoi* I shall increase the city. And now making a proclamation I have a decree brother to these [*nomoi*] for the citizens about the children of Oedipus" (191–93).[40]

Creon speaks with a view towards the future, towards the city that he shall increase and preserve with his pronouncements and decrees. His laws need no other origin than his own speech. With his speech directed to the "setting straight" or "keeping upright" of the polis, Creon, however, denies his own family ties, his own religious responsibilities to the child of his sister.[41] Although he acknowledges that his own power depends on the

---

39. In Antigone's next speech, forms of *kērugma* appear three times, at lines 27, 32, 34.
40. On the use of *kērugma* here, cf. Ostwald (1986:154).
41. There is a considerable disagreement about Creon's responsibility to bury Polyneices: Segal (1964:49, 49 n. 10) says that Creon disobeyed the religious laws, while Ostwald (1986:151) emphasizes the piety of Creon's actions by finding divine support for his edicts and indicating that even Antigone acknowledges Creon's piety (923–24). Ostwald comments that "an Athenian *nomos* prohibited burying traitors in Attic soil" and that, "in championing the cause of the city, he also champions the cause of its gods." Ostwald here does

"nearness" of himself to the family of Oedipus and to his two nephews who have perished by mutual slaughter, he nevertheless abstracts with speech from biological creativity and birth, worrying only about that which is created and preserved by the speech of law-enacting men. The chorus had sung of the passions of the laws of the city in the same breath that they sang of capturing the birds of the air and taming the animals of the hills. The wonder of man is that he can imagine a world all of his own creation, a world that, after giving the gods their due and attributing to them both the success and the failure of cities, denies the gods and denies nature.[42]

Only Antigone, from the opening moments of this play, denies the efficacy of human speech, scornfully dismissing the spoken decrees of the city's leader, mocking Creon as a tyrant who can do and say whatever he wishes, unrestrained by a people whose "tongue fear confines" (505–07). Ismene had urged Antigone not to act against the speech of Creon and of the city (as she equates Creon and the city), but Antigone scorns the laws that come from human speech. The laws that she follows are worthy of obedience precisely because they are unwritten and unspoken. As she says in her famous speech to a Creon who cannot accept that she had buried her brother, knowing full well of his speech-become-decree forbidding such a deed (*kerugthenta me prassein tade*):

> Not at all for me was Zeus the announcer (*ho kēruxas*) of these things, nor did Justice who lives together with the gods below define such laws (*nomoi*) for humankind (*anthropoisin*). Nor did I think that your decrees (*kērugmath'*) were so strong that you, a mortal man, could overrun the unwritten and unfailing laws (*nomina*) of the gods. For not at all now nor yesterday, but always do they live, and no one knows from when they appeared.
>
> (450–57)

Always existing, with unknown origins, the laws of the gods were never the creation of human intellect. They are part of a nature that always is, which Creon in his sense of potency feels he can ignore through speech, and which the chorus praises man for conquering. The uncreated, unwritten laws of the gods stand, in Antigone's vision, opposed to the spoken, created decrees of the city over which Creon rules.

The conflict between the two protagonists may, on one level, be seen as

---

not acknowledge the tension that may exist between the traitor and the kin, between the gods and human effort.

42. Knox (1979:171) notes that man "'taught himself'—no Prometheus or Zeus was needed—and the list of what he taught himself does not include . . . sacrifice and divination."

the debate about whether it is art or nature that is the source of unity in this world. Both view the world as uniform, making unequivocal demands on the individual. For Antigone, that unity is there in nature, and the human being following his or her impulses, sense of piety, and sense of outrage knows it. For Creon, that unity does not exist in nature. Many are the forces, but most of all selfish greed, that tear the man-made unity apart.

The external threats to his island of security were vanquished with the death of Polyneices; now the internal threats that distract individuals from devotion to the city must be rooted out as well. Creon must create that unity by exercising his intellect and expecially by speaking against a diverse natural world where one man can be both friend (*philos* as in "relation") and enemy (*echthros*). Antigone's unified world emerges only by denying a creative human intellect and defining a uniform nature where a brother is unambiguously *philos*, whether he attacked or defended the city. Only human speech (such as that coming from Creon), not nature, can make him *echthros*.

Antigone, perhaps recalling for us the Parmenidean "One," focuses on this uniform and unchanging nature, on what always has existed and what always will exist in the changeless halls of Hades; she denies to nature as well as to humans any creative powers, preferring a death beside her "dearest" brother to a life beside a living husband.[43] "Beloved I shall lie beside him, beside him who is dear, myself having accomplished what is holy . . . Since for a longer time it is necessary that I please those down below rather than those here, for I shall lie there forever" (73–76). In contrast to the eternity of death, biological creativity is instantaneous. By this attachment to the uncreated, uncreating, eternal, and unmoving dead, as well as to the unmoving, ungenerated laws of Zeus, Antigone neuters herself; she is neither male nor female. Her name itself captures her stand: *anti-gone*, against birth, against generation. Though female, she describes herself in male language, language that Creon in his turn uses when he refers to her.[44] In

43. Benardete (1974–1975:8.1): "Oedipus' confusion of generations so that succession is replaced by togetherness finds its proper extension in Antigone's refusal to think of any future apart from the dead." As Peter Euben has pointed out to me, though, Antigone changes. "Immediately before she is led away, she recognizes the costs of her stand; she develops a more complex sense of herself and her world, of what she has excluded . . . confronting death she recognizes the limits of her conception of life" (letter dated September 15, 1991).

44. As Pomeroy notes (1975:100), "Antigone refers to herself with an adjective in the masculine gender (464). Creon, in turn, perceives her masculinity and refers to Antigone by a masculine pronoun and participle (479, 96)." Benardete observes (1974–1975:8.6): "She never uses the word *gunē*, though it occurs eighteen times in the play. . . . She fully acknowledges consanguinity as she denies generation." See also 27.5. Cf. Segal (1964:51), who discusses Antigone's "full acceptance of her womanly nature" and her absolute valuations of blood and affection.

her devotion to what cannot be created through human efforts and human speech, she fails to understand her difference from and her dependence on that which is other—the city and the male.[45]

By contrast, Ismene, as the far weaker of the two sisters, as the one who can have no impact on either Creon or Antigone and who is unable to avert the forthcoming tragedy, acknowledges the tensions and the multiple dimensions of human life. Thus, unlike Antigone, Ismene is torn between the love of her sister and the force of the city by which she is protected and by which she lives. Ismene holds no attachment for the immobile dead, for the eternity that draws Antigone to seek a death joined with her brother and other members of her family. Ismene cares for those who live as well as for those who will be, but not for those who have died. Antigone is the one who is beloved, not the dead brother. Ismene, to the dismay of many current feminists, reminds Antigone that she is a woman, not a man, that she cannot act as a man in the city. It is Ismene who must raise with Creon the relationship between his son and the bride he is condemning to death. It is Ismene who says, "But will you kill the bride of your own child?" (568) and who exclaims, "O dearest Haemon, how your father scorns you" (572).[46] Antigone does not speak of marriage for the first half of the tragedy. Marriage entails creation and the attachment to another; the piety Antigone espouses is an antilife piety and, like the male Homeric heroes, she becomes the warrior whose glory can be achieved only at the moment of death, in the very act of denying life and change, not in birth.[47] In the cruel mixing of images, marriage is death: "Not yet has any song celebrated me in bridal ceremonies. . . . I shall wed Acheron"(815–16).

In an ode almost as well known and just as powerful as the "Wonders" ode, the chorus sing curiously of *erōs*. They sing of the power of *erōs*, of "unconquered *erōs*," wandering the seas and fields, which neither immortals nor humans are able to escape. And those whom love fills become mad

45. The portrait of Antigone as devoted to the unchanging and uncreated is supported later in the tragedy by her own recollections of the sufferings of Niobe. Strangely, she sees in Niobe's sufferings an analogue of her own. But Niobe's suffering entailed the slaughter of her many children. The antigenerational Antigone focuses not on this aspect of Niobe's fate, but on her transformation into a rock, incapable of animation or generation, yet always weeping. It is precisely in Antigone's stone-like aspect that she resembles the suffering Niobe.

46. There is debate on whether this is the line of Antigone or Ismene. See Winnington-Ingram (1980:93 n. 7). He concludes, "The weight of argument inclines strongly towards Ismene." I accept his conclusion because, apart from the textual evidence, Antigone could not use *philos* of one who is alive in this play, betrothed or otherwise.

47. Benardete (1974–1975:9.3), with reference to line 73, notes that, "Antigone borrows the language appropriate to the patriotic soldier whose dying on behalf of his country coincides with his fighting."

(781–90). The goddess Aphrodite plays, unconquered in battle, while Eros rules over the sacred laws (*thesmia*) (799–801). This ode follows the interchange between Haemon and Creon. Again, the choral ode seems slightly off target with reference to the immediately preceding action. Haemon did not come to plead for his bride, driven by an erotic desire for her—at least not openly. The focus of the interchange is rather the nature of political rule within the family and within the city. The politics Haemon espouses, in contrast to that proclaimed by Creon, acknowledges diversity of opinions and requires an openness to discourse or dialogue, that is, the admission that the city is not one man but many men. He does not claim to know that his father "does not speak correctly," but "to another man also there might occur some [thought] of value" (685–87). Haemon is open to diversity of opinion, to an other, to the admission that one is not whole but depends on others. Even if one is wise, "there is no shame in learning many things" (710–11). Such openness means for Creon disorder; he rejects Haemon's claim that a city does not belong to one man (*andros . . . henos*) (737–38). "You would rule well alone over a deserted land," responds Haemon (739).

We must read the choral ode on love as describing not so much Haemon in love, but a Creon (as well as an Antigone) who denies *erōs*, who refuses to submit to its unconquered power.[48] Neither of the main characters acknowledges that either as individuals lacks anything. Creon, sure in his own knowledge, does not need to know the opinions of his subjects. A mere thirty lines later, the chorus describes Antigone as "living, alone, a law to herself (*autonomos zōsa monē*)" (821). *Autonomos*, a term usually applied to a city rather than to an individual, underscores her isolation and independence. Neither Creon nor Antigone needs another; they experience firmness in their unified world view. They speak of *philia*, attachment to relatives, or to the city, but they do not speak of *erōs*. They both understand *philia* as separate from erotic desire, but beyond this they differ. Antigone uses *philia* for her attachment to her dead brother (not her living sister); Creon defines *philia* as loyalty chosen to the polis that has replaced the family. Neither can yield to *erōs*, that sense of incompletion, that acknowledgment that one is not whole, that disruptive passion disorders the world and leaves one uncertain about the unity and structure of one's vision. It is not only, as has been suggested before,[49] that Antigone ignores the city or forgets that one brother was an invader and traitor, the slayer

---

48. See further Nussbaum (1986:65); Winnington-Ingram (1980:97) reads the ode in part as a mockery of Creon "who fights the power of Eros and Aphrodite." But Antigone does so as well.

49. For example by myself, Saxonhouse (1980:65); see also Knox (1964:76–90); Nussbaum (1986:56).

of the brother who was defending the city against the foreigners' invasion. This is certainly true, and the absence of any reference by Antigone to the recent war is indeed striking. But it is her attachment to a family that is dead that is critical for our understanding of her role, for it defines the static nature of her vision. Just as Creon will allow no alternative opinions to upset the unity of his city, so Antigone will allow no living person, no love, to destroy her pursuit of a unity in the world below. Each in his or her drive for a unity that is unchanging simply dismisses from consciousness whatever may be different.[50]

Antigone's rejection of *erōs* in favor of *philia* for those who are dead entails a denial of creativity and birth; Creon thinks too much of human creativity and the power to unify a disordered nature. Even so, his is a creativity of speech against nature or biology, as abstracted from the creative powers of the family as Antigone's piety towards the dead. From the biologically grounded family we find the city built and preserved through human effort. Throughout the tragedy, the author plays on the ambiguity of the terms *philos* and *echthros*, with Antigone understanding these words only in reference to the family that lies dead beneath the ground, while Creon applies them only to the city and its defenders and its potential destroyers (Segal 1964:52; Winnington-Ingram 1980:129–33). Incorporating language traditionally associated with the family, Creon remarks: "Not would I ever set as friend (*philos*) to myself a man ill-minded to the land, knowing this, that when she is the one who saves and if we sail on her upright, we make those who are dear (*tous philous poioumetha*)" (187–90) (Benardete 1975:1.26; Nussbaum 1986:57; Winnington-Ingram 1980:123, 129, 148). We create our friends through the city; we do not inherit our friends or our loved ones from our parents or our family. Thus, Creon can ignore his religious responsibility to bury Polyneices. If family has been replaced by polis, he can only know Polyneices as an enemy and not as a friend.[51] He thus gives to the city the creativity that Antigone has denied to the family. Creon's assertion of his own creative powers is set off by his pride in his masculinity, a masculinity he feels is threatened by Antigone's resistance. She has denied meaning and efficacy to his creative endeavors by ignoring his speech, by disobeying the decree openly pronounced to all the city. "I am not the man (*anēr*), but she is the man, if

50. Vernant (1988a:102) speaks somewhat oddly of the "'uncooked' element in her [Antigone's] character," but means her inability to accept or "become accessible to 'an other,' that is to recognize Eros and, by entering into union with a 'stranger,' herself to transmit life in her turn."

51. Sorum (1982:204–05) sets this transformation into the historical context of the changing position of the family in relation to the city.

this rule rests with her impunity," he says (484–85). Later in the discussion with Haemon, he asserts, "While I am alive, no woman shall rule over me" (525). He creates by himself—as free of woman as of others.

Throughout the play Creon and Antigone stand in opposition to one another. Antigone seeks and then laments her death. Creon finds that the city is not an adequate replacement for the family as he confronts the death first of his son and then of his wife. Their opposition to one another brings on the suffering that would not have occurred had either yielded to the powers of *erōs* that, according to the chorus, controls all men, all women, and all immortals. Antigone, rejecting creativity, relies on "what is" and thus must turn to death itself; Creon, looking only at what comes into being through human choice, ignores—according to Antigone—the demands of "what is," what is eternal.[52] Creon's political action aims at a conventional unity that arises from subjective choices, a man-made unity with no foundations in nature, which is, indeed, opposed to nature.

While the tragedy arises because neither Antigone nor Creon in their exclusive visions of a world unified by nature or by choice can accommodate the other, Ismene and Haemon vainly offer to each character the opportunity to see the world as complex. Antigone may alert the audience to unchanging laws that exist independently of the city and to the paltry role of human speech, but Ismene alerts us to a world far more intriguing and ultimately far more demanding. Ismene speaks of both love for her sister and submission to male authority in the city. She accepts the tension between them, while Antigone, seeing no possible compatibility between them, chooses one to the exclusion of the other. Ismene speaks to both Creon and Antigone of life (548, 566) and of the processes of birth, that is, of the dependence of both on the diversity of nature that each wishes to deny. Ismene's focus on diversity, the meshing of opposites, indeed, the necessary *erōs*, also alerts us to the particularity or specificity of the individual rather than the uniform and exchangeable. During the confrontation with Creon, Ismene asks, "Will you kill the bride of your own son?" (568), to which Creon coarsely replies, "There are arable fields of others" (569). The vulgarity is not in the image of "plowing."[53] Rather, the vulgarity is in his refusal to acknowledge the particularity of Antigone (Benardete 1975:35.1). Antigone differs no more in Creon's mind from other women than the money-grubbing prophets differ from one another (1055). Ismene tries to remind him of the unique harmony between

52. Antigone's focus on what does not come into being bears a striking relation to the city that Socrates creates in the *Republic*, a topic to which we shall return in chapter 6.

53. Nussbaum (1986:57–58) notes that this is the language of the Athenian marriage contract.

Haemon and Antigone, that Antigone cannot simply be replaced by another female. However, Creon, the political leader, categorizes and simplifies. One female equals another, one prophet equals another.

Here, as elsewhere, we see in Creon's actions and statements themes that remind us of the growth of democracy in Athens. The emphasis on interchangeability rather than particularity is part of the democratic perspective; as with the phalanx and with the reliance on lot for political office, individual qualities recede in importance and equality surfaces. Some may read an appeal to democratic values into Haemon's speech urging his father to listen to what people are saying in the corners and backstreets. To do so anachronistically introduces into ancient tragedy modern democratic theory of consent and constitutional limits to rule. Ancient democracy entailed participation, not approval. Creon, in his abstraction from the family, in his refusal to notice the particularly "appropriate fit" (570) between his son and Antigone, in his attempt to equalize all without attention to family background, is in his tyrannical way an embodiment of the democratic ethos as it came to be understood in Athens. With reference to Creon's first grand speech articulating his conceptions of the role of the political leader and the security of the city, Bernard Knox has pointed out (1979:167), "[T]hese were thought of as the epitome of democratic patriotism." And Martin Ostwald (1986:156) goes so far as to say that "Creon starts out as a constitutional ruler, whose convictions, far from being tyrannical, conform to the principles of Athenian democracy." In a perverse way, Creon's refusal to distinguish, to particularize, to see differences, may make him more the democrat than the tyrant.

Ismene's pleas that Creon attend to the unique fit between his son and his niece fail to move the self-assured male leader of the city. Nor is Haemon more successful in his attempt to bend his father's will. Though he speaks to his father of his own loyalty—"I am yours," he says (635)—and of the multiple "voices" in the city that question Creon's decree, Creon sends Haemon away, admitting no compatibility between claims of loyalty and the questioning of his rule. The sister and the son try to understand and function within a world that is multiple, one driven by *erōs* where individuals acknowledge needs and incompletion, where the world is neither static in the eternity of death nor infinitely malleable by a human intellect capable of abstracting from all particulars and from bodily creation. And so the two protagonists of the play, each defending opposing visions of certainty, destroy each other. Ismene preserves her own status as female, standing between Antigone and Creon, reminding them of marriage and the family, yet unable to move the adamantine will of either. Each preserves his or her own vision of the simple and the uniform. Haemon and Ismene offer a world that grows and is multiple. The offer is refused.

Into this world of conflict and failure comes the seer Teiresias, one who knows the ways of the gods and interprets the auguries and sacrifices for the leaders of Thebes. As a seer, he is an intermediary between the gods and men, but he is also an intermediary between the male and the female for, upon killing the female of a pair of coupling snakes, he was himself transformed into a woman for part of his life. Teiresias thus understands the perspective of both the male and the female and his role as an intermediary between the gods and men is in part dependent on this double vision. Unlike Antigone, Teiresias does not deny the value of the city. Rather, he helps to guide. When Teiresias first appears, Creon comments that previously he has never deviated from Teiresias's advice. Teiresias responds that Creon has therefore kept the ship of state upright (993–94). Unlike Creon, Teiresias does not assume too much for the capacity of human rationality to simplify our world and remove from it complex and conflicting demands. Human intelligence must accept diversity in the world—the gods of the dead as well as the gods of the living, the male as well as the female, the *erōs* that tells us we are incomplete, not autonomous—and it must not attempt to transform that diversity into simplicity. Creon has made into one what is multiple, failing to acknowledge the difference between what is above and what is below: "You have thrust one of those from the upper world below scornfully making a tomb a house for a living soul, while you hold above a corpse . . . which belongs to the gods below" (1068–71). So intent on the difference between friend and enemy was Creon that he disregarded the difference between the dead and the living. In his drive to assimilate all, he confuses life and death, just as Antigone had done by treating a dead brother as if he were alive and a live sister as if she were dead.[54]

Teiresias offers to Creon escape from the suffering he is about to endure: recognize the distinction between the living and the dead; do not make the religious and the political replacements for each other; and acknowledge both the gods and human creativity. Creon had, in effect, ignored the gods, making the political the only standard for his actions. Thus, in his refusal to distinguish the realms of human existence, he had politicized the burial. At first, Teiresias's advice, or rather warnings, are dismissed as Creon, arrogant in the power of his own intellect and his ability to understand human motivations, forgets the particular help that Teiresias has given to the city and simply assimilates the prophet into the general category of "prophet," concluding, "The race of seers all love silver"

---

54. Benardete (1974–1975:1.3) comments on the first line of the play: "Antigone refers twice more to someone's head: Eteocles's and Polyneices's (899, 915). . . . That Eteocles and Polyneices are dead in no way changes Antigone's manner of address."

(1055). Refusing to accept the vision of the prophet until too late and then meekly submitting to the advice of the townspeople, Creon must endure the tragic destruction of his world, a destruction speech cannot prevent; he learns through the death of his son the powerful attachment to an irreplaceable child, who simply cannot be assimilated into the category of citizen. Likewise, he must learn that Antigone as niece, as betrothed of his son, as woman is not only subject. The seer demanded acknowledgment of distinctions. Antigone was the other Creon refused to acknowledge.

Antigone and *Seven against Thebes,* in very different ways, suggest how women stood as threats to the masculine image of potency in ancient Greece, reminding men of what they must escape in order to found and preserve the city, namely, the fundamental diversity of nature, which did not yield easily to the imposition of rational simplicity. For Eteocles, there is the chorus of Theban women. For Creon, there is Antigone, though Antigone herself becomes genderless in her longing for the same simplicity of vision as he desires. Nevertheless, she threatens Creon with her different status, with the reminder that the family is not the city, that the living differ from the dead, and that any other woman is not simply a substitute for Antigone. Creon wanted to create a seamless city, the same sort of unity that Antigone imagines that by nature awaits her in death. Such unity, however, creates within the city the same sterility as that found among those forever consigned to the land of Hades. The simplicity that Eteocles, Creon, and, despite her sex, Antigone desire depends on the denial of the female, of that which is other and which creates within nature, not against it. These two tragedies suggest that such a denial is destructive of the polis, which cannot survive without the processes of birth that depend on the commingling of opposites, the erotic attachment of male to female.

Euripides' Ion

We will leave for the moment the somber tone of these tragedies and turn to what has been called a Euripidean comedy where, though the playwright mocks the male's desire to ignore the female, he nevertheless allows such a dismissal to serve as the mythic foundation of the city—without the tragic consequences we have seen above. The unity of the city (and of the family) in *Ion,* though, comes from deception and lies. No arrogant, self-assured heroic political leader tries to impose an unattainable unity. Rather, the comedy reduces the claims of completion to a series of manipulative acts in which men and women, gods and mortals engage so that the unity of the city may not be fractured by interlopers male or female, real or imagined.

Written while the Athenians were debating the proper grounds for citizenship status in Athens (Walsh 1978), *Ion* looks to questions of origins and the meaning of preserving an imagined purity. Undoubtedly, contending claims to political power were at the heart of the debates about who could vote in the assembly, but Euripides builds his play, *ad nauseum,* as one critic has said (Knox 1979:267) around the city's autochthonous origins and the meaning of such origins for inclusion in or exclusion from the polity. The Theban tale of autochthony emphasized the masculine powers of generation, the sowing of dragon's teeth from which spring fully grown and armed men. The story in Athens is somewhat more ambiguous. While the female was not necessary to bring forth the early kings in Athens, she does nurture these earthborn progenitors of the Athenians. The myth prominent in *Ion* recalls Hephaestus's pursuit of Athene, the virgin goddess: as Athene escapes from Hephaestus, his sperm lands on Athenian soil. From that seed Erichthonius is born from the earth, and handed over by Ge to Athene. The earthborn here, unlike his Theban counterpart, is not one armed and fully grown, but one still in need of nurture.[55] Nevertheless, the myth still finds the beginning of the Athenian line in a denial of heterosexual mutuality. Athene remains a virgin and Hephaestus drops his seed aimlessly.[56] As Euripides uses this myth in *Ion,* however, he keeps the female prominently before us despite the attempt of the mature male characters in the play, both mortal and immortal, to exclude her. He, the playwright, thus works against his characters. As the Athenians worried about the preservation of their purity, Euripides places on stage a perhaps novel tale[57] about Athens's dependence on the female. In his version, a purity is maintained, but only through the female Creusa[58] and the deception of the male.

Euripides' most powerful plays, of which *Ion* is certainly not one, open up the human psyche to show its multiple elements and to dramatize the tragic consequences that occur when characters, for example, Hippolytus and Pentheus, try to deny the irrational forces that exist within them. Characters who take pride in their own rationality and fail to acknowledge their psychic multiplicity suffer tragic destruction. In *Ion,* Euripides moderates this lesson as he applies it to the polity. The city, eager to preserve

55. Loraux (1979:9) discusses this myth and the asexual/sexual implication entailed within it *in extenso,* raising questions about whether Erichthonius was a child or a baby when handed over to Athene. This has implications for whether Athene was responsible for the child's nurture or just for his education. See the discussion in Burian (forthcoming) as well.

56. Segal (1978:191). I will discuss the same story with a different emphasis when we turn in chapter 5 to the tale that Aspasia tells in the *Menexenus.*

57. See below note 63.

58. As Loraux (1981:202) states, "Tout, dans l'histoire d'Ion, mène donc vers Creuse. Vers une femme."

its purity against interlopers of any kind, tries to dimiss with its tales of its autochthonous origins the female from its mythic and political conscious-ness. Nurture may be theirs, but not the all important founding or gen-erating act. Euripides, by making this play a "comedy" rather than a tragedy, allows this exclusion for the city as he does not for the psyche. At the same time, he reveals the artificiality of such exclusion that can only be maintained through deception. The young temple boy Ion yearns for his mother and laments that he has never known a mother's breast (319, 1372). A city of males may scorn such a yearning and encapsulate that scorn in the myth of autochthony, but Ion reminds us that, while that scorn may preserve the city's sense of unity, it also becomes self-destructive. Creusa is the only means to preserve the autochthonous line that founded Athens. Denial of her and of heterosexuality in this case becomes the denial of autochthonous unity.

"*Amētōr, apatōr,* without mother, without father," sings the young temple boy Ion of himself at the beginning of the play (109). A foundling left at the steps of the temple of Apollo at Delphi, "ignorant of the father who begat him and the mother from whom he sprang" (49–50),[59] he keeps the god's sanctuary clean; he cares for the temple, nourishes it, as the temple had cared for and nourished him. As the sun rises, he sings of how he preserves the purity of the holy place, cleansing it of the bird droppings that befoul the sacred offerings, but more than his broom of laurel branches is needed. With a bow and arrow he sets to flight those birds who dare to land within the temple walls (102–112, 170–75). Vio-lence thus preserves the purity of the temple. He grieves that he must kill the birds, but he is a servant of Phoebus Apollo, and "I will not stop caring for those who nourished me" (182–83). In the midst of Ion's gentle, lyrical song we learn of the purity maintained by the threats of slaughter, albeit of little birds.

The parable is striking. Ion, we know from Hermes' prologue to the play, is the issue of a violent rape of Creusa by the god Apollo. Creusa, the daughter of Erechtheus, born of an earthborn king of Athens, kept the rape secret and abandoned the child to an expected death in the cave below the Acropolis where the rape took place, an evocation of the earthborn ancestors of Ion. Preservation of the purity of descent from Athens's au-tochthonous kings depends on the violence of Apollo and the deception perpetrated on Creusa's husband Xouthos to make him accept as his son one who is not. As Euripides presents it, violence and deception are nec-essary to preserve the seamless mythic unity of Athens. Euripides, as play-wright behind the play, reminds us that it is only through such deception

---

59. See Kovacs (1979:112) for this reading and its application to Ion rather than to the priestess who finds him.

and lies-become-founding-myths that women can be excluded.[60] Creusa, though, rebels against such an exclusion that is acceptable to her husband and the god Apollo and, as the medium through whom the autochtho-nous origins of the city are continued, demands that her own role as mother be respected. The violence that the young temple boy willingly employs against the birds to keep the temple pure parallels the violence Euripides' men are willing to accept to keep the city of Athens pure. Even Creusa, as she plots the death of the young temple boy (before she recog-nizes him as her son), is willing to employ such violence to keep her own house pure and free from the invasion of what is not her own.

Despite the violence, the rape, and the planned murders of son by mother and of mother by son, *Ion* is not a tragedy. Knox, for example, has argued persuasively that this play is the precursor of new comedy beginning a long line of comedy extending through Menander to Molière. It "leaves us with a sense that the standards of this world, though not perfect, are sound: there is no flaw in the universe, only misunderstand-ings, maladjustments" (1979:266).[61] Such "comedy" entails a "restora-tion to normalcy," the reaffirmation of traditional values. Whereas the two plays dealt with above explode the unity pursued by a myth such as autochthony, Euripides forces his audience to consider not whether the first ancestors of Athens were indeed earthborn, but rather the value, benefits, and deficits of such a tale. He allows the myth to stand as a "political truth," a mechanism to ensure the "restoration to normalcy." Throughout the play, Euripides does not deny or mock the notion that men can be born from the earth. It is the non-Athenian Xouthos who does this (542). Rather, Euripides suggests how such a myth limits the city with the false goal of purity, no more accessible to human action than the power of Pentheus's reason to conquer the disruptive, divisive forces of Dionysus.

Ion ends happily for the characters within it. Each has the mother or child he or she desired, and Athens has assured itself the purity of succes-sion for its autochthonous line of rulers. No basic beliefs have been over-turned. No brothers, sisters, sons, or wives lie dead off or on stage, and thus we may have our comedy, but the audience has been discomforted by the action. The unity achieved by the city is in the end artificial, dependent on the denial of natural desires and natural diversity. At the same time that Euripides has accepted the traditions of the past and returned us to a con-dition of normalcy, he has also asserted a new vision, one that introduces the female into the origins of cities and reveals the city's contradictory

60. I deal extensively with the role of foundation myths in this play in Saxonhouse (1986a). I draw heavily on that essay for my discussion here.
61. See also Burian (forthcoming).

need for mutuality and openness as well as for exclusiveness.[62] In opposition to the action of the play, Euripides has emphasized heterosexuality (and thus the female) that lies at the foundation of the city, but which is ignored or consciously dismissed. The suppression of heterosexuality and the deception required to maintain that suppression reveals the tragic content of this early comedy.

Let us now turn directly to the play. Euripides has taken an unknown foundation myth as the basis for his story line. Creusa, having kept secret her rape and the birth of her child, marries the foreign adventurer Xouthos, a son of Zeus, but they remain childless. They go to Delphi to inquire of the god about their childlessness, Creusa secretly also eager to discover the fate of the baby she had left in the cave. Apollo tells Xouthos that the first person whom he meets upon leaving the temple is his son; Xouthos meets Ion, claims him as his child, and plans to bring him back to Athens as the future king. Creusa becomes jealous of the child to be brought into her house and reveals to the chorus and her tutor her suffering at the hands of Apollo. The old tutor suggests that she burn down Apollo's temple, kill her husband, and kill the youth. She rejects the first two proposals but plots, albeit unsuccessfully, Ion's murder. A recognition scene takes place, and Ion returns to Athens as the son of Creusa and Apollo, while Xouthos believes that Ion is his son by some maid he impregnated years before at a religious festival he scarcely remembers. The only source for this version of the myth is Euripides; most likely he made up the story from scant references in the mythological history.[63] Euripides

62. Although the ending of this play may be "satisfying" on the political level (the race of Erichthonius continues to rule Athens), this does not mean that all questions are resolved; in particular, Apollo's role in the events is not resolved (he appears as a violent rapist, a deceiver, and one unwilling to take responsibility for his deeds), and thus the antagonistic relationship between gods who act execrably and humans who look to them for moral leadership remains.

63. The scholarly literature on *Ion* agrees that Euripides' version is unusual, but there are debates as to whether he made it all up; see, e.g., Grote (1851–56, 1:273, n. 1): "I conceive many points of that tragedy to be the invention of Euripides himself; but to represent Ion as the son of Apollo, not Xuthus, seems a genuine Attic legend." Conacher (1967) says that there is no evidence that Apollo was considered the father of Ion before Euripides. He doubts, however, that it is a Euripidean invention. He also quotes H. Gregoire from the introduction to the Budé text, who claims that both Ion and Xouthos were strangers to the Attic Ionian tradition: rather, they were created for specific political purposes by the geneologizing epic of the seventh century. Xouthos was inserted into the Homeric catalogue, he claims, to establish an affinity between the Ionians and the Achaeans, while the function of Ion was clearly to associate the Ionian patronym with the state of Athens. Owen (1939:xiv) remains an agnostic on when and how Ion entered Athenian legend and on the paternity of Apollo. See also Nilsson (1951:61–67).

thus revises for Athens her foundation myths, making the female the necessary participant in the city's struggle for unity. Inclusion, though, also entails the acceptance of the violence of her rape.

The story of Creusa's rape is repeated several time. By the end of the play, though, the violence so prominent earlier is forgotten in the pleasure of her reunion with the son she bore and abandoned. Hermes in his prologue offers the first version. He tells of Apollo's passion for Creusa, how Phoebus yoked (*ezeuxen*) her with violence (*bia*) in marriage (*gamois*) (10–11) (a phrase often used to describe an irregular union) (Owen 1939:68), and how in secret she bore the child of that union and abandoned him in the same cave where she had been violated by the god. Creusa first tells of her rape obliquely; it is the tale of a "friend," not her own tale that she recites to the sympathetic, but incredulous, temple boy she meets outside the oracle. "A friend of mine says she was sexually united with Phoebus" (338). To Ion, who has asserted that the god would be ashamed by the injustices of men, Creusa affirms simply that this friend has suffered many griefs. The pain described by Creusa here comes not only from the violence of the act itself, but also from ignorance about the fate of the child. Is he alive or dead, torn by the ruthless claws and beaks of wild animals and birds? Need she raise a tomb for the child who has died? Ion's longing is matched by that of his mother. Creusa pities him: "O suffering one, I being sick have found one also sick" (320). Creusa's "friend" hopes that the oracle will reveal to Creusa the fate of the child. The pain that arose from the initial rape then would cease as mother and son find one another.

In the middle of the play, after she learns that Xouthos has found a son, Creusa reveals to the chorus in a song of lament what befell her, and not her friend, by the lust of Apollo. She denounces both men and gods, betrayers of the marriage bed (879–80). She describes for the chorus how Apollo led her to the infamous cave, how his violent hands grasped her wrists as he, heedless of her cries for her mother, acted without shame "for the sake of Aphrodite" (896). To the sympathetic old tutor she recalls the spot: "There the dreadful conflict (*agōna deina*) we fought" (939). Again there is repetition; there was not only pain from the conflict, but also from the loss of the child born of the violent rape. The action of the play resolves the latter pain for, by the end, after all the near tragedies, mother and son are united. The joy achieved by this final unity erases the pain of the rape that had been so prominent before, and the attitude towards Apollo changes. Creusa again repeats her story at the end of the play; this time she recalls simply that Apollo enjoyed her bed (1484). The violence of the act is forgotten in the delight of finding her son.

I revere Apollo whom I did not revere before;
No longer is he unconcerned about the child he now returns
    to me.
These gates are fair to look on for me, as is the seat of the
    oracle
Now that the anger is a thing of the past.

(1609–12)

Creusa had first appeared lamenting the suffering of women (*o tlēmones*) (252) that was brought on by the gods. Euripides transforms her role from the suffering maiden to the fulfilled mother in her role as the preserver of Athenian purity.

Myths of autochthony obscure the agony of origins. As men spring from the earth they cause no pain and suggest no dependence. No *agōn*, conflict or struggle, need precede their emergence. Apollo does not appear at the end of the play lest his presence call forth old recriminations (1557–58). Scholars have wondered at Apollo's apparent cowardice and either try to explain it away or see it as indication of the play's criticism of the Olympians.[64] But Apollo's absence here is important for understanding what must be forgotten as cities are founded. The city must forget the internal conflicts, the *agōnes* that gave it birth, and thus the female.

Stories of autochthony, though, intrigue Ion. When he first meets the woman whom he knows only as the queen of the Athenians, he asks at once: "By the gods, tell me truthfully about the stories spoken (*memutheutai*) by mortals. Did the earth bring forth the (grand)father of your father?" "Erichthonius, yes. . . ." "And Athene raised him from the earth?" "Into her maiden hands, but she did not bear him" (265–70). The questioning continues through the violent deaths of the daughters of Cecrops and those of Erechtheus, the sisters of Creusa slain by their own father. Creusa explains their deaths, violence perpetrated *pro gaias*, for the sake of the earth (278); that is, the city is identified with the earth from which the founder was born. As in the vision put forward by Eteocles, birth from the earth allows unambiguous devotion to the earth, rather than to children or brothers, who may have been the issue of heterosexuality.[65] Forgetting the female here enables the complete devotion to the *chthōn* and the capacity to kill one's child *pro gaias*.

Euripides, filling his play with these persistent references to autochthony, reacts against its principles by illustrating the inadequacy of all at-

---

64. For the former view, see Burnett (1962); for the latter view, see Rosenmeyer (1963: 113–22).

65. The agony that characterizes the killing of Iphigeneia by Agamemnon, putting on "the yoke of necessity," is completely absent here.

tempts to exclude the female and even expresses the humor of such attempts. Xouthos, in particular, becomes the comic character: he has asked the god for a son and has been told that one awaits him outside the temple. He rushes out and throws himself upon the bewildered Ion. Appropriately, Ion asks: "Are you thinking well? Or has some harm from a god driven you mad, stranger?" (520). Ion can see the approaches of Xouthos only as lascivious disrespect for the god's servant. Finally understanding the meaning of Xouthos's actions and words, Ion asks a question that neither Xouthos nor Apollo are prepared for: "From what mother was I born to you?" (540). Xouthos did not inquire—"Delighting in the discovery of a son, I did not ask" (541)—and Apollo did not supply this information. Ion pursues the question: "Perhaps I was born from the mother earth" (542). (The precedent of Erichthonius is vivid in his mind as suggested by the earlier conversation with Creusa.) Xouthos, a foreigner to Athenian myths, is scornful of such an idea. "The plain (*pedon*) does not give birth to offspring" (542). Ion, innocent, young, and more susceptible to such stories must thus push further. How could he be born without the benefit of a woman? How could he be the son of the man who stands before him without a woman involved in the process? His search for a mother belies the self-satisfaction that Xouthos feels. Xouthos is not at all interested in this question. Ion urges him to speculate: perhaps it was some Delphian maid encountered years ago at a religious festival, but Xouthos shows no sustained interest. Ion is not so easily distracted: "O beloved mother, when shall I see your form? Now I long more than before to know whoever you are" (563–64). Xouthos gladly leaves such questions to some later time when perhaps (*isōs*) they will find her (575).

Xouthos's willingness to forego the search for Ion's mother is almost a comic parody of the powerful trial scene at the end of the *Oresteia*, where the arguments for the conquest of maternity by paternity are given full expression. As Apollo says there, the woman only nurtures the child. Her role is, as some have suggested, like that of the flowerpot. Athene, the female embodiment of masculine virtues, the goddess who is no female, sprung from the head of Zeus, defends the principle of asexual birth.[66] No female participated in her birth. Nor does Ion need the involvement of a female in his birth—at least according to Xouthos and Apollo. Ion's demands for his mother, his longing to know who gave him birth, flies in the face of this, as does the plot of the play itself: rather than denying the importance of the female who can be summarily dismissed as Apollo tries to do, Euripides establishes that it is only through the female that the

66. The chorus in *Ion* ironically prays to Athene, "born without the pangs of labor" (452–3), as they pray that their mistress may give birth to a child.

Athenians are able to preserve the purity about which they seem to care so much. Like Apollo, Xouthos cares little about the role of the female in the process of procreation. He searches for a son and finds one; where the seed is planted matters not at all.

While the comic interaction between Xouthos and Ion undermines masculine pride in powers of generation, Creusa enacts the female version of the myth, scorning her husband—an outsider—as irrelevant and rejecting the "son" of her husband as a threat to her own purity (1302). She rebels against a story of birth that would exclude herself. Athene, the virgin goddess, voted on behalf of paternity. Creusa, who has experienced childbirth, demands acknowledgment of the role of the female in the processes of generation. According to Apollo's plan, Creusa would accept the apparent interloper as her own, that is, he inaccurately predicts that she will be able to do what the city itself cannot do—accept freely a foreigner into its midst, one who brings diversity rather than unity into the fabric of the city. Creusa rebels and refuses to accept an auxiliary role, to be the mere nurturer rather than an active participant in the creation of the next generation and the race that is to give rise to so many of the Greek cities. Urged on by the chorus, who desire to preserve the purity of their city against Xouthos and Ion, she plots the murder of the interloper who would deny her a place in the creation of children. To do this, though, she must, ironically, return to the autochthony myth at the base of the play, for the poison to be used in Ion's murder comes from Erichthonius, who, as the tutor again recalls, was "first of your race the earth brought forth" (1000). Creusa's father inherited from his father two drops of the Gorgon's blood; one drop heals, the other poisons.[67] The poisonous drop is now to be used to protect women from again being excluded. The plot is the catalyst for the series of events that lead to the recognition scene. Without Creusa's rebellion, though, without her refusal to be simply the passive receptacle excluded from "delighting in things which are common" (358), and without her rejection of the stranger from outside the household, Apollo's plan to have Ion return to Athens as the son of Xouthos would have succeeded. Against the god, Euripides asserts the importance of mutuality—and thus of the female.

The primary exponent of the myth of autochthony and its demands for purity is Creusa's tutor, a mindless instigator of evil actions, beginning with his sacrilegious proposal to burn down the temple of Apollo and then to kill Xouthos. With the tutor and the women of the chorus as the defenders of the values incorporated in the myth, the tale loses much of

---

67. Whitman (1974:98) notes that only in this version is the Gorgon referred to as being autochthonous.

its seriousness. It is worthy of those who are servants to others and who are tied to antiquated notions of a purity in which they themselves do not directly participate. However, while the myth as the foundation for exclusiveness may find its defenders in the comic characters of the play, the playwright nevertheless allows the story to stand—with important modifications. Ion, the son of Creusa and Apollo, is the new Erichthonius. Creusa preserves the custom of her ancestors and the earthborn Erichthonius: Ion, like Erichthonius, is placed in a circular cradle (19–21) and, again like Erichthonius, is handed over to another to be cared for. Despite the snakes adorning his casket, Ion, unlike Erichthonius, did not emerge from the earth as his predecessor had. The race of Ionians, in Euripides' version, can now trace their origins back to one of woman born.[68] Indeed, it is she who gives to Ion his ties to the Athenians. The descent from Zeus that Xouthos claims does nothing to elevate his stature among the Athenians; he remains an outsider. It is Creusa who has born in her womb the eponymous hero of the Ionians. Not only is woman brought back into the foundation myth of the city, but she is placed securely at its center in this play extolling the attachment between the mother and the son. The denial of heterosexual reproduction inherent in the myth of autochthony is rejected by Euripides, though not by the characters in the play, most of whom have a limited vision of the diversity necessary to create and preserve the family and the city.

Throughout the play, there emerges from Euripides criticism of the exclusiveness that characterizes his characters and even the Athens that stands behind the play. Creusa finds fault with an Apollo who might have taken her fictitious friend's child and raised him by himself: "He did not act justly enjoying alone what was common (*koina*)" (358). Nonetheless, both Creusa and Xouthos are willing to enjoy individually what is a common endeavor. The intricacies of the whole plot and Apollo's botched plan depend on Xouthos's expected refusal to accept into his own house that which is not his own. He must be tricked into believing that Ion is his own son in order to welcome him. Creusa is no less parochial in this regard than Xouthos. The thought that she might have to nurture in her home an alien child, the son of another mother, and that her husband could find a child while she herself remains barren leads—with some help from the tutor—to those thoughts of murder. It is her antipathy to the acceptance of one who is not her own that brings about the crisis of the play. Ion, in

68. Burnett (1962) also sees Ion as the new Erichthonius, but suggests that Apollo as the father replaces Athene as the "mother." Although Burnett emphasizes the glorious divinity of Apollo, I find the negative portrait of Apollo as presented by Rosenmeyer (1963) far more convincing. By keeping Apollo outside the action of the play, Euripides emphasizes the maternity of Creusa far more effectively than the paternity of Apollo.

contrast to all his parents (imagined and real), urges Xouthos to show compassion for the woman Ion does not yet recognize as his mother. "Before she shared in common your misfortunes" (608–09). Now she suffers alone. How could she not hate the newly found son? (607–15). The gentleness of Ion, who deeply feels a woman's anguish, stands in marked contrast to the boorish warrior Xouthos—sensitive to neither the female's passions nor to the city's own need for myths about earthborn ancestors.

Ion is critical not only of Xouthos. Athens too is excessively exclusive, hostile to any outsider. Ion at first resists the return to Athens with his new-found father. "They say that the famous Athenians are autochthonous and not from a race drawn in from outside." Thus they will scorn and hate him, a bastard and son of a father from outside (*patros epaktou*) (589–92). The speech that follows praises the apolitical life;[69] his gentleness, his sensitivity to the emotions of the barren wife, and his openness to the visitors at the oracle all make him resist the life of the polis where gentleness, sensitivity to female feelings, and openness are worthless attributes. In his present role, as servant to the god, he says goodbye to some visitors and then new ones come. It is pleasant, he claims, to welcome the new (640–41). Athens, the political world, does not welcome the new. It preserves its identity by excluding the new and maintaining the old. The open, welcoming Ion, servant to the god who serves all, resists at first the restraints that political life would entail. This resistance, admittedly, does not last for long. A brief speech from Xouthos convinces him.

In his prologue, Hermes recalls how Creusa placed Ion's cradle in Apollo's cave and how he carried it to Delphi where the priestess of Apollo found it. At first she removed the cradle from the temple, assuming that the child within was the product of the shame of some nymph in the vicinity, but then she took pity on the child in the cradle and nurtured it to manhood. The priestess is the only character who is able to accept something that is not her own. She is not part of the city that tries to preserve its exclusive purity. Her role allows her to transcend the particular and moves her to the universal.[70] By contrast, the Athenians, just as Xouthos and Creusa do within the family structure, pay constant homage to visions of purity, a purity associated with nobility of birth. The interloper, the foreigner, threatens and debases that nobility and can be accepted only under duress—as was Xouthos, the adventurer whose military force bought an Athenian princess as his bride, a war prize (298), she who is *engenē* (293).[71] Creusa speaks of her husband as "not of the city, but some-

---

69. Kovacs (1979: 121) disputes the authenticity of these lines as "inorganically stuck into a deliberation to which they do not contribute."

70. Burian (forthcoming) remarks on the priestess's sacrifice of private life and family.

71. Loraux (1981: 217) comments on the difference between *engenēs* and *eugenēs*. Xouthos, the descendant of Zeus is *eugenēs*, but not *engenēs*.

one brought in from another land" (290). He is a guardian (*epikouros*) but not of the land (*chthōn*) (1299). There is an apologetic tone: she had to marry him because the military weakness of Athens made the city dependent on the strength of foreign princes. It is the fear of yet another interloper into the pure city, into the pure line of the autochthonous Erechtheids, that incites Creusa, abetted by her tutor, to plot the murder of Ion. The foreigner, be he king or serving boy, cannot easily enter the unity of the city that finds its origins in the autochthonous birth of its kings; or, as Ion comments, a stranger (*xenos*) who enters the pure city (*katharan polin*) has no freedom to speak (673–75). The chorus confirm Ion's fears: "Never let the child come into my city; abandoning his gentle youth, let him die . . . the present ruler sprung from King Erechtheus is enough" (719–24).

The play, like several others by Euripides, suggests finally the inadequacy of male arrogance, Xouthos's self-satisfaction as well as the city's sense of purity. In the other plays, this inadequacy is often expressed in terms of the arrogance apparent in war, the arrogance of power or brute strength. *Trojan Women* is perhaps the most familiar exposition of this theme. Here in *Ion*, the arrogance is simply the belief in male genesis. It is a belief characteristic not only of men but of the gods as well. Euripides does not delve into the biological aspects of heterosexual reproduction as Aeschylus allows his Apollo to do. For Euripides, the psychological aspects are powerful enough. The child demands, longs for the maternal breast; the father ignores that demand, thinking that any substitute for the womb or the breast will do.[72] Creusa's plot to kill Ion, and Ion's own sensitive fear of the hostile reception that awaits him as a foreign interloper into Creusa's home, give the lie to that vision.

The most powerful, though unacknowledged, attack on the superiority of the male as father comes in the form of Xouthos's ignorance of the fact that he is the dupe of both Apollo and Creusa. He accepts without question as his son one whom he has absolutely no recollection of fathering. In the better known versions of the myth, Xouthos is indeed Ion's father (Herodotus 7.94, 8.44). By making Apollo the father, Euripides turns Xouthos into a comical character satisfied with an ignorance to which he admits (*ouk oida*) (544). At the end of the play, when all has been revealed to Creusa and Ion, Athene bids Creusa, "Be silent now regarding how this child is yours in order that the opinion may pleasantly hold Xouthos" (1601–02). Xouthos's ignorance parallels the ignorance and susceptibility to deception with which all men must function. As Telemachus has already pointed out in the *Odyssey*, paternity depends on inference and speculation. Maternity needs no inference; it is easily observable in the growing

---

72. Remember here Creon's ready substitution of any other woman for Antigone.

belly and the actual labor of birth. It is the definitive statement of the male's dependence upon the female. It is a dependence that the males, Apollo and Xouthos, and myths of autochthony try to deny, but one that Euripides as playwright asserts. Xouthos would not bring Ion back to Athens did he not believe that Ion were his son. The importance of that belief for Xouthos is asserted throughout the play. The control Creusa has over that belief raises her from the status of an irrelevant individual to the very source for the founding of cities. Euripides' play irreverently suggests a revision of the autochthony myth and in so doing exalts the role of both women and of motherhood. The foolishness of autochthony is transcended by the lyrical and sensitive relation between mother and son, and by the more human focus on birth from the mortal female.

The autochthony myth, so powerful in the Athenians' self-conception (at least as presented by Euripides here), becomes a limiting, stifling influence—it is antithetical to Athens's vision of itself as an open city (Thucydides 2.39). Foreign influences, indeed foreign benefits, the sons of gods, are likely to be excluded for what has become a petty concern with citizen purity.[73] The search for unity and purity can extend so far that it destroys what it seeks to protect. The autochthony myth rooted in this desire for purity must be modified. As the city grows, it must acknowledge the female and it must accept the son of a god. Refusal to accept the other is characteristic of the old fool of a tutor. He illustrates the dangers of the myth on which the city is built, the danger of forgetting its fragile origins, and the mutuality of male and female necessary for the creation of a race of heroes. *Ion* presents to the Athenian audience their own myths, not those of the family at Thebes, and it suggests how those myths are necessary for the survival of the city. The play also questions myths that create unified wholes incapable of penetration, which are satisfied with simple definitions of who is friend and who is foe. The city as constituted in ancient Greece must have its boundaries, its citizenship laws, its ability to exclude the other. Yet, at the same time that those laws give order and stability to the city, they can also limit the possibilities of the city and deny the fullness of human experience.[74]

While the ending of this play does not leave us crushed as the curses of gods and of men are fulfilled, it nevertheless is perhaps more sinister because the playwright, and now the audience, know the central role of the female in the processes of succession of the royal family from its autoch-

---

73. See further Walsh (1978).

74. Burian (forthcoming) discusses how even Ion's fantasy of pure devotion to the god Apollo must be shattered by the knowledge that must be revealed to Ion, by no less than Athene, of the rape perpetrated by his father. Early in the play he had refused to believe that such a deed would be possible. Burian develops the play's mixture of beauty and violence.

thonous origins;[75] yet, for the sake of the city and for the preservation of
the myth, the lie maintaining the irrelevance of the female follows Creusa
and Xouthos back to Athens. Athene demands that the secret be kept.
Thus, the king and his "son" return, while the female, excluded from
the celebrations, must be satisfied with the unacknowledged role that she
plays. Unspoken of, for good or for evil, she nevertheless is critical to the
founding of the city.

Seven against Thebes and Antigone set before an Athenian audience the
destruction of the Theban royal family. That destruction is marked by
the drive for excessive unity in the incestuous family of Oedipus and in the
excessive simplicity of perspective pursued by the main characters. The
latter goal is captured perhaps most vividly in Seven against Thebes by
the emphasis on autochthonous origins. Allowing the city to replace the
human female with the land, the myth helps to obliterate the tensions that
may exist between demands of family and the city. Eteocles exists to slay
his brother for the sake of the land. Though autochthony is not present in
Antigone as it is in Seven against Thebes, Creon's (and Antigone's) ill-fated
attempts to eliminate any concern with the multiplicity of human relations
expresses in less mythical dress the same principles of political foundation
as does autochthony. The structure of the plays and the poetic language
used by the tragedians, however, undermine the viability of such uniform
perspectives, whether they arise from autochthony myths, the "wondrous/
dreadful" power of human speech, or a Parmenidean vision of nature; the
playwrights move the audience towards a more varied understanding of
our political world. This larger understanding, though, must lead to the
acknowledgment of incompatibilities and tensions. The playwrights' tragic
vision entails the explosion of the uniform; it leaves us torn, in a frenzy
(tarachē), like Haemon as he comes to his father, tragically recognizing
our eternal, mortal incompletion, our distance from divine wholeness, and
thus our subjection to the erōs that Eteocles, Creon, and Antigone try
to deny.

75. Loraux (1981:232ff) develops this theme well.

Part Two

Plato and the Ambiguous Pursuit of Unity

Although Platonic criticism over the last two and a half millennia has found many different Platos lurking behind the dialogues, Plato has stood securely, heir to Parmenides' *kouros,* as the founder of "idealist" philosophy, asserting the existence of a world beyond the senses, one comprehensible only to the intellect, one that unifies by abstracting from the particulars of the world that we experience with our senses. The city that Socrates founds in Plato's *Republic* is the political expression of that unity: particularity is removed and the city becomes one. The following chapters raise questions about this understanding of Plato and suggest that lurking behind at least some of his dialogues is less a fear of diversity and more an ambiguous pursuit of unity.

4

Socrates and the City of Athens

The Education of Euthyphro

A young man "wise in the ways of the gods" encounters Socrates as he waits at the porch of the *archon basileus* in 399 B.C. The young man has come to Athens to indict his father for murder. Socrates in his turn awaits indictment on the charges of corrupting the young and introducing new gods into the city. Euthyphro, as the young man is known, in common with many of the youths with whom Socrates discourses, is certain of the rightness of his actions and beliefs. Socrates' task, as they both wait on the porch of the *archon,* is to reveal the complexities of the issues that Euthyphro sees as simple. Euthyphro wants to abstract from the particulars of who is father and who is not. He wants to discover—indeed, he believes that he has discovered—universal laws that apply in all times and in all places, and he turns to the city as a realm of universality to implement those laws. He finds in the city the abstraction from the particular. Socrates forces Euthyphro to hesitate (we never learn for how long) by suggesting the difficulty of applying abstract principles that come from a unified vision of the moral universe, which are captured by the laws of the city, to one's action with regard to particular individuals with whom one lives, be it father, mother, son, or daughter.[1]

1. Most studies of Plato's *Euthyphro* categorize the dialogue as an early, aporetic work, in other words, one that asks what a particular virtue is, be it courage, moderation, or piety, and then fails to answer, at least directly, the question posed. *Euthyphro* is often seen as particularly interesting because, although supposedly written early in Plato's career, we find in it glimmers of the "later" theory of the forms. See,

Although Euthyphro sees himself as joining Socrates in scorning the common mass of men (3b–c), the principles of universality that he espouses conform to the development of the democratic polity in Athens. A focus on equality before the laws and a citizenry of equals bound to the city by their uniformity rather than their individuality lie at the heart of the Athenian polity.[2] To achieve the unity of the city, the traditional bonds to the family needed to be fractured and the individual released from those ties that bound him to the private rather than to the public.[3] Aristotle, describing Cleisthenes' reforms of 508–507 B.C. that were considered by the Athenians to be the beginning of their peculiar political regime, notes: "[Cleisthenes] first distributed all into ten tribes instead of four, wishing to mix them up so that more of the citizens might have a share in the *politeia*. From which it was said: 'Do not judge by tribe.' . . . And he made those living in each *deme* fellow *demesmen* of one another, so that they were not called by their father's name . . . but named according to their *deme*" (*The Constitution of Athens* 21.1–4). Euthyphro is there on the porch of the *archon basileus* ready to indict his father for the sake of what exists above and beyond the bonds that can be created by the family, that is, beyond the divisive particularity of the family. Jean-Pierre Vernant has suggested that, "with Cleisthenes, the egalitarian ideal was directly linked to political reality . . . it inspired a reshaping of institutions. The world of social relations thus formed a coherent system, governed by numerical relations and correspondences that permitted the citizens to declare themselves 'the same,' to enter into relations of mutual equality, symmetry and reciprocity." (1982:100–101). While the breakdown of the old tribes and the institution of the new *demes* became the basis for the identity of

---

e.g., Allen (1970) and Blitz (1980:19, especially the references in his footnote 2). The dialogue becomes interesting in these interpretations because of subsequent developments, rather than on its own. I wish to take seriously the dialogue on its own and to show that, rather than foreshadowing the theory of forms or *ideas,* the dialogue raises questions about the political implications of a philosophic drive towards abstraction such as entailed in the theory of the forms.

2. For a fascinating and often brilliant exposition of the development of these themes as expressed in the funeral oratious of the fifth and fourth centuries, see Loraux (1986), especially chap. 6. Loraux, using the language of Plato's *Parmenides,* refers to the "quasi-Parmenidean aim of establishing the nonexistence of the multiple which," she claims "was also the subject of an ideological struggle in Athens" (279). I am making no claims about what went on in the city, only what we find in the philosophic and dramatic writings.

3. Debates continue about whether the preservation of the structure of the household supported or undermined the stability of ancient Athens. See the contrast between Glotz ([1929]1969) and Fustel de Coulanges ([1864] 1980). Glotz emphasizes the need of the individual to break out of the ties of the family, while Fustel de Coulanges stresses the importance of the family as a source out of which the city and its institutions develop.

the citizens, the institution of the lot or selection by chance for all except certain military offices and financial appointments (Aristotle, *The Constitution of Athens* 43 ff.) led to a society "in which each citizen, because he was like all the others, would have to cover the entire circuit as time went round, successively occupying and surrendering each of the symmetrical positions that made up civic space" (Vernant 1982:101). The polity transforms any one individual, set in a particular series of relationships with particular traits, into a member of a group of individuals abstracted from those ties and traits.

Accompanying this new vision of social and political relations expressed in the democratic reforms of Athens we see a new picture of the individual removed from his past; thus, for example, Orestes stands, almost irrelevant, in Aeschylus's *Oresteia,* shorn of all individuality, as others debate abstract principles of maternity and birth, ignoring the particularity of the son who has murdered his mother. Justice has moved from the web of familial particularity of the father killing the daughter, the wife killing the husband, the son killing the mother, to the abstract city that tries Orestes' case before a group of strangers chosen by lot, that is, by the mere fact that they were citizens and had no particular relationship to Orestes or to the individuals who were murdered. A focus on the family forces the individual away from such abstractions of the polity and towards particular relationships and individual traits. It is for this that the Furies, as guardians of household justice, fight—and lose.[4] While I certainly do not want to make an analogy between the Furies and Socrates, I do want to suggest that we can see both the Furies and the Socrates of the *Euthyphro* as resisting the abstract unity of the city that draws individuals out of their particular familial ties.

It was the role of the *archon basileus,* the magistrate on whose porch Socrates and Euthyphro meet, to handle legal cases having to do with religion, including homicide cases, by assigning them to one of the particular courts charged with prosecuting cases of impiety or of homicide. For instance, the *archon basileus* must determine whether a case is to be heard in the Palladium, the appropriate setting for cases of unintentional homicide "and anyone who kills a slave or a metic," or at the Areopagus for cases of deliberate homicide or wounding (Aristotle, *The Constitution of Athens* 57.3). The setting of this dialogue on the porch of the *archon basileus* has further significance, however. It was here that the laws of the city stood inscribed on the stone tablets for all to see in their physical manifestation. In a movement foreshadowing Justinian's sixth century A.D. codification of Roman law, the Athenians appointed "inscribers" in

4. See further Saxonhouse (1988c).

410 B.C. The inscribers were responsible for reinscribing the laws of Solon and Drakon. Any law not so inscribed lost its force; the validity of the laws depended on their physical presence at the Stoa Basileus (MacDowell 1978:46–47). Thus, as Euthyphro and Socrates discuss the meaning of piety, they are surrounded by the laws of the city, laws that are physically present and visible on the stones around them. These are the laws that will speak to Socrates in the *Crito*.

Let us turn first to the *Euthyphro* itself. As readers of Plato, we know why Socrates is present on the steps of the porch of the *archon basileus*. He has been accused of corrupting the young and introducing new gods into the city. Euthyphro, however, does not know why Socrates is there. Plato would have us believe that the prosecution of Socrates was a major political event of the time. Euthyphro is somewhat befuddled, removed from the day-to-day life of the city, unaware of the events that have brought Socrates to the porch of justice. Like Socrates, Euthyphro seems a stranger in the political world of Athens (*Apology* 17d), though it is to this world that he appeals in his pursuit of what is just.

In the first interchange, Euthyphro assumes that Socrates does not have a *dikē*, a private case, "as I do." Socrates responds, "A *graphē* the Athenians call it," indicating that he was there for a public crime, a crime that threatens the community at large. Such a case can be brought by any citizen supposedly concerned with the welfare of the community as a whole. Euthyphro, in contrast, arrives as a private citizen bringing a suit against another private individual (who, as we later discover, happens to be his father). A *dikē* must be brought by those affected by the crime, those who use the institutions of the city to resolve private conflicts as Apollo and the Furies do in the *Eumenides*. *Graphai* are brought by those who claim to care to preserve the institutions themselves against those who threaten them.

Euthyphro has come to prosecute his father for murder in a case so ambiguous as to make law school moot court cases look simple. A hired hand had struck and killed a slave belonging to Euthyphro's father. Euthyphro's father then bound the hands and feet of the hired hand and threw him into a ditch while he, the father, sent to Athens to inquire of the *exēgētēs* (interpreters of the law) what he should do with this murderer of a slave. Meanwhile, since the hired hand was a murderer and not worth much, the man died "from a lack of care" before the answer came back from the *exēgētēs*. Euthyphro is to indict his father for the murder of the hired hand. The major question, seldom asked, that must introduce a consideration of Euthyphro's case is, What is the incentive to bring this case to trial? What motivates the young man to go against his father with far less reason than Orestes has to act against his mother, or her Furies against

him? Socrates, who appears in Aristophanes' *Clouds* as justifying the beat-
ing of one's father, is shocked (4a–c). Euthyphro's relatives are angry at
him as well (4d). No one can understand Euthyphro's actions except Euthyphro himself. As he himself admits, by bringing "this man" to trial he
"seems to be mad (*mainesthai*)" (4a).

To understand the full extent of the difficulty with Euthyphro's decision
to prosecute his father, we must review what is known about homicide
law in the Athens of this time.[5] The primary source for this is the inscrip-
tion of Drakon's homicide law. The problem with homicide law is unique,
since for all other private cases the one harmed is the one to bring suit
against the accused. Obviously, this is impossible in the case of homicide.
The question then, in a society in which there is no public prosecutor, is
who is to bring homicide cases to court on behalf of the deceased? According to Drakon's law engraved on a stone and placed at the Stoa Basileus around 409–08 B.C.: "The basileis are to adjudge responsible for
homicide either the actual killer or the planner; and the ephetai are to
judge the case. If there is a father or brother or sons, pardon is to be agreed
to by all, or the one who opposes is to prevail. . . . A proclamation is to
be made against the killer in the *agora* by the victim's relatives as far as the
degree of cousin's son and cousin."[6] Scholars have debated whether one was
required to prosecute. One scholar suggests that a relative might feel an
obligation, but that there was no sanction should he not bring a case
(Gagarin 1979:303). Others, not quite knowing what to do with the
Euthyphro but referring to a case described by Demosthenes, argue that
no one *but* a relative could bring a case (Hansen 1981:13, passim). However, Euthyphro acts neither as kin of the murdered man, nor as master of
a slave who was killed. In no sense can we assume that he is legally required to act. The man who has died, who was bound and thrown into a
ditch, is explicitly a *pelatēs*, a hired hand, neither property nor kin. We are
not informed as to whether this man had a living father or any relations,
even so far as a cousin's son.

When Euthyphro informs Socrates that it is his father whom he intends
to prosecute, Socrates assumes that it must have been for the sake of a
relative, not a stranger. Euthyphro's response is significant: "O Socrates,
that is laughable, that you think there is any difference whether the dead
man is a relative or a stranger" (4b), even though Drakon's reinscribed law
acknowledges that there is a difference. For Euthyphro, the only question
is whether "the killer killed in justice [*en dikēi*] or not, and if with justice,
let him be, but if not, to bring a case against him even if the killer shares

5. My main sources are Gagarin (1979, 1981); Hansen (1981); MacDowell (1963, 1978).
6. Cited in and translated by Gagarin (1981:xvi–xvii.).

one's hearth and one's table" (4b–c). Euthyphro desires a concept of righteousness that is absolute and can remove him from the complexities of familial ties. The murder was either just or not; the nature of the rela-tionship to the murderer or murdered man is irrelevant. Euthyphro wants universal prescriptions without complexity. For this he turns to the ab-stract institutions of the city, to the public realm for a case that tradition-ally was handled as a private crime.[7] He has an abstract notion of *dikē*, justice or right and wrong, that moves away from any particularity of relationships. The puzzle set up by Euthyphro is the contradiction be-tween the justice premised on universal gods, for which he turns to the city, and the piety that is demanded by the family.[8]

Euthyphro desires a concept of righteousness that removes him from the complexities of familial ties; to find them he searches first in the laws of the city—giving them a greater universality than they may have had. He must also expand his abstract notion beyond the city to the gods. Although the preserved provisions of Drakon's law are "entirely secular and contain no indication of any religious origin or purpose" (Gagarin 1981: 164), Euthyphro perceives his actions as "pious." "The pollution (*miasma*) is equal if you knowingly associate with such a man and do not purify him and yourself by prosecuting him" (4c). The purification Euthy-phro seeks is to come from the laws of the city, not from the religion of the family. But his relations, including, not surprisingly, his father, are angry at him, saying that it is *not* holy for a son to go against his father. Euthyphro reacts with, "They don't understand (*kakōs eidotes*) how the divine thinks concerning the holy and the unholy" (4e). Yet, despite his own professed antipathy for the masses, Euthyphro finds this understand-ing in the laws of the city and what the many in fact do say about their gods (5e–6a). We should note, however, that it was Euthyphro's father who had sent to the *exēgētēs*, the religious interpreters, to inquire as to what he should do with the murderer and that the murderer died while the father waited for the answer.[9] The father was willing to acknowledge the complexity of a case in which a hired hand unintentionally kills a slave. Euthyphro assumes that the still more complex case with which he is con-fronted is simple.

Euthyphro longs for a simplicity of moral precepts that can include all:

7. Bonner and Smith (1938:210–11) note that "It is possible that the early attitude towards homicide as the affair of the relatives persisted in the fifth and fourth centuries to such an extent that no legislation was ever passed which permitted the homicide to be dealt with directly by others than relatives of the victim."

8. See also Lewis (1984).

9. MacDowell (1963:11) explains: "The rules of religion . . . were not published; knowledge of them was a prerogative of the *exēgētai*, ('expounders') and in the cases of doubt these officials had to be consulted."

family members, the city, and the gods. Distinctions of relations to each must be transcended by those "who know well" the nature of things. He, in seeing the world as simple, turns to the laws, the abstract institutions of the city that with the creation of democracy have moved men away from familial relations to equal individuals. Socrates draws out Euthyphro's desire for simplicity and plays up to him in this way in order to make him fall. Thus, Socrates marvels that Euthyphro knows these things so clearly (*akribōs*), that he has no fear that by prosecuting his father he may be doing something that is unholy. Euthyphro assures Socrates that he, Euthyphro, would be worth very little, hardly different from the many,[10] if he did not know all such things clearly (*akribōs*) (4e,5a). He, Euthyphro, with the arrogance of a Heraclitus, can see the unity of all, whereas others see only what is complicated. Citizens, though they depend on the universality of their principles, do not always recognize that need.

When Euthyphro is then asked by Socrates to define the *idea* of the holy, he gives this definition first: "To bring a case against anyone doing an injustice (*adikonti*); either in the case of murders or thefts of sacred objects or going astray . . . whether he happens to be a father or a mother or anyone else, and not to bring a case against them is unholy" (5d–e). Support for this "definition" comes not only from the laws of the city, but from the gods; indeed the best and the most just of the gods, Zeus, proceeded against his father for unjustly devouring his children (6a). Now, Euthyphro complains, men are angry at him for going against his father "and thus they say opposite things about the gods and about me" (6a). Apart from Euthyphro's assumption that the world is so ordered that the same rules apply to the gods and to himself, that the divine laws are identical to those inscribed on the stones around him, Euthyphro here is searching for a consistent standard, for uniformity of principles of actions for gods and for men, for son and for citizen. Again, the particularity or difference between a man and a god, between a citizen and a stranger, becomes irrelevant.[11] Euthyphro functions under the impression that there is no complexity in piety.[12] He simply has to do what is right, and the city offers him the context within which he can apply his straightforward prin-

10. We see here the complexity or incompatibility of Euthyphro's vision—on the one hand, universal principles that ignore distinctions between, e.g., a father and a hired hand, and on the other, superiority on his own to the many equals within the city.

11. Lewis (1984:253) phrases the problem in somewhat similar terms: "Euthyphron's zeal for *dikē* . . . or interfamilial justice has all but obliterated his concern for *themis* or justice within the family group . . . there is obviously a tension between loyalty to one's own and the principle of fair and equal treatment for all. Euthyphron's action can in part be understood as a working out of the 'logic' of impartial justice."

12. We should note that Socrates pushes him in the direction of admitting this: "Did you say that by one *idea* the unholy things are unholy and the holy things are holy?" (6d–e).

ciples, uncluttered by the complexities introduced when one thinks of the multiplicity of relationships that arise as the result of one's existence as a member of a city as well as of a family.

Socrates' task here, I believe,[13] is to force Euthyphro to understand complexity, to raise questions about attempts to impose abstract definitions and principles, *ideas* of right and wrong, just and unjust, pious and impious, on a complex world. At the beginning of the dialogue, Euthyphro is prepared to act against his father and his relatives for the sake of what is right, but he learns under Socrates' guidance that turning principle into practice is made difficult because of the various levels of one's existence—as a member of a household, a tribe, a city. The Athens of 399 B.C. is not Praxagora's Athens, nor is it the Thebes Eteocles wishes to exist, nor the Callipolis of the *Republic*. Euthyphro is not an autochthonous individual for whom there is no conflict between family and polis, nor can he be considered only a *demesman* or an Athenian. Thus, Euthyphro exists on a multiplicity of planes, and definitions of justice may differ and change from one level to the next. The attempt to turn to the laws of the city is in this case the questionable use of the unified to deny the multiple.

Indeed, we soon learn from Euthyphro's and Socrates' explorations that a definition of piety such as that which is dear to the gods fails because, as Euthyphro admits early on, the gods themselves are at war, with great hatreds between them (6b). They are, as is reiterated frequently, in conflict (*stasiazousi*) (7b for the first reference). The term is a political one. As for the gods to whom Euthyphro turns for a consistent model of piety when humans themselves are inconsistent, even these gods fail him as he searches for precise principles. Thus, he abstracts, trying to claim (as the Socrates of the *Republic* will do in his reformed poetry) that there is no difference among the gods, that they all would agree that he who kills unjustly must pay the penalty (8b). Euthyphro makes this a statement of general principle that Cronos and Uranus along with Zeus would accept, but Socrates again draws Euthyphro onto the level of particulars. Give me proof, he asks, that the gods think it correct for a son to bring a case of murder against his father (9a). Euthyphro, relying on his general principles, is certain that when someone knows—as he does—what is pleasing to the gods, to *all* the gods at *all* times, and acts according to that principle, he saves the private household and the community of the city; if he does otherwise and admits conflicts among the values of gods as among the values

---

Socrates helps him to articulate the perspective that underlies his decision to prosecute his father.

13. I admit that I am arguing here against the preponderance of scholarly work on the dialogue, cf., e.g., Neumann (1966a) for one of the better expositions from the opposite perspective.

of humans, if he admits the existence of stasis or factions, he destroys all (14b). Euthyphro claims that he will be able to convince the judges of this view, "if at least they listen to me speaking" (9b).

Euthyphro assumes an obviousness, a simplicity to the world, a world that he, though perhaps he alone, is able to comprehend. Socrates makes him see a world of gods and of men that is multifaceted and not uniform, a world in which context and not abstract principles must apply, a world in which gods as well as men differ. The family ties that Euthyphro was so eager to ignore at the beginning of his encounter with Socrates must be acknowledged. The laws of the city seemed to allow Euthyphro to escape from his bond to the family to which he was born and to find abstract principles. "Let any man . . ." begin the inscriptions on the stones at the Stoa Basileus. Euthyphro had come to the institutions of the city as a realm of universality, to escape the particularity of the family. He thought that he was being pious by turning to those abstract principles that make the identities of the dead man and the murderer irrelevant for the pursuit of justice. Through Socrates' manipulation, that piety and simple justice is questioned. The way to the truths of the gods is not through the city, with its attempt to focus on citizen over father or city over son. Perhaps by making piety an aspect of justice, as Socrates suggests in his final discourse with Euthyphro, Socrates is universalizing piety beyond Euthyphro, beyond the city, and even beyond the Greek gods. For the implications of such a move, we would have to go beyond *Euthyphro* at least to the *Apology* and *Crito*. The abstractions based on the city's democratic principles with which Euthyphro was working, both Socrates and Euthyphro show us, lead in circles to arguments that will walk away, as do the statues of Daedelus.

Euthyphro runs away at the end of the dialogue. To where, we do not know. Indeed, we do not even know whether Euthyphro was on his way in or out of the magistrate's office at the beginning. If Socrates' questions were successful, perhaps Euthyphro is returning to the complex world of multiple ties rather than the simple world of precise rules. It may also be that precisely by returning Euthyphro to this world, Socrates is indeed the corrupter of the young that the city of Athens is about to indict.

Meletus and the City's Defence of Unity

The counterpoint between Euthyphro and Socrates that marks the entire dialogue appears in the first few lines, as one is the object of a *graphē* and the other brings a *dikē*. Euthyphro has come to the *archon basileus* to use the laws of the city in what was considered a private matter; Socrates is there to be indicted by those eager to protect the city itself, to protect the laws and institutions of Athens from his alleged corrupting influence. Upon hearing that Socrates is accused, Euthyphro, gossip that he is, wants to know "who" before "what." Thus, before hearing from Socrates the charges against him, we learn about the man with the name meaning "care," "concern," or "attention to," a man who is young and unknown. We learn his *deme*, Pittheus, which has replaced the older, aristocratic patronymic; we thus learn first of the priority of his ties to his city over his ties to the family.

This man is Meletus, with a hook nose and scraggy beard, who recognized, according to Socrates, the importance of educating the young but, in his devotion to the city, fails to understand the means of this education, means that Socrates, through his attention to the particular, has discovered. Describing Meletus's charges against him, Socrates admits that the charges themselves are not ignoble. "For one so young, Meletus understands a matter not at all paltry" (2c). Indeed, Socrates even praises him: "He alone of the citizens appears to me to begin correctly (*orthōs*). It is correct to care for the young first of all that they be the best that is possible" (2d).[14] Such concern can only lead to the greatest good for the city. The dripping irony of the passage depends on our awareness of Meletus's youth and his uncertain knowledge, not on our questioning the principle of making men as good as possible, a principle Socrates himself often articulates as his own goal.

Socrates develops his portrait of Meletus's concerns by introducing the image of the farmer who attends to the growth of young shoots before all else. The image draws forth no specific response from Euthyphro—but are the young of the city similar to the green shoots springing forth from the earth that the farmer tends as he weeds out those bad shoots that are not up to the standards of others? The seemingly reasonable image of the farmer reminds us again of the myths of autochthony at the basis of the Athenians' self-conception of their own origins; these men, sprung from the earth with neither father nor mother, are related to one another by a common parentage in the earth itself. In such a world, Euthyphro's prosecution of the murderer might be, at the least, somewhat more pious since the hired hand would be a brother and there would be no particular father. The complexity imposed by a world in which Euthyphro does have a particular father raises questions about the piety of his deeds. In the world that abstracts from particular ties by setting all only in relation to the city and not the family, there can be no impiety.[15] Euthyphro would not

14. Jennifer Clarke pointed out to me that the use of the infinitive *archesthai* rather than the participle *archomenos* after *phainetai moi* indicates that Socrates implies appearance rather than reality here.

15. Here it is important to consider the criticism that Aristotle makes of Socrates' proposals for the destruction of the family in the *Republic*, and, in particular, that they will allow for the grossest kinds of impiety. *Politics* II.4. I will consider this in more detail in chapter 8.

be subject to the kind of questioning that Socrates engages in here. In the *Republic*, according to the noble lie, the citizens of Socrates' city are fashioned in the earth in part to establish a hierarchy, but also to ensure unity and devotion to their common mother. It is Meletus who now wishes to impose this vision of the unified Callipolis on the city of Athens—not Socrates. It is Meletus who wants to treat the young as without father or mother, who desires a uniformity that excludes a Socrates. It is Meletus who wants to create a city in which Euthyphro would indeed be pious.

Thrasymachus, in Book 1 of the *Republic*, well understands the threat that the pursuit of justice and virtue poses for the family of the just individual in a world composed of both family and city: "And when it is the turn for the just man to rule even if he suffers no other punishment, his household on account of a lack of care (*ameleian*) suffers hardships and from the people there is no benefit on account of his justice, and in addition to these things," he adds, almost as if he were thinking of Euthyphro, "his relatives and acquaintances are angry when he does not wish to serve them against what is just" (343e). Socrates as much as admits the validity of Thrasymachus's claims in his speech before the court of the Athenians. His devotion and service to his god leave him time neither for the activities of his city nor his family. Thus, he lives in deep poverty (*penia muria*).[16] In response to Thrasymachus, Socrates in the *Republic* eliminates the family, eliminates poverty and wealth, and eliminates private gods or daemons in order to found the just city. The exigencies of the trial in 399 B.C., however, allow no opportunity to transform Athens into Callipolis and to obviate the conflict between public and private. Socrates instead must show how his life—unique in the experience of Athens— accomplished what the institutions of the city cannot, that is a binding together of family and city that Meletus cannot comprehend. At the basis of this integration is Socrates' understanding of the piety that he and Euthyphro had with difficulty tried to define. It is a definition of piety particularly at odds with that offered by Meletus.[17] Meletus is concerned with a piety grounded in the needs of the city, a city that he wants to see as whole, unified, and uniform, that is, a city like that in the *Republic*. The threat of new gods such as Socrates' daemon suggests cracks in the unity

16. *Apology* 23b–c. This reference to poverty, of course, refers to the conventional notion of the task of the household as the protector of the wealth of the family. As Mary Nichols has pointed out to me, though, "his neglect of the affairs of his family would not preclude his caring for the virtue of his wife and children. Couldn't his statement that he neglects the affairs of the city and of his family mean only that . . . Socrates 'cares naught for wealth or power, but for each individual'?" (letter dated January 7, 1986).

17. It is unclear what the law against impiety entailed. In 403–402 B.C. a law was passed that no uninscribed law was to be enforced, but no law specifying what impiety was remains. MacDowell (1978:199) speculates that the law probably went "'If anyone commits impiety, let anyone who wishes submit a *graphē* . . .' without offering any definition of impiety."

of the city—as does the presence of Socrates himself, the one corrupter among all the others who improve the young. In Meletus's city, there is no room for loyalty to one's father, much less one's own god. There is no room for the particularity of a Socrates.

In the *Apology*, we find a Socrates who, from the moment he describes himself as a stranger in the law courts (17d), constantly points out how he differs from other men, how he values truth and virtue as the citizens of Athens do not, how he scorns the political power the citizens of Athens pursue. This unique Socrates, this peculiar gift of the god, stands outside the democratic equality of the city. As such, he puts himself into the position of not participating with them on an equal basis in the assembly nor before the law and paints himself not as an equal, but, as I read the *Apology*, as a father to the members of the city.[18] We may have to revise somewhat our image of Socrates giving his speech to the city: instead of visualizing the old, stooped philosopher with receding forehead and bulging eyes, opposing the city, let us imagine Socrates as an old father scolding his children—the men of Athens whom he never dignifies by calling "judges" or "citizens," with the exception of those who have acquitted him (40a). Socrates stands before the Athenians chastising them, not defending himself (Brann 1978). In so doing, he blurs the distinction between public and private, for in becoming like a father to the citizens of Athens he transforms the city into his family—and, indeed, his family into his city. He accomplishes this not as Praxagora had done, nor as we shall see him do in the *Republic* through fantastical myths and forced expulsions, but through individual action as private being, caring naught for wealth or power, but for each individual. He speaks to all, "whether young or old . . . having wealth or not" (33a). His relationship to the citizens is not impartial interaction, but personal care. Political life for him reflects the relationships of the family in which differences are acknowledged rather than suppressed.

Socrates' explanation for his unique behavior depends in part on his claim to be given to the city by the god. As evidence that he is such a gift, he refers to his inhuman lack of concern with his own affairs. For so many years he has not attended to the affairs of his family, but always "attending to yours, going to each one of you in private (*idiai*), just as a father or an older brother persuading you to be concerned with virtue" (31b). That he

18. Euthyphro describes his father as a man who is very old, indeed *eu mala presbutēs* (4a). Socrates at seventy may not be *mala presbutēs*, but he certainly lacks the youthful impetuosity of Euthyphro or Meletus. In the *Apology*, Socrates reminds us of his age frequently: a well-wrought speech will not issue from the plain-talking defendant, for "it is not at all fitting, O men, to go among you at my age fashioning speeches like a youth" (17c). See also his diminution of Meletus by commenting on his youth (25d) and his comments to the jurors who have condemned him that he will die soon anyway (38c).

receives nothing for this effort—no drachma, no appreciation—is evidence that there is not any reason (*tina logon*) behind it (31b). Clearly, he comments, it is not part of human nature (*ou gar anthrōpinōi*) to act thus, with no reason behind it. But is it not? Do not the analogies of the earlier part of the phrase belie the assertion? Do fathers or older brothers receive pay for their care of the young?

Indeed, in the earlier part of his speech, Socrates explicitly tells of fathers who pay enormous fees to others so that their sons will have the best teachers in virtue (19e–20b). Socrates' lack of care for his family is inhuman only if one separates family and city. Socrates has conflated them, going to each citizen as though that citizen were a son or a younger brother. Socrates tries to introduce to the city ties that govern relations within the family—ties that Meletus, from the deme of Pittheus, and Euthyphro, in his prosecution of his father, choose to ignore in their adoration of the city as the abstract equalizer. Socrates, through his care for the education of the citizens as individuals, transforms the city from such an abstract unity of equals to one made up of diverse citizens to whom he must go in private.

Socrates' life as a father draws him away not from the city into the private world, but to the city as the expansion of that world where he, the philosopher, the exhorter to virtue, cares for the young as a father for his son. The city, as an abstract unit with its laws engraved in stone, tries to educate all at once and to punish according to its principles without attending to the peculiarity of each individual. Meletus has argued that Socrates corrupts the young. Who, Socrates wishes to know, makes them better? Meletus, taking the question to be "what," responds, "The laws (*hoi nomoi*)." Socrates is not satisfied with the abstract notion to which his accuser turns, for Meletus has referred not to a person (who) but to a concept (what), to the joint speech of citizens engraved on the inanimate stones of the Stoa Basileus. Socrates wants to know, "What human being (*tis anthrōpos*) who first knows also this very thing, the laws?" (24e). The laws do not act by themselves; they must be concretized in the body of an individual who can use, enforce, and educate according to them. Meletus, in his pursuit of abstract unity and perfection, had wanted to bypass the particular and the concrete. Socrates will not let him do so. Socrates thus puts Meletus in the apparently absurd position of saying that all the judges, listeners, and council members, everyone except Socrates, make the young better.[19]

However absurd Meletus's responses may seem, however much he may

19. Socrates' refusal here to accept laws as acting without the particularity of individual enforcers must, of course, be contrasted to the willingness to talk to the abstract laws of the *Crito* and thus alert us to the different texture and aims of the two dialogues.

melt before Socrates' sharp intellect, Meletus is defending the unity of the community against the defiantly unique Socrates. We can see here the parallels with the *Republic* in the apparent desire to create a perfectly uniform city, only this time it is Socrates' accuser who argues for it. Meletus, so quickly able to forget the recent oligarchy that ruled in Athens, asserts the unity of the city, the absence of conflict that Socrates had forced Euthyphro to admit existed even among the gods. It is Meletus who wants to view the world as simple and whole, and especially the city within it, whereas Socrates sees them both as complex.

The problem with acknowledging differences and complexity plagues Meletus again when he fails to recognize the difference between Socrates and Anaxagoras. After Meletus insists: "He [Socrates] says that the sun is a stone and the moon earth," Socrates asks, "Do you think you are accusing Anaxagoras, dear Meletus?" (26d). Meletus sees no difference between Socrates and Anaxagoras, between individuals or cases of impiety brought before the city.[20] Again, concerning Socrates' beliefs in the gods, Meletus insists that Socrates believes in "no gods, none at all, by Zeus" (26e). As Socrates develops his argument, however, it becomes clear that Meletus's uniform perception of the atheistic Socrates must be modified by Socrates' belief in his daemon and in demigods, those complex creatures born of gods and humans. The belief in the gods is neither a clear yes nor no, but a complex integration of the relation between actions and actors, children of the gods and their parents.

Socrates refers specifically to his own sons in the third section of the *Apology,* in the last few words of his speech, when he asks of those who have condemned him to care for his children: "My sons, when they become young men, punish them, O men, causing them the same grief such as I caused you, if they seem to you to be concerned with either money or anything else before virtue, and if they being nothing appear to be something, rebuke them just as I did to you—that they do not tend to those things they should tend to and that they think themselves, being nothing, to be worthy of something and if you do these things, both myself and my sons shall have had justice from you" (41e–42a).

It may seem surprising that Socrates asks those who have condemned him to care for his sons, but the justice referred to at the end of the passage indicates the parallel between Socrates' treatment of the city and the treatment he asks for his sons from the city. Justice will be accomplished when the city becomes a surrogate father to Socrates' sons as Socrates had been

---

20. MacDowell (1978:200–201) suggests that the law according to which Anaxagoras was perhaps prosecuted lapsed in the rewriting of the laws in 403 B.C., especially since the procedures for a trial of impiety differed substantially between the two cases.

father to the citizens of Athens. The transformation that Socrates, as a gift of the god, had tried to accomplish in the city was based on his going from one to another—trying to make each one as good as possible and not treating them, as Meletus would, as young shoots to be tended and weeded by a farmer, abstracted from the particularity of their growth and birth. Socrates' death will have been repaid and his sons will receive justice should the city adopt for itself the same task of education that Socrates had practiced in the city of Athens. This is not the uniform education that Socrates prescribes in the *Republic,* but rather the education that comes from "going among you as a father or as an older brother" (31b). By condemning Socrates, the Athenians have shown as little understanding of the meaning of piety, respect, and loyalty for those who have made one—or made one better—as Euthyphro did in the dialogue that precedes the *Apology.* The reaction we see on the part of the city arises from the desire to eliminate the one who acts against the principles of abstraction, who introduces particularities and differences, who raises questions about the principles of Athenian democracy. The justice of the city, in repayment for the death of Socrates, will be for the city itself to take over the role of Socrates, to act as Socrates with regard to the young and to learn the meaning of piety to the old. It is unclear whether Socrates expects this transformation to take place, indeed whether he ever expects that it can, but the story of the *Crito* explains why he must let the city try, why he supports the city when it did not support him, why, like Strepsiades, he continues to love his son though he causes him grief.

The Laws Speak

The laws that stood silently inscribed on stone while Euthyphro and Socrates discussed the meaning of piety speak to Socrates as he and his aged friend Crito discourse on whether Socrates should escape from prison. Socrates had tried to calm the anxious and eager Crito down, urging him to look at the *logoi,* the arguments, before precipitously arranging for the prison guards to be bribed and the cart to be brought to spirit Socrates away to Thessaly. When the *logoi* that Socrates presents bring Crito to an impasse, and Crito, unable to answer Socrates' probing questions, must admit, "I do not know," Socrates introduces the speech of the laws and the community (*hoi nomoi kai to koinon*) of the city (50a). They speak as one, the unified expression of the city's existence, and they draw Socrates and Crito as well into the unity of city so that they become part of, rather than distinct from, the city.

The autochthony myth as the unifying force binding together the citizens belongs to a mythical past; it is not the earth, the mother that Eteocles, for instance, desires to defend, but the laws that now claim to have borne Socrates and Crito and bind them to that abstract notion of community, *to koinon*. The language and the imagery may change. For Eteocles and for the characters in *Ion*, the original unity of the city depends on birth from a maternal earth. In the established city of Athens whose laws speak to Socrates, the unity takes on a masculine image captured in the language of *patris*[21] (51a–d). "Did we not first give birth to you?", the laws ask of the two old men (50d), as if the abstraction of the laws could replace the eroticism of human bodies. The evocation of the ancient myth is modified when the laws continue, "Through us, your father took your mother and begat you" (50d). The laws have established dependence on themselves for the existence of citizens; fathers and mothers are only accidental. It is a world Eteocles and Euthyphro would envy. No ambiguity nor impiety would shade the certainty of decisions to attack one's own brother or prosecute one's own father. One should here remember as well the passage in the *Apology* where Socrates announces that he will not bring forward his sons. He introduces this comment with a quotation from the *Odyssey*: "And these are the very words of Homer: I have not been born 'from oak or stone,' but from human beings, so that there are relatives (*oikeioi*) and three sons to me" (34d). Penelope, eager to learn the ancestry of the handsome stranger who has come to Ithaca with news of her lost husband, uses these words to probe the stranger's background (*Odyssey* XIX.163). Men are not just washed up upon the shore as messengers to ladies waiting there—nor, indeed, are they simply given to a sleepy city by "the god." The laws in their speech to Socrates would like the citizens not necessarily to see themselves as "born of oak or stone," but at least born of the laws.

The laws in their speech to Socrates then attribute to themselves Socrates' education in music and gymnastics, an education, they claim, given to Socrates by his father only at the direction of the laws of the city. The father, as the laws portray it, would not be a father without the laws to direct his paternal actions. Crito, in his appeal to Socrates earlier in the dialogue, had criticized Socrates for betraying his role as father to his own sons, deserting them and allowing them to become orphans in a world of chance. "Either it is necessary not to make children," he admonishes Socrates, "or else to endure the hardships of nourishing and educating them" (45d). When the laws speak through the voice of Socrates they respond to Crito's concern: they, the laws themselves, not the biological fathers, take care of the offspring of the city. Socrates, in the laws' version

---

21. We might note that though *patris* clearly derives from the masculine *pater*, father, the noun itself is feminine, *he patris*.

of paternity, appears not so much as a father to his own sons, but only as an intermediary in the city's creation of offspring. Thus, they say to Socrates, "Would you be able to say first that you are not ours—as both offspring and slave, both you and those born before you?" (50e). Socrates here merges into the city-become-family but not as a father, as distinct, as unique, as he was in the *Apology*. Rather, the universalizing laws of the city of Athens incorporate him and his sons into the unity of the city.

The image of the laws as father, as begetter of the inhabitants of the city, is not fully convincing, for Socrates has his laws slide over the very obvious distinctions between physical and theoretical birth. The laws of Athens may have made Socrates a legitimate child, a citizen of the city of Athens, but they did not give birth to him any more than the earth could give birth to the inhabitants of a more ancient Athens or a fantastical Callipolis. A lie is a lie. A fatherland (*patris*) is not a father (*patēr*). The laws speak of what is understood through the mind, the intellect, and of what is created through speech or *logos*. They go beyond the senses that divide cities into fathers and families, into individuals and friends, and create a unity that we cannot experience with our senses. Like Zeno with his arrow, the laws ask us to ignore what the senses perceive and to accept what the mind tells us.[22]

Socrates has the laws of the city respond further to Crito's claim that he, Socrates, is deserting his children. The laws assure him that his friends will care for the children. In other words, Crito's argument that Socrates would be deserting them is replaced by the notion that friends can take over his post as educator of his children. Socrates, at least as the laws present it, is no longer the unique individual who dominates the speech of the *Apology*. Rather, as in a democratic society run mostly by lot, he is replaceable. In Meletus's argument, all the citizens educated the young of the city except Socrates, who stood alone. Now, in the laws' version, Socrates is no longer special, not the expert horse trainer he implies that he is in the *Apology*. In yielding to the speech of the city, Socrates yields his uniqueness, and any other may take his place.

Towards the end of his presentation of the speech of the laws, Socrates compares their speech to the music of flutes. The simile is not entirely flattering, for flutes play a less than noble role in the Platonic dialogues. In the *Symposium*, for example, they accompany the drunken Alcibiades as he appears at the dinner party, disrupting the ordered discourses on love. In the *Republic*, Socrates favors the instrument of Apollo, the lyre, over

---

22. An irony throughout this section is that Crito is the friend who cares most thoroughly for the body of Socrates and has difficulty rising above the concern for the body to more abstract concepts. See especially the *Phaedo*.

the flute of the satyr Marsyas; the flute is thus banished from Callipolis. Socrates listens to the arguments of the laws as if he were a Corybant; their words echo in his ears. They are not his speech, for they enchant rather than convince him. Now Crito would speak in vain; so loud is the sound of the laws, that Socrates is unable to hear the speech of others. The once silent laws to which Socrates gives voice speak of a unified city that Socrates, at least in the *Crito,* accepts. But he does so only after the two earlier dialogues have revealed to us his hesitations about such a vision.

5 Autochthony and Unity in the *Menexenus* and *Statesman*

> Human beings were poured forth from the earth in the manner of worms with no author and with no design.
>
> Democritus

In the *Euthyphro, Apology,* and *Crito,* Socrates stands outside the city and its laws, questioning the unity of the city and its goal of comprehensiveness. As the gift of the god, Socrates had escaped incorporation into the city so unified by its laws and its equalizing democracy. In each of those dialogues portraying Socrates' confrontation with the city, Plato gives the speech pursuing unity to another character, namely, Euthyphro, Meletus in the *Apology,* and the laws themselves in the *Crito.* In each case, though, Socrates mocks those claims and makes us question the pursuit of a unified polity. In the dialogues under discussion in this chapter, Plato again gives the claims of political unity to interlocutors other than Socrates, but Socrates does not in these works take on directly the role of critic. Indeed, in the *Menexenus,* he himself recites Aspasia's speech, a funeral oration and, in the *Statesman,* where the myth of Cronos is told by a stranger from Elea, he is barely visible. The claims for unity may seem less challenged, but the structure of the dialogues works again, I shall argue, to raise questions that Socrates as a character within the dialogues had raised for us in chapter 4.

In both the *Menexenus* and the *Statesman,* myths of autochthony provide the foundation for a unified vision, in one case of the city, in the other of the cosmos itself. As discussed in chapter 3, autochthony myths can unify a political regime by eliminating the disruptive forces of family ties and differentiating one city from those around it. The earth as mother appears, through autochthony, to defy a natural world empty of natural cities, a world where natural boundaries are not articulated. Autochthony can give the patina of that which is ancient to the city and thus, at a time when age and nature fuse (Strauss 1953:1, chap. 3), it can give to the city the appearance of being in accord with nature. The questioning that surrounds the legitimacy of the modern state explicitly founded in opposition to nature through a social contract or through conquest is not an issue here; the city born from the earth appears to be the natural unit demanding men's devotion and allegiance. Autochthony, though, need not only give birth to a distinct city; it can also be the gift of a bountiful earth (duBois 1988:42), a mother who sends forth men as well as the fruit by which men shall live. In this version, autochthony does not divide men, for there is no scarcity, no conflict, and men live united as one "herd" nourished by the mother that bore them. In yet another version, autochthony can suggest the chaotic world of Democritus's first men who appear "without design." Plato's characters, however, reject the Democritean version and explore instead the meaning of a unity created by autochthony, in the *Menexenus* for the city, in the *Statesman* for all humans.

As the pedagogue in Euripides' *Ion* taught, myths of autochthony that unify the city exclude that which is other, those not born of the land, or those not necessary for the beginning of the city (i.e., the foreigner and the human female). The unity engendered by this form of autochthony depends on the exclusion of difference. In *Ion,* this appeared as a profound xenophobia on the part of the Athenians, a fear that foreigners would upset the comprehensive unity based on a common ancestry from those born from the earth. Further, claims to autochthony on the part of the inhabitants of the city can have aristocratic connotations: those born from the line of autochthonous ancestors have a close association with the land and thus rank higher in the city's hierarchy. But democracy can also draw on autochthony, as we see in Athenian funeral orations,[1] for in democracy the equality of the individual directly faces the laws of the city without the intermediary force of the family, at least theoretically, if not historically.[2] An autochthony that bypasses the family unifies the community of individuals; they inhabit the city as the children of one mother rather than live divided by birth from many different mothers and fathers. In such a world of unified citizenry, tragedies disappear and the conflicts faced by an Eteocles or a Socrates, by an Antigone or a Euthyphro, never arise.

In the ironic discourse of the *Menexenus* and the *Statesman*, we find two strangers—one of whom is a woman—who give expression to the

1. See especially Loraux (1986).
2. Loraux (1979) distinguishes between autochthony "sans mediation," where autochthony "accordée collectivement à tous les Athèniens" and an autochthony "derivée," one where the focus is on what is inherited.

autochthony myths that might work to remove them from the unity of the city of Athens. They both, however, transform the myth so as to make it hospitable to their peculiar station in life. In Aspasia's version in the *Menexenus,* the earth as mother is emphasized so that the city's unity originates from the reproductive female, not from the speech of such men as Pericles. In the *Statesman,* the Stranger's myth portrays a prepolitical world in which there are no cities that might exclude him, branding him as other, as a foreigner. Rather, the rise of cities and the development of boundaries mark the fall from a primordial (Parmenidean, I shall suggest) unity. Only after that fall can the term "stranger" have any meaning. It is in the transformation of the myth that the difficulties surrounding the unity created by autochthony emerge. Thus, at the same time that Plato introduces this myth into his dialogues, he reveals its inadequacy and leaves us to question any society whose unity is based on myths of autochthony.

Aspasia: The Birth of a City and the Death of Its Citizens

In their engagements with Socrates, Meletus and Euthyphro were passionate about the city and about their principles of right and wrong. Through the laws of the city, each pursued a unity and eschewed diversity. In their search for wholeness, they dismissed Socrates as the importer of complexities, such as gods who disagreed with one another or daemons who were neither gods nor men. In the story recited in the *Menexenus,* engagement and commitment are lacking, and we see instead the almost joyful pursuit of excess and bad taste. The funeral oration Aspasia taught to her "student" Socrates belongs to the genre of speeches that looks to sorcery (235a). Through magic, it moves the soul and unites a city fractured by war and death.[3] The playful tone mocking the rhetorical power of seductive speeches that introduces the oration must alert us to the ironies that pervade the text.

Pericles' funeral oration had included those notorious words urging women to shun the glory sought after by men and to accept that she who is least spoken of, whether for good or for ill, falls least below her nature. In a perverse response to this, Plato has Pericles' mistress, a woman much spoken of, pose as the author of Pericles' famed funeral oration, as well as of an alternative oration replete with references to the original Thucydi-

---

3. Loraux (1986) has given us an exhaustive study of the role of the funeral oration in the creation of the city as an abstract unity, born in the imagination. For the purposes of this study, I will turn only to the speech of Pericles as presented in Thucydides' *History* in addition to Aspasia's speech, although as Loraux illustrates, the genre as a whole has a critical role in establishing the identity of a "city" separate and independent from the particular individuals who are its citizens.

dean version.[4] They both exalt the city and understand its greatness in terms of its unity and wholeness. For Pericles, in the funeral oration at least, this unity comes from the incorporation of the individual into the community. "We alone think the one who does not share [in political life] not as one who keeps to himself, but as one who is useless" (Thucydides 2.40.2). There is no such thing as the uninvolved citizen. The eroticism that could define the love of one's own, that could isolate one from the community of the city, is transferred to the city as Pericles asks his citizens to gaze upon Athens (as if there were an "Athens" upon which one could gaze in the same way that one might gaze upon a beautiful young woman or man or even statue),[5] so that they might become her lovers (*erastai*) (Thucydides 2.43.1). To do this, they must create in their minds an "Athens," for she, the city, does not exist except as the object of the human intellect and emotion.[6] For Aspasia, speaking as a woman and a foreigner who is drawn into the city of Athens through her sexual relations, unity in Athens comes from a feminized understanding of autochthony, not from the creative intellect of the male politicians who abstract from the bodies of men both living and dead to "see" the city.

Before we pursue this contrast, though, we must consider the context of Aspasia's speech. The dialogue is so curious that the temptation to remove it from the corpus of Platonic works has led many scholars to dismiss it as unPlatonic, but Platonic it is.[7] Like the *Gorgias*, this dialogue is outrageously anachronistic. Aspasia and Socrates die long before many of the events described in Aspasia's speech take place; thus, their conversation (and Socrates' conversation with Menexenus) must occur after the main characters are dead. As Loraux suggests, the dialogue "blur[s] the frontiers between life and death" (1986:265). Indeed, the very act of listening to a funeral oration puts one on that "frontier." Socrates admits that funeral orations leave him unable to recall who he is or where he is (235c).[8] After "speech from the speaker enters [his] ears" (235c), he believes himself

4. Kahn (1963), along with others, raises the question of whether the reference in the *Menexenus* to the funeral oration of Pericles is to the one attributed to him by Thucydides or one that he might actually have given at the end of the first year of the Peloponnesian War. In what follows, I will treat it as the Thucydidean version, convinced as I am that Thucydides' *History* looms large behind the Platonic dialogues. For further discussion of my views on this, see Saxonhouse (1983a).

5. This language should actually work to make us aware of the relationship between Thucydides' presentation of the city in this speech and the forms or ideas in the world of being as we learn about them in the *Symposium* or the *Republic*, for example. See further chapter 6.

6. Loraux (1986: conclusion) calls this the "Imaginary Athens."

7. See, e.g., Allen (1984:319); Taylor (1956:41); Shorey (1933:185).

8. See here the beginning of the *Apology* in reference to the speeches of his accusers.

living on the Islands of the Blessed, not in Athens. For four or five days
after hearing a funeral oration, Socrates continues in his state of confusion,
not knowing the difference between the deathly perfection of the Islands
of the Blessed and life in the city of Athens. The oration confuses life and
death, as does the dialogue in which it is embedded. In a sense, the oration
and the dialogue working their magic obliterate the boundaries between
the living and the dead. The speech transforms the dead into the living by
making them part of the city that is praised by the speaker, and it transforms the living into the dead by transporting them to the Island of the
Blessed.[9] The speeches glorify those who have died by glorifying the city
and, like the laws of the *Crito,* they leave the audience unable to respond
for the buzzing that goes on in their ears. Citizens seem nobler to themselves, or as Socrates says of himself, better born (*gennaiteros*) (235b)
(Maletz 1976:32), and instead of grieving for those who have died, the
dead whom they are commemorating, they focus on their birth, the birth
of Athens, and the birth of citizens.

The recitation of Aspasia's speech by a Socrates who must have died
long before the dramatic action of the dialogue is prefaced by the question
of Socrates' relation to the city, the city that killed him and sent him to the
Islands of the Blessed for far longer than four or five days afterwards. The
Crito shows us a Socrates yielding his uniqueness (so evident in the *Apology*) to the speech of the laws. In the *Menexenus,* he admits his enchant-
ment with the language of the speeches over the dead and adds that, by
making him part of the city, they make him grow bigger, better, and more
beautiful along with the city. Socrates the outsider, the one executed by
the city because he fractured the city's wholeness, presents to us the speech
of those who through language would unify the city, exalt the city, and
make those within it (even Socrates himself) think of it as greater and
more noble than it is (235b). The anachronisms of the dialogues keep this
irony before us, as does the fantastical image of a foreign woman reciting
a funeral oration for Athens. The rhetorical power and brilliance of Pericles' supposed speech, the male voice in the city, recorded by Thucydides,
contrasts with the female voice speaking not only for the dead, but from
the dead and through the dead.

Socrates recites the speech of Aspasia at the behest of his young friend
Menexenus. Although we know that Menexenus was present at Socrates'
death (and thus heard a very different discourse about death then) (*Phaedo*
59b), we get a better sense of this young man from Plato's brief dialogue

9. Loraux (1986:268) points out that the Greek has Socrates distinguish between himself and the city when he says: " 'For they [the foreigners] seem to have the same impression
of me as of the rest of the city.' " I see assimilation here rather than differentiation. The speeches
are such that they unite rather than separate out one individual, even Socrates, from another.

about friendship, the *Lysis*. Menexenus is Lysis's closest friend, though this does not mean that the friends do not have their rivalries. To be friends is not necessarily to be one. Menexenus, in the dialogue that bears his name, meets Socrates on his return from the *agora*. He is excited. The *boulē* is about to select the speaker who is to deliver the funeral oration for this year's soldiers killed in battle. Menexenus sees the city as a realm of competition: who will be chosen among those who contend for the honor? Socrates' response is that it does not much matter who is chosen, for all funeral speeches are basically the same. Socrates dismisses the contention for political glory that arouses Menexenus's interest.

Part of the tension in the dialogue on friendship arises from the question of how unified friends really are or can be. While the dictum that friends share all alike is being expressed, Menexenus is called away and thus does not share in his friend's conversation with Socrates. Nevertheless, when he does return he is certain of the unity and, indeed, the identity of friends, even if he is not certain of the unity of the city composed of friends. When questioned about who is lover and who is loved in the *Lysis,* Menexenus says that there is no difference between them. Friendship, as he sees it, is based not on the needfulness of one and the fullness of another. The Periclean request that the citizens gaze upon the city until love of her fills them has no analogue in Menexenus' understanding of the mutuality of friendship.

In the *Menexenus,* Socrates moves this young man to a relationship with the city that contrasts with the friendship between two young boys. In this relationship with the city, we can no longer say that there is no difference between the beloved and the lover. The city cannot love back. It can only be a "beloved." By praising the city rather than the dead individuals, the orator makes the city the beloved and the citizens lovers who gaze longingly at her, themselves elevated by their love and forgetful of the personal losses that they may have suffered. The death of citizens in battle exalts the city so that the death of individuals is immersed in the beauty of the city. No special praise of actions that might separate one actor from another is offered. All are enclosed in the city. The praise is unified and unifying, enchanting the listeners, Athenian or foreign, with the magnificence of the city. It "enables the living to identify with the andres agathoi [good men] whose funeral the city is celebrating . . . since, like Socrates, every Athenian takes the praise to apply to himself and immediately transforms himself into an epic character" (Louraux 1986:265).

Menexenus had appeared on the scene coming from the *agora*. Socrates teases him: he, Menexenus, having shown his interest in politics, thinks that he has reached the completion of his education and philosophy and now isready to rule over those who are older than he. Though Menexenus pretends to submit to Socrates' rule—"if you allow it and advise it" (234b)—Socrates' goals appear to be to transform the politics of Menexenus fromcontention and striving for rule to a politics of unity and incorporationof self into the city. It is through the speech of Aspasia, as absurd as it is, that he can accomplish this.[10]

Funeral orations may be powerful, but every speaker in Athens, Socrates contends, has one or several already prepared, ready to give at a moment's notice. Nor are they difficult speeches to compose, Socrates claims. Praising the Athenians before themselves requires no great oratorical skills. Menexenus takes up the bluff: "Well then, do you think you would be able to speak yourself, if necessary and if the council would choose you?" (235e). Socrates himself has no speech ready to offer, but just yesterday he learned one under the strict discipline of his teacher in rhetoric, Aspasia. Would he recite it? Menexenus asks. Socrates hesitates: he is an old man (we might add, a dead man) behaving like a young man, playing games. He compares the forthcoming recitation of the speech to his dancing naked for Menexenus, should it give Menexenus pleasure. As we read the speech, we must also remember how neither Socrates' age nor his form could turn this into a pleasing simile. The speech he would give to the city to honor its dead by praising its city is as ugly as a naked, dancing Socrates—and perhaps just as seductive. At the end of the recitation, Socrates elicits a promise that Menexenus will not speak openly of the oration Socrates had just recited. The public speech of the dialogue is to be kept private, out of the *agora* from which Menexenus had just come when he meets Socrates, that is, it must be kept within, like a woman would be kept—spoken of neither for praise nor for blame in the city at large, though the men may talk of it in private, like women, among themselves.

It is with all these qualifications that we must now consider the content of Aspasia's speech—a speech to commemorate the dead citizens by unifying the living and the dead, just as the anachronisms of the dramatic setting bring together the living Menexenus, the dead Socrates, and the dead Aspasia. The contrast with the publicly recited speech of Pericles recorded in Thucydides' *History* dominates any reading of the beginning of Aspasia's speech. Whereas Pericles begins with the laws of the city and then questions the law that requires speeches that can never be adequate to the deeds of men, Aspasia's private oration begins with the individuals who died and their families. Pericles had begun with the irreconcilable conflict between word and deed, mind and action, a conflict to be resolved later in the speech as the citizens through death become one with the city.

---

10. Clavaud (1980) divides analyses of the dialogue into those which take seriously the speech and those which see it as farcical. It is, of course, both.

Aspasia alerts us to the tension between family and city, a tension that can only be resolved when, as in Praxagora's plan, city becomes family. The men who have died, she claims, sent forth "in common (*koinei*) by the city, in private (*idiai*) by the household members" (236d). Pericles had tried to exclude the private; the family appeared only at the end of the speech and then only to be merged with the city, or to be dismissed as the women were sent within. Aspasia expresses the tension immediately, but she resolves this by praising first the origins of the Athenians and recalling the unifying autochthony of Athenian myths. The men whom she praises are good men because they were born from good men. And where did these good men come from? Their ancestors arrived not from foreign places as settlers in a strange land; they were "*autochthonas* inhabiting and living in their true fatherland and being nourished not by any stepmother, as other men, but by their mother, the land in which they lived" (237b).

Having questioned the laws of Athens, Pericles turns to the ancestors; it is just and proper, he claims, but the praise offered is rather modest. "It is just and also proper that this honor of remembrance be given to them [the ancestors] on this occasion." They have inhabited the same land and handed it on to their off spring until the present (2.36.1). The allusion to autochthony is hard to discern (though commentators on this passage are often quick to point it out) and quickly passed over. Praise for the ancestors in Pericles' speech is undercut by the still greater (*eti mallon*) praise for our fathers, as Pericles moves quickly towards the present with each generation enhancing Athens's greatness. Aspasia, by contrast, in private and in her female voice, lingers over the ancient world of autochthony (237b–c). For her it is most just (*dikaiotaton*) to praise their mother (237c). Pericles had yielded: "It is just and also proper to give the honor of remembrance," but he turned quickly to the true glory of Athens, not its ancestry but the unifying force of its *politeia*, the constitutional structure or the "regime." Aspasia focuses on the land, worthy of praise by all men (237c), and on the origins of Athens in ancient history, rather than on the imaginary unity created by the *politeia*.[11]

Aspasia, returning to the oldest history, talks of how the gods loved the land, how Athene and Poseidon fought over the land long before a *politeia* established by men gave theoretical birth to Athens. While other lands gave birth to wild and strange beasts and living things, the land of Attica was pure and unblemished by monsters. "This land gave birth to the ancestors of those [who died] and of ourselves" (237e). Once they were born she, the earth, like all bearers of children, nourished what she bore. In

---

11. Maletz (1976:68) comments on the piety of Aspasia's speech and Pericles' focus on the acts of humans rather than of gods.

what might seem a perverse use of logic, Aspasia argues backwards: since the land provided nourishment, she must also have given us birth. Thus, the land as mother, Aspasia analogizes, could only provide the abundance of fruits if she had indeed generated the Athenians. Since the land, Aspasia claims, is bountiful, she must have given birth to Athens' ancestors. As Aspasia develops the conceit, the human mother appears only as a weak imitation of the earth. "For the earth does not imitate the female . . . but the female the earth" (238a).

This same maternal earth established the gods as the organizers of their lives, as the teachers of their crafts, as the guardians of their land. This ancient history defines the Athens of the present. Pericles, who offered few lines to acknowledge that which was old as he raced to the present, envisioned citizens unified by their adoration of the current city. He turned the city into a beloved object. Indeed, Pericles' speech abstracts the city from the land just as his wartime policy, bringing the farmers within the city walls and relying on the navy, depended on making Athens free from her land. The unity Pericles envisions is one that transcends the senses that see the hills and the acropolis; he turns instead to memories and passions sequestered in citizens' hearts. Aspasia's unified city depends on the land that one sees and on the city's origins from that land. She is turning the city, as did Praxagora, into a unity based on the family, but for the Platonic Aspasia it is a family defined by generation from the soil—and generation defined only in terms of the mother. The story of Hephaestus pursuing the virgin Athene that embellished *Ion* is nowhere to be heard in Aspasia's speech.

Only after the maternal earth has received her extended praise over several pages does Aspasia turn to the *politeia* devised by those ancestors nourished and raised by the gods. Here she speaks briefly (*dia bracheōn*) (238bc); this was the topic on which Pericles based most of his speech. For Pericles, all Hellas imitates the *politeia* of Athens. It is the model of how one must live in a great city. For Aspasia, the *politeia* is the nurturer of men (*trophē anthrōpōn*) (238c); the nurturing *politeia* must now take on the role the earth had in the past and make the men of the city good. It is not the "democratia" that Pericles praises, the regime that looks to the welfare of the many; it is an "aristocratia," both then, when the ancestors lived, and now as we live as citizens in the city (*politeuometha*) (238c). Aspasia does not make much of political typologies; instead, she blurs the boundaries between political regimes.[12] The unity of Athens comes from the political organization, certainly, but it goes deeper; since autochthony is the source of the unity, it does not really matter what particular form

12. Or, as Maletz (1976:127) suggests, she ignores the history of political transformations, e.g., from monarchy to democracy to oligarchy to democracy.

the *politeia* takes. Thus, while she may call it an "aristocratia," another (Pericles? Or she herself as the author of Pericles' speech?) may call it a "democratia" and yet another whatever pleases him. The uniting element is not the structure of the *politeia*, but the common birth of those governed by the *politeia*. While other cities are composed of various individuals, of masters and of slaves, "we are all brothers born from one mother (*mias metros*)," neither slaves nor masters of one another (238e–239a). In Pericles' speech, such equality comes explicitly from the *politeia* (Thucydides 2.37.1), rather than from the ancient birth of ancestors out of the earth many generations ago. By contrast, Aspasia claims that the cause (*aitia*) of the *politeia* is the equality of birth (*he ex isou genesis*) (238e). That birth from the land, the mother, continues, in a sense, to the Athens in which they now live and for which the dead have given their lives. Thus, she reiterates: "We do not think it worthy to be slaves and masters of one another, but the equality of birth according to nature (*isogonia . . . kata phusin*) forces us to pursue an equality (*isonomia*) according to the law (*kata nomon*)" (239a).

The recollections of the birth of Athens in the soil of Attica, a birth that united and continues to unite (and thus create) the city of Athens, attends to what is past; Aspasia leads only slowly to the present as she recounts in some detail the history of Athens, moving from ancient events to the treaty signed between the Persian king and Athens long after her death, the Peace of Antalcidas. The Periclean funeral oration is virtually absent of history. The present, an immortal present where past and future are one, where death is meaningless because the soldiers killed in battle live on in the memory engraved in the hearts of the citizens, dominates the Athenian leader's speech. It is a speech that virtually denies the death of the dead by making them one with a vital and vibrant city that lives. Aspasia's method is one of unity, not through the denial of death, but through a focus on birth, nurture, and growth, the growth of a city and then only later of *politeia*. Thus, history from antique times is recalled, back to the Amazons and other early threats, though Aspasia admits all these tales are better told by the poets. After learning the central facts of Persian history, she takes us to the "offspring of this land" (239d), who prevented the enslaving of the Greeks at Marathon, and on through selected incidents in the Peloponnesian War down to 386 B.C. and the King's Peace. She, a woman, replaces these tales told by male poets and male historians, citing one incident but omitting another. The conflicts that tore Athens apart at the end of the Peloponnesian War were, she claims, handled with moderation because of the "common birth" (*suggeneia*) that provided a sense of friendship and because Athenians came from "the same stock (*homophulon*) not in word but in deed" (244a). None of this history intrudes into the world of Pericles' speech. His Athens remains present, not past. He ignores generation as he ignores death. His city exists in the realm of speech, the creation of male intellect. Aspasia's city is the product of the generative, creative act of the female body, the land that has borne the Athenians and nourished them. Aspasia's is a lesson in rhetoric offered from behind closed doors.

The final consolation, such as it is, in Pericles' speech urges further identification with the present and the beautiful city; private loss is turned into support for the city, and parents still of childbearing age are urged to bear more children to help them forget those who are no longer with them—and to help secure the safety of the city that has lost her soldiers. Aspasia's consolation urges instead that grief not overcome the parents. They must identify with the children who were willing to die for the city. Excess grief would raise suspicions about their difference from brave sons and thus about their own paternity. More important, however, are the comments about the children and parents of the dead. The city has set up laws that they must be cared for and, in particular, the city will nurture the children. Indeed, as this passage continues, the language of the *Menexenus* forces us to recall the conflation between the city and the family we noted in the speech of the laws at the end of the *Crito:* "And while they are still children, she[13] stands in the shape of a father and when they have arrived at manhood she sends them away in full armor" (249a).[14] These children the city will nurture "so that their orphanhood will be as unclear to them as possible" (249a). As in the *Crito,* the city can easily replace the family, and tensions fade.

Thus Aspasia speaks, or so Socrates says. Menexenus is suspicious. Of course he admires Aspasia and is grateful to her for such a speech—or to whoever gave it. Mostly, he thanks Socrates, who in the process of reciting the speech became Aspasia. As a male Socrates offered the female version of the city and the death of citizens. It was a story in which the feminine force dominates. She, Athens, as mother of all, creates a unity out of diversity based on a commonality of birth. The Athenians molded within her become one because of her deeds, not because of language used by an articulate leader of the city who can hold up a vision of beauty before an enthralled citizenry. The deed of creative reproduction here dominates the speech of the *politeia* and yet, like the autochthony of the plays, earth as mother means that the human female as mother is unnecessary. Aspasia can honor the female force that gave birth to citizens, but when the citizens die it is the city as father who buries them, who protects their young and their old. The female forces are left far behind in an ancient unifying

13. The pronoun *autē* (feminine) is used for *polis,* which creates the curious mixing of "she" as a "father," *patēr.*

14. Loraux (1986:27) explains the significance of this "send[ing] them away in full armor" or "endow[ing] them with a complete set of armor" in her translation.

history. Aspasia's speech—or Socrates'—is in many ways a rejection of the principles of Pericles' speech. There it was *logos,* reason, word, speech itself, that could transcend the material world, that could rise above the deeds and incorporate, unify, and elevate them. The *Menexenus* presents a world that tries to create a unity without the dependence on the sorcery of words, a unity that derives from the material world of procreation. Thus it must be a speech kept within, in secrecy away from the public world of the city that it claims to commemorate.

Menexenus was about to enter the political world of competition. He was entranced by the question of who would be chosen for the special honor of delivering the funeral oration. The speech that Socrates gives via Aspasia will moderate that competitive spirit; naked Socrates, dancing before Menexenus, dampens any desire for public glory. Instead, the feminized unity born from the ancient soil leaves the city whole, divided neither by political strife nor the competitive pursuit of glory.

The Statesman: *A Retelling of Parmenides' Voyage*

Hesiod tells twice the story of Pandora, she who was the gift of the gods who brought suffering to men. Zeus of the *Theogony* has her fashioned, "an evil thing (*kakon*) for men" (570). Men must now marry, lest they arrive at destructive, ruinous old age with no one to tend their needs (604–5). Before, perhaps, they worried neither about old age nor about procreation. Did they live as youths forever? Were they like the gods? Sexual reproduction is not a joy or a delight, but a burden for men who now must live with the evil of womanhood. *Works and Days* portrays a Pandora enjoying all the gifts bestowed upon her by the gods, the fine clothing, the golden necklaces, who, as she opens the famed jar, releases cares and griefs for mankind (95). She is the cause of all sorrows. Before her fashioning by the gods, men lived in a golden age, a period of abundance and joy. She transforms the life of men into that of suffering and of work.

The tale told by the Eleatic Stranger in the *Statesman,* the so-called Myth of Cronos, offers a new version of this story. The god (or gods), not woman, transforms the life of man from one of undivided happiness into one of sexual reproduction and toil—and politics. Woman is exonerated as it is the god, like the captain of a ship, who lets go of the rudder that controlled the revolutions of the earth. From the perfection of autochthonous, asexual birth, men are thrust cataclysmicly into a world of sexuality and aging.

We must, however, put this story of transformation into the context of the dialogue as a whole.[15] The story follows a failure of intellectual pursuit.

15. I shall certainly not attempt to analyze the entire dialogue nor the importance of its connections with the *Sophist;* for such analyses, see the extensive studies by Benardete (1984); Klein (1977); Miller (1980); Scodel (1987).

The Eleatic Stranger and his companions, including the Young Socrates (who serves as the primary interlocutor), the relatively silent Socrates, and the mathematician Theodorus, are searching for the *politikos*, the one who truly understands (though he need not practice) the political art. To find him, the Stranger has engaged the Young Socrates in the process of separation or division down the middle, the so-called "diacritical" method, each time casting aside the useless half. They have asserted the identity of the science that rules over household and over city. "It is clear that there is one science about all these things" (259c). Such a science must have an object, however; in the case of the statesman it is obvious that it must have a living object or objects. And here begins the process of separating out the object of political science from all other living things.

The Young Socrates, unsophisticated in the complexities of mathematical divisions, wants simply to separate out men from beasts (262a). His verve and his courage the Stranger admires, but he warns that they can not "suffer again" the same mistake. Young Socrates learns that they must not separate out small parts from the whole. Rather, they must cut through the middle. In this way they are more likely to chance on the *ideas* (262b). The Stranger compares Young Socrates' division to dividing the human race into Hellenes and all others, the barbarians. But barbarians cannot constitute a class; they "do not mingle[16] and are at variance with one another" (262d). All that the barbarians share is their "otherness" to the Hellenes. So too with beasts and men. All that beasts share is that they are not men. According to the Stranger's method, equal divisions are required, such as we find in numbers between odd and even "and in the race of human beings between male and female" (262e).[17] Thus, they cut through the middle, not separating men out at once. They divide according to whether these living creatures live in herds or individually, whether they live on the land or in the water, whether they walk or fly, whether they have horns or not, and so forth, until we are left with the featherless (bare) chicken (266e) and the two-legged pig (266c) as the object of the statesman's rule.[18]

Missing from this pursuit of the object of statesmanship is any sense of cities in the plural, or what might separate one herd from another herd (Benardete 1984:III.87). By focusing on the objects rather than on the

16. This is an awkward translation of *ameiktois*, which later in the dialogue (276a) will mean "do not interbreed."

17. Miller (1980:21) adds the explanatory comment: "And since what each distinguished form *is not* (does not combine with) is definite and positive, they are genuinely informative; to know what each *is not* illuminates what it *is*."

18. We cannot ignore here Glaucon's city of pigs, where there is no ruler necessary, where everything simply functions according to nature; Miller (1980:31 n. 32) reminds us as well of the passage in the *Theatetus* (161c), where man is also compared to a pig.

divisions within the object, the Stranger eliminates "strangeness." The dia-critical method, in fact, seems to unite rather than divide. No one who is human, a two-legged pig, is foreign. We might see two foundations for the separation of the human species into herds. Men divide themselves, define one realm as their own territory and property and exclude others from entering into and participating in that world. Or nature might divide the species into herds based on origins, on birth, so that the unity of the city does not come from the conscious act of human choice but from birth according to nature. Such is the tale Aspasia tells in her funeral oration. Nature, the earth herself, divided Athens from all others. Athens's glory in Aspasia's version depends mostly on the natural birth of Athenians from the soil of Attica. She makes a cut not allowed by the Stranger's diacritical method.

The Stranger has created by his divisions a world without strangers or foreigners, a world without war, and, thus, a world with the gentle rule of the statesman over his two-legged pigs. We do not here need rulers who are war-leaders or generals. Indeed, he talks of kings as nurturers and care-takers, barely distinguishable from nurses and midwives (267e–268a). We seem to find ourselves in the peaceful age of Cronos before the tale of Cronos is told. Thus, the statesman is he who cares for and who tends to the physical welfare of the objects of his rule, just as a shepherd tends to the welfare of his sheep (or, as Thrasymachus reminds us in another con-text, tends to their welfare until he becomes a meat eater).[19] The myth enters the dialogue, though, only after further efforts are made to distin-guish the statesman from others who care for the featherless chicken; he must stand apart from those who feed, those who clothe, those who cure. This effort, however, leaves the statesman undefined and so we must leave—only temporarily, we are assured (268d)—the imported, sophisti-cated methodology of mathematical divisions and begin anew (268d) by openly going back to the ancient myths. We must turn our minds to this tale, as if we were children. The Young Socrates is indeed young, not many years away from childhood (268e); he need not pretend much in order to listen to the story as if he were a child. The tale is complex, though, even to an adult.[20] Time frames meld into one another, chronology wanders, rotations return upon themselves.

19. One could argue that what we see here is the "feminization" of politics; no war, no realm of masculine glory, only the activities of the female who cares for the body, activities that will be captured when the Stranger uses his paradigms of weaving and breeding later in the dialogue.

20. Rosen (1988). In particular, scholars have confused the period of the cataclysm when the earth reverses its revolutions with the Age of Cronos, as Vidal-Naquet (1981:208), e.g., does when he writes that, in the Age of Cronos, "Men are born greybeards and die babies."

The Stranger begins with a strange appearance (*phasma*) of the sort that has occurred before and will occur again, one that happened during the time when Atreus and Thyestes lived. (Earlier, those who interpreted the messages from the gods were eliminated from the practice of statesmanship; apparently, this does not mean that we who pursue the statesman are limited to the qualities required by the statesman.) The young interlocutor thinks of the *phasma* as a sign, a *sēmeion* (268e), specifically of the golden lamb, possession of which was to determine who inherited the estate of Pelops. Atreus appeared to be the one favored by the gods. The youth interprets the *phasma* in relation to determinations of inheritance, of disputes about the boundaries between one man's possessions and another's. The stranger whose diacritical method had led to the unity of men does not view the world as divided by boundary stones that separate one man from another, or one herd from another. Rather, he interprets the sign cosmically and thinks instead about the motions of the sun. The *phasma* to which he refers is when the sun stood still and then changed directions so that it sets where once it rose and it rises where once it set. The cosmological transformation dominates the petty inheritance disputes of a pair of Argive brothers in the Stranger's analysis.

The Stranger also ignores the Hesiodic tale of the overthrow of Cronos. There is no rebellion against the father, no violent castration; thus, there can be a cycle that takes us back again to what once was. History is not linear in its telling nor in its chronology. It presents the unity of the world as its different aspects are revealed or uncovered for us.[21] We move from an epoch of divine rule to one when men must rule over themselves, from a golden age of unity to an age of diversity, conflict, and sorrows, and then back again. The cause of this transformation, the significance of the sign, comes from the inborn nature of necessity and the letting go or taking control by the gods of the revolutions of the cosmos, not from the evil that is womankind.

The first detail introduced about the Age of Cronos is that, when Cronos ruled, men were "born from the earth and not from each other" (269b). The stories are old and the stories are many from this period, but "no one has spoken what experience (*to pathos*) was the cause of all these things. Now [in the search for the statesman] it must be stated" (269bc). The Stranger is the one who will tell it, and so he speaks of the cataclysmic transformations when much human life is destroyed. When the god's hand

---

Or Rosen (1988:70): "Death in the counternormal cycle is then not a return to the womb since there is no sexual reproduction; it is instead a vanishing." This is true only in the transition period. See below p. 126.

21. See Rosen (1988) for a more extreme statement of this.

limits the revolutions of the cosmos, men spring from the earth. The Stranger's version of autochthony differs greatly from that of Aspasia, however. For Aspasia, autochthony identifies the peculiar and the particular, separating out a subset of humanity attached to a specific land. The Stranger's autochthony unifies the whole species who live in the golden age when Cronos rules; these men need not depend on sexual reproduction for the human species to survive.

The story is not so simple as it appears; that is, it is not just the Age of Cronos and autochthony, the Age of Zeus and sexual reproduction. There is a transitional period as well, when everything reverses itself, "when the revolution becomes the opposite of what is now established," at which point there is "from necessity the greatest destruction" (270c) of animals and of the human race.[22] Of the latter, only a small part was left. These humans endured many marvelous and new experiences. Time stops and all creatures stop aging. Instead, they become younger and younger as the gray hairs darken, bearded faces become smooth, and bodies grow smaller until they become infants and then "entirely disappear" (270e). As the Young Socrates realizes, such events would leave the earth depopulated by all living creatures. So, whence come those from whom we ourselves are sprung? "It is clear, O Socrates, that the birth from one another was not in that time by nature (*phusei*) as it was at that time, but the earthborn race (*gēgenes*) . . . was the one which came out of the earth again at that time" (271a). Those who had been alive when the cosmos changed its course reversed their motion and retreated into infancy and finally disappeared, but those who had died and were buried in the earth were brought back to life (*anabiōskomenous*) (271b) and grew up (*phuomenous*) as the *gēgeneis* "according to this story out of necessity" (271bc). The earth is thus re-populated autochthonously, not necessarily according to cities or communities. There is no mention of Theban heroes or Athenian kings. All remains one. The Age of Zeus in this telling seems to precede the Age of Cronos.

The Stranger turns now to the life of those men descended from the *gēgeneis*, when the god cared for the whole and when "according to regions and in the same way all parts of the cosmos were distributed under the ruling gods" (271d).[23] Divine daemons distributed animals according to race and flocks, and each daemon was entirely self-ruling for each one of those which he shepherded. "There was no wildness, nor eating of one

22. Note that the Stranger here divides in speech men and beasts, which he was unwilling to divide according to the method of *diakrisis* earlier in the dialogue.

23. As Scodel (1987:81) observes, the language here is reminiscent of the diacritical sections, but the divisions seem not to extend as far, e.g., there is no distinction between wild and tame since there are no wild beasts in the Age of Cronos.

another and there was no war among them nor conflict at all" (271de). Thus were the animals governed and thus were men governed "according to race." For the god established shepherds over them all, just as men, being now a different and more divine being, shepherd the races (e.g., sheep and pigs) inferior to themselves. During this age there was no *politeia* nor possession of women or children. All men came to life out of the earth remembering nothing of those before. The past (and along with it ancestors and piety) plays no role in this world. All families and cities are absent, but "they had bountiful fruit from the trees and much other stuff not being produced from agriculture, but by the earth itself (*automatēs*) giving forth." Shelter they did not need: "they grazed naked" and slept in open fields of grass (272a). Thus was life in the paradise of the Age of Cronos.

We should note that during this period there were no divisions among men, no regimes that distingushed a Sparta from an Athens nor political leaders drawn from the inhabitants themselves. Rather, there was the tending and caring of flocks by the demigod. There were no divisions according to families, nothing to define that which was close (*oikeios*) and that which was distant or foreign. There was no reproduction that might lead to family exclusivity or private property. It was a world Praxagora would have loved, the luxury of plenty and the life of the eternal festival.

During this golden age of abundance, when men lacked nothing, there was the opportunity for men "to be together . . . through words" for the sake of philosophy, not only with other men but also with wild beasts (*theriōs*) (272c). The Stranger was right to reject the Young Socrates' cavalier distinction between animal and man. In the Age of Cronos, they form a unity capable of the highest human activity, philosophy. The Age of Cronos has no barbarians—neither the speech of men nor animals is incomprehensible. Whether men and animals did indeed spend their time discoursing about Anaxagoras or Parmenidean theories of unity or the right life for man is not at all clear. Since there were no tensions in their lives, nothing that was unsatisfied, no choices to be made, they may just as well have sat around being fattened, as did the men in Glaucon's city of pigs. Most likely, men did not take advantage of the ability to discourse with the animals in order to philosophize.[24] Possessing all, existing in a state of completion, they would not have been driven to question and to pursue the unknown. In a linguistic equality with animals they become animals. The initial proposal that men might philosophize with animals is

24. Scodel (1987:81 n. 9) focuses on the process of forgetting that characterizes the Age of Cronos and the impossibility of philosophy under such circumstances. Rosen (1988:72) also comments, "we may find it easy enough to conclude that in the absence of memory, experience, Eros, and work, there can be no philosophy."

curious. It reduces the activity of philosophy to a bestial activity rather than being a divine one. Although in the Age of Cronos unity and order control the cosmos and boundaries that separate man from animal can be destroyed, the transcending of these boundaries suggests, as did the dia-critical method, the reduction of man to the level of animal rather than the raising of animal to the level of man.

The differences between the flocks of animals and the flocks of men is acknowledged in their different caretakers, but there are no conflicts among the various flocks. In particular, there is no meat eating and thus no kill-ing. Nevertheless, despite its apparent idyllic perfection, it was an age that, because of matter's necessary imperfections, could not last: "For when the time of all these things was completed and it was necessary that there be a transformation and in particular all the race of the earth (*gēinon . . . genos*) was used up . . . then the ship's captain of the whole, just as if letting go of the rudder, withdrew into his own place to observe" (272d–e). At that point the cosmos turned back on itself, and those who ruled over the different races, like the gods, let go, unleashing yet another cataclysm as we enter the Age of Zeus.

The cataclysm initiates a world of temporality, of generation (*tēn gene-sin*) (273e), of change. At this point there is a certain confusion in the myth for we are back in the Age of Zeus, which we left earlier to enter the Age of Cronos. Let us call this period Zeus[b]. This epoch continues to deteriorate with no apparent resistance until it reaches such a state of con-fusion (*aporia*) that the god, caring lest the world "storm-tossed by chaos dissolve into an endless sea of dissimilarity (*anomoiotētos*)" (273d), asserts his role as the ship's captain, reverses the chronology of deterioration, halts the invasion of "dissimilarity," and makes the cosmos deathless and age-less, without generation again; the cosmos is thus rescued and brought back to the perfection of the Age of Cronos. During Zeus[b], genesis had dominated and with genesis came diversity, change, and multiplicity. It is a vision of the universe horrifying to the Eleatic Stranger, whose intellec-tual mentor, Parmenides, had written his great poem to proclaim and to prove the untruth of genesis, of differences, of multiplicity. Thus, the god rescues the cosmos, almost, it appears in the breathless treatment of the myth, at the last minute. Because nothing made of matter can be "death-less and ageless," the god lets go yet another time, and we are now located in the third Age of Zeus, Zeus[c]. This time, men resist and need not depend only on the gods stepping in at the last moment to prevent the chaos of dissimilarity from taking over.

The world does change with the second rudder released: beasts who are by nature harsh, but who conversed with men in the Age of Cronos, now become wild and vicious, while mankind, weak and unprotected, is destroyed by them. Men in this early period of Zeus[c] (and in this age we can now talk of historical transformations, of coming into being, of dying) are without crafts or arts and they suffer, for nourishment no longer appears *automatēs*. Though the gods no longer rule over them and the other beasts, the gods do give to men skills, fire from Prometheus, crafts (*technai*) from Hephaestus, which will enable them to survive and thus rule over themselves. Men, not gods, have put together the human life (*anthrōpinon bion*) (274d). On their own, men themselves prevent the deterioration into a "limitless sea of dissimilarity." They must do this not by recreating on their own the world of Cronos as a unified whole; rather, they divide and join—much as the Stranger and the Young Socrates did in the earlier section of the dialogue and will do in the later sections. Now, during Zeus[c], we find families, the possession of children and wives, that is, the introduction of the concepts of mine and thine, concepts irrelevant during an age of perfection when there was want of nothing. We find men working the fields and, most specifically, we find political regimes where men must rule over men, that is, equals must rule over equals, create their own order, and make their own distinctions.

What has this elaborate and confusing myth taught to the participants in the dialogue? They were searching for the wrong ruler. They had been looking for the ruler over men in the period of Cronos and thus, for them, all humans were one. Now they must look for statesmen who order against the physical deterioration that plagues all living things. They no longer rely on autochthony to repopulate the earth. Instead, the ruler, as we learn later in the dialogue, must attend to the blending of opposites as he joins male with female and courage with moderation.

The Eleatic Stranger has told a Parmenidean tale. The Age of Cronos is the mythologized Way of Truth; it is being, whole and one. "What is not" does not exist, and so men and animals can converse with one another. Their dialogue disappears, though, when we do distinguish between man and beast, as Young Socrates does automatically and precipitously early in the dialogue. But this can only happen in the world of seeming when Zeus reigns. The Eleatic Stranger is faithful to his Parmenides, for he tells of both the Way of Truth and the Way of Opinion, or of "what is" and of what comes into being and therefore cannot be. To offer the political portraits of Parmenides' two ways of knowing, the Stranger offers his listeners two opposed understandings of nature. The Ages of Cronos (there appear to be two at least) offer a natural world of wholeness, of completion, of limits. It is a world where nature has no *erōs*, no lack, and thus no need to generate; all is one and all is whole. Divisions are the result of faulty senses. The Ages of Zeus present a nature that is multiple and manifold, a nature that is divided within itself, that is comprised of multiple races of animals who do not discourse with one another, a world of male and female who reproduce. This is a natural world that must preserve itself by generation, the mixing of opposites; it does not survive by simply being, as does "what is" for Parmenides. Whatever unity there is in this world of genesis must come from the activities of men, from the rule they set over themselves. The human being must act with crafts (such as the political craft) and skills against a natural world that seems to be moving inexorably towards the "sea of difference." The crafts, as the model of the second half of the dialogue indicates, must weave together the opposites with which the Ages of Zeus have left us. In turn, weaving together opposites, that which is dissimilar, characterizes human rather than divine care. The world of the god is one of unity. The Eleatic Stranger takes us into the world of men when the cosmos, tempest-tossed, is left in human hands. We know not whether the god will need to step in again, concerned that all will dissipate, whether he will need to take control and lead us back to autochthonous births, or whether, in this third Age of Zeus, we will be able to stand firm against the god, unifying ourselves into cities, armed with our feminine crafts of weaving and control over generation. Parmenidean unity is not what we must now see with our minds; it is an historical past or historical future. The Stranger, despite his strangeness and his teacher, tells the senses to focus on the present and the many, to work with divisions that unify and not to unify by excluding divisions. The myth has shown us these two worlds, and it has left us focused on the world of motion, cities, and sexual generation.

Conclusion

Autochthony for the Stranger marked a period of cataclysm and of perfection—a period when human life vanished and had to be brought back to life again from the souls that were in the earth, a period that, being whole and complete in itself, eschewed sexual generation. For Aspasia, autochthony became the basis for what was unique, what was divided off from others. Focusing on the life of her city and eschewing tales of cosmological transformation, she gives a funeral oration in which we find the maternal appropriation of war by the female; she speaks more of birth than of death. The Stranger relegates the myth of autochthony to a prepolitical period. The unity that accompanied his autochthony eliminated the need for all cities, for all conflict. There were no wars in the Ages of Cronos. Sexual generation allows for divisions; a city that arises from autochthonous origins will have no understanding of the human crafts that combine and work together that which is opposite. As the dialogue between the Stranger and the Young Socrates proceeds, that is the theme that keeps emerging—the weaving together of opposed elements—moderation and courage in particular. This is the political craft. For Aspasia the woman, autochthony allows her to take a stand against the masculine war, to assert the primacy of birth. In so doing, she must emphasize a unity that seems to exclude the male as the male had previously excluded the female. It is the Eleatic Stranger, a moderate man himself (*Sophist* 216b), who can include difference within the community as Aspasia the female cannot.

Autochthony myths in each of these dialogues serve as correctives on each other. Aspasia imagines that autochthony can unite a city, that tales of past generation can serve as the basis for current glory and unity. The *Statesman* makes of autochthony an apolitical myth, one that characterizes a world without cities when all is one and "what is" is. His myth demands that we move beyond autochthony to understand the political as integrating a multitude of phenomena.

In the *Republic*, Socrates tells his own autochthony myth, a Cadmean tale he calls it, of men and women fashioned by the god in the earth. With it, Socrates begins the process of unifying the city he is founding in speech, of making the Stranger's Age of Cronos the model for the best city. The question we will have to pose is whether Socrates can conjoin the perfection of the Age of Cronos with the temporality of political life found in the Age of Zeus in his Callipolis, his "beautiful city."

6

Callipolis: Socrates' Escape from Tragedy

> . . . so that each man, practicing that one task that is his own, will become not many, but one, and thus the entire city will grow by nature (*phuetai*) to be one, but not many.
>
> *Republic*

We turn now to the *Republic*. No longer does Socrates allow others to express the city's dream of unity and uniformity. No longer does Socrates stand aside and in a way undercut the dream of a polity that is undivided, comprehensive, and complete. In the *Republic*, he speaks forth forcefully as he founds his Callipolis, his beautiful city, that lives for a moment in time before it dissolves into many disparate pieces.[1] The tension in Socrates' presentation must be understood from the Platonic perspective, for here it is Plato giving speech to Socrates, not Socrates giving speech to the laws of Athens, to Aspasia, or, as we shall see in the next chapter, to Diotima. The story of the *Republic*, from Socrates' descent into the Piraeus to the nightlong discourse to the final myth of resurrection, is well known and I need not rehearse it here. Likewise with the characters, Glaucon's enthusiasms, Adeimantus's reserve, and Thrasymachus's taming have all become part of our discourse about the dialogue.[2] Instead, I shall focus in this chapter first on the politics of interpretation expounded in this dialogue, a style that serves as a pref-

1. The name Callipolis is given to Socrates' city only in Book 7 (527c), but for ease of expression I shall refer to the third city founded by Socrates and his interlocutors as Callipolis throughout this chapter.

2. Strauss (1964: chap. 2) perhaps most powerfully made these points part of the interpretive discourse about the *Republic*, and Bloom (1968) helped to popularize this, but others who would not see themselves as students of either still pay attention to such characteristic aspects of the Platonic dialogues as the personalities of the interlocutors. See, e.g., Clay (1988); Lee (1989); Nussbaum (1986: 127, especially chap. 6).

ace to the uniform political community towards which Socrates draws his young interlocutors. I shall then focus on the actual community founded in speech by Socrates and his friends where the city becomes one and not many. At the beginning of Book 2, Glaucon tells the famous story of Gyges' ancestor, a shepherd, who upon descending into a chasm discovers the ring that could make him invisible, that is, be unseen. Such power enables him in storybook fashion to kill the king and marry the queen. The movement of the *Republic* in some respects parallels the tale of Gyges' ring. Socrates searches for (and perhaps sometimes creates) the unseen unity behind a world of multiplicity. That unseen unity is not to allow him to seduce queens and kill kings, but rather to escape from the tragic conflicts that plagued the lives of those for whom nature is multiple and varied.[3]

The Politics of Interpretation: Poetry and Narration in Callipolis

Poetry

In Books 2 and 3 of the *Republic*, Socrates censors the poetry that is to be recited in Callipolis. To censor, Socrates must interpret, and interpret he does as he excises passage after passage of Homeric poetry. The method of interpretation that leads to these excisions is related directly to the structure of the city he and his young friends are founding. Each passage to be excised has only one dimension, just as the men and women in his city are to have only one dimension and one job. Interpretation and the subsequent censorship become a process of flattening the text under consideration. As such, Socratic censorship becomes the countermodel to the multiplicity of levels of interpretation to which the Platonic dialogue drives us. The Platonic dialogue thus works in opposition to the Socratic poetry of the *Republic* and, in the very process of discussing poetry, Socrates, as participant in a dialogue, undermines the interpretive model he is proposing. By counterposing the internal Socratic interpretation of the poetry he censors to the multidimensional levels of interpretation to which Socrates' own words (through Plato) lead us, I hope to indicate not only how Plato

3. This chapter is based on an unpublished paper delivered at Virginia Polytechnic Institute and State University at a conference on Methodological Approaches to Plato (1988) and is an expansion of ideas originally expressed in Saxonhouse (1986b:411–13). The literature on the *Republic* is so vast, the debates so varied, the disagreements so profound, that a chapter dealing with the *Republic* runs the risk of being weighted down with endless footnotes concerning arguments, disagreements, qualifications, etc. Let me note here simply those works that have most profoundly influenced my reading of the *Republic* and leave aside the critical apparatus that would, I believe, distract rather than add to the arguments: Benardete (1989); Bloom (1968); Clay (1988); Nichols (1987); Nussbaum (1986); Strauss (1964).

opens up his texts to us, but also how the process of interpretation practiced within the dialogue will raise questions about the beauty of the polity
founded there.

Socrates is at a loss (*aporēsas*) (375d). His true city, his city of pigs, is
not good enough for Glaucon. To satisfy the fevered desires of Glaucon,
who longs for that which makes life satisfying to the aesthetic vision, Socrates has increased the size of his original city—so much so that we must
now have warriors, men whose one task is the protection of the city from
internal and external enemies. According to the very principles articulated
at the first moments describing the first city, each individual is to perform
that task for which he or she is best suited by nature. Nature appears
beneficent, giving to each man one, and only one, skill. No man will be
able to build houses and cobble shoes equally well. No "career choices"
need to be made. However, the very concept of the warrior sets Socrates
at a loss, for the warrior must violate this principle and be double-natured
rather than uniform with one specialized skill. Socrates has built his city
on the principle of unidimensionality: one man, one art. The warriors
who will indeed be only warriors and not shoemakers or housebuilders,
must, however, be gentle towards those they know and harsh towards the
unknown. Where to find such men?

The solution to Socrates' self-confessed confusion lies close at hand, in
the philosophic dogs, those animals combining in one nature the gentle
and the fierce. Socrates sees this as a thing worthy of "wonder," and questions Glaucon as to whether he too had not "wondered" at it; Glaucon
admits that he had not given it much thought at all before now. Nevertheless, having discovered this wondrous unity of gentleness and fierceness in
nature, Socrates has his agenda set. The combination is possible *in nature,*
however wondrous such a unity may be. How, then, do we take this very
special canine model and transfer it to the warriors in his city? This time
there is no *aporia,* no *thauma,* as the interlocutors change and Adeimantus,
the one least filled with wonder, takes over the job of responding to
Socrates (376d). The two of them together turn to storytelling: "Come
now, just as storytellers (*muthologountes*) in a story (*muthōi*) and enjoying
our leisure, let us educate in speech the men" (376d). This education in
speech becomes the interpretation of poetry and its censorship.

It is here that the city of Callipolis begins. The city of pigs emerges
from the forces of nature,[4] and has no need of the poet's constructive arts.
As the city grows, artifice enters and we are able to mimic nature (as in
the unity of the fierce and the gentle in the philosophic dogs) through the

---

4. Derivatives of *phuo* recur frequently in the passages describing the first city: e.g., 370a,
370b, 370c.

crafts of the poet. By nature, men are unable to combine ferocity with gentleness; poetry accomplishes what nature does not. Poetry is thus the mechanism that brings the city into being; so potent is it that it must be treated like a dangerous drug, administered only by those with special skills and not by the *idiōtes,* the private men (389b). Those gathered at Cephalus's house become specialists in the founding of cities and the interpretation of poetry that must go along with it.

Socrates, reporting on his night in the Piraeus, sets himself into a story within another story: there is the story he tells to the unnamed auditor who sits through the recitation of the long discourse from the night before and, within that story, he and his interlocutors, especially Glaucon and Adeimantus, fashion yet another story of the political foundation of a city. Within the second story, they are now to tell more stories, stories that have the explicit pedagogical purpose of training men to hold within themselves the qualities of philosophic dogs. Socrates alerts his cofounders that they must pay special attention to the young for "the beginning (*archē*) is the most important of every action (*ergon*)" (377a). It is at that point, the *archē,* that it (whatever "it" may be, a child, a city, a story) is molded and takes on the stamp (*tupos*) (377b) that anyone may wish to give it. Socrates here is explicitly discussing the young who are to be molded as members of the city, but the city that he is founding is also in its youth, waiting to be given form, to be stamped by the storytellers. The work they engage in now, as they begin the founding, is the greatest be-cause at this point in time they set the stamp on the whole enterprise. The city to which he gives birth through *muthos* is to be shaped and molded into the form of a man. Just as the young are molded (*plattetai*), so too are the poems. The stories, the young, and the city are all fashioned by the speech of Socrates and the assent of his companions.

The poems that the young hear as they are molded with the proper stamp must be fashioned so as to bring into being the model warrior, the man (or woman) who loves his (or her) city, obeys its rulers, and is fierce and hostile to those outside the city. "Shall we thus easily allow the young to hear whatever stories they happen upon, stories molded by just anyone and to take into their souls those opinions for the most part which, when they mature, we think to be the opposite of what is necessary?" (377b). Not in anyway whatsoever, responds Adeimantus. Thus, they practice the politics of interpretation, standing over the makers of stories, accepting the ones nobly made and rejecting those that are not so well made, those that might lead to uncertainty, and, in particular, those that might lead to an awareness of the multidimensionality of human life. For the city with-out conflict, for the beautiful city, he must exclude any works that allude to the problem of choice or that suggest that a nonbeneficent nature may make men multifaceted, forcing them to make choices that often reveal the tragedy of human existence. The poetic interpretation and censorship performed by Socrates removes from his city the tragedy of choice. The world is to be made simple: no enemies who are in fact friends, no friends who are in fact enemies, and later no families that are not cities, no citizens who are not brothers. Such complexities must be removed, for they interfere with love of the city and hatred of enemies. Since this city is to be founded on the principles of simplicity from the very moment of its birth, so too must the young men in the city be trained to view the world as simple and uniform from the very moment of their own birth.

The standards of interpretation that are imposed under these conditions require that the complex stories from the past, composed by unsupervised poets who saw the world in all its varied and ambiguous splendor, must be abandoned. The Socratic reading of those stories portrays them not only as lies (which some, in fact, may not be), but as harmful. They may suggest that there are cases where the gods, and Zeus in particular, may be the dispenser of evil as well as good, where they may be the cause of the breaking of oaths, where they punish those who least appear to deserve punishment (379e–380b). Such stories present the gods themselves as multifaceted, the source of both good and evil, rather than as uniform and simple. Complexity in the heavens will undermine the simplicity at the foundation of the city of Callipolis. The interpretation and subsequent purging of poetry is to ensure this simplicity and uniformity.

First among the tales to be excised is the biggest lie about the biggest affair: the castration of Uranus. As Socrates reads the story as it appears in Hesiod, it is an ugly tale, an offensive tale, far too suggestive to be recited to the young. It tells of the son's revolt against the father. But Socrates ignores the other aspects of the tale, for example, the devotion of Cronos to his mother, his pity for her suffering, and the violence of the father, for, as Ge says: "For he first sought to do unseemly (*aeikea*) deeds." Cronos's promise to his mother that he shall accomplish the deed she requests includes the same phrase: "For he first sought to do unseemly deeds" (*Theogony* 165, 172). In Socrates' interpretation, presented before the young men founding the city and molding the young who are to inhabit the city, the justice of Cronos's deed is ignored. Nor does Socrates note that from the castration, beauty in the form of Aphrodite, along with *erōs*, desire, are born (*Theogony* 188–206). The interpretation leading to the censorship of this part of Hesiod's version of the birth of the gods considers only one aspect of the tale: the revolt of the son. All else is omitted, as Socrates excises threats to authority and the possible justifications for those threats—as well as the benefits that may accrue from those threats. The tale of Uranus is one of unspeakable secrets; the beauty and the ambiguous status of justice would be misinterpreted, Socrates assumes here, by the young who would understand these poems only as a justification for harshness to their parents. In the castration of their own fathers, the young would see only a fine imitation of the oldest of the gods.

There is in this story within within a story within yet another story only one interpretation that matters; it is the interpretation that supports obedience and subordination to authority, irrespective of the validity of the claims to rule. After all, our interlocutors are founding a city in which the warriors must protect and preserve. There is no need for them individually to learn about the complexity of the beauty of Aphrodite being born from the ugliest of deeds or about the complexity of justice and decisions concerning who deserves what and how we distinguish between attachments to Mother Earth and Father Sky. The multiple interpretations that one can apply to the experience of the human being in the actual city or to the tragedies that are performed on the Attic stage or to a Platonic dialogue have no place in the Socratic city of strict demarcation between jobs and roles. The attempt to combine fierceness and gentleness had left him originally at a loss, resolved only by the philosophic dogs for which he now interprets and legislates the tales that are to be sung.

At the start of Book 3, Socrates has completed his purge of the lies that the poets tell about the gods; he has eliminated any stories that might suggest that the gods differ among themselves; that Hephaestus might be called upon to defend his mother against the violence of Zeus (378d; *Iliad* 560–660); that Zeus can be the distributor of evils as well as goods (379c–e); and that the gods can change form and thus deceive mortals. He now can consider the next level, the heroes, those models of human behavior (mostly in the form of Achilles) set forth for the young to imitate. While the poetic presentation of the gods must develop their uniformity and remove all the ambiguity that might arise in the world of the divine, we study the heroes by concerning ourselves with courage. But the question of courage leads immediately to the issue of death, and Book 3 turns to seven brief passages from Homer. These passages are quickly interpreted as presenting an unpleasant portrait of the underworld and subsequently are excised from the tales to be sung in the city of Callipolis. The seven passages follow hard and fast upon one another. All deal with Homer's presentation of Hades, that realm of shadows where everyone and everything lacks substance, a world resembling the darkness, the dampness of caverns where the ghost-like cries of bats make us tremble in fear. The images of Hades are powerful, the scene in Hades uninviting. All would make the readers or the hearers shrink from acting so as to release their souls into such a place; they lead us rather to prefer, like the dead Achilles, the life of a serf of a lotless man to an existence where one is the king of all the dead (386c; *Odyssey* 11.489–91). So depressing is the portrait of Hades included in the poets of old that Socrates fears it might prevent the young from fighting willingly and enthusiastically in defence of their city. They would, he suspects, do anything rather than face an existence of endless darkness where souls float aimlessly. Socrates interprets the poems from the perspective of the founder of a city. Such images will not be useful (*ōphelima*) (386c) for those intending to be fighters. They will turn men away from the pursuit of manly glory in battle. Such is the power of poetry.

We, however, outside the structure of the dialogue, peering into, perhaps we may say eavesdropping on, the conversation in Cephalus's house, can see more in these excised passages. We are the ones who have not been molded to understand the poets from a single perspective. We have learned that poetry (and dialogues) can have many levels of interpretation. When we first meet Achilles, though not by name, he is lamenting his existence in Hades, admitting a desire to live as a serf of a lotless man on earth. As the descriptions of Hades culled from the poetry of Homer continue, we can well understand why the young men training to be warriors for the city must not listen to the sad tales of the existence that awaits them in the land of Hades. It is a land of shadows, rather than substance. It is a land where not much seems to happen. At the same time, however, that we read the passages with regard to their relationship to the city of Callipolis, we must also ask whether Socrates sees the parallels between his own and Achilles' situation. In his speech before the jury at Athens, Socrates will compare himself to the son of Thetis, replacing the courage of Achilles on the battlefield with his own courage in the courtroom: neither man flees. Both willingly face death when circumstances require such courage (*Apology* 28a–d). Here, in the passage cited from the *Odyssey*, Achilles appears most eager to flee death. Do the parallels between Achilles and Socrates hold here as well? Is Socrates too eager to flee from Cephalus's house, which may have become for him a Hades?

We must not ignore the dramatic setting. Dinner is long overdue; the only foods to enjoy are the insubstantial words of Socrates. Thrasymachus, knowing the very substantial benefits of tyranny, scornfully mocks Socrates at the end of Book 1: "Let that be your feast at the festival of Bendis" (354a). All Socrates has offered are words; Thrasymachus can offer feasts, meat, wine, and all the relishes and delicacies Glaucon is soon to demand. Night has by now come to the Piraeus, overtaking the bright light of a Mediterranean seaport. Within the house of Cephalus, stomachs grumble and lamps must cast shadows on the walls. Only the bats are missing. In this world of shadows and insubstantial words, Socrates rules. He has overthrown the various opponents who are contenders for the rule: Cephalus, the old man himself; Thrasymachus, the man who clearly prefers meat and relishes to words; and the poet Simonides, for whom young Polemarchus speaks. Socrates has thus taken over the leadership role in the house of Cephalus and the young men gathered there follow him. But like Achilles, is he wondering as he enjoys the adulation of the young, Who wants to have power here? Is he as scornful of his role here as Achilles is of his existence in Hades? After all, Socrates remains down in the Piraeus only because he was caught and restrained by the war leader. He himself was eager to go back to the city (327a–c). Rule among the babbling souls may mean as little to him as it does to Achilles. Is he perhaps like the Tiresias of the central of the seven quotes who, though dead, retains his senses and has a mind that can "understand" (386d; *Odyssey* 10.492–95) while the others are just floating shadows? Is he an Orpheus, lulling his audience with his music[5] so that he can return to the world of Athens where he lives as a multifaceted human being and not as a uniform and unvarying member of the community he pretends to found?

Socrates wishes to give us only one reading of the passages that introduce the third book. He sees them as disincentives to martial valor. We who are outside the dialogues and the stories told within it are able to glance at these quotes from a variety of perspectives and see in them a multiplicity of interpretations, including, perhaps, even Socrates' mocking presentation of his own role within the story. The famed Socratic hubris may indeed shine forth in this subtle comparison with the unnamed hero of the *Iliad*.

Also in this series of seven quotations at the beginning of Book 3 is the undermining of the very premises of the city Socrates is in the process of founding. Throughout the quotes and the subsequent discussions of lamentation, the relationship between Achilles and Patroclus surfaces. In particular, the third and sixth quote both come from the same section of the *Iliad* (23.100–104) where Achilles grieves after seeing the ghost of Patroclus in a dream. Death is dreadful in this case, not because it brings one to a world of insubstantial shadows where the soul of Patroclus now resides but rather because death separates friends and precludes the physical embracing of those we love. "So saying, he reached forward with his own arms, but could not hold him" (23.99–100). Death destroys the possibility of the physical expression of love. While we read about the caves and the gibbering souls, it is the relationship of Achilles and Patroclus that continues to haunt us and carries on into the next section in which the poet's depiction of lamentation by renowned men is censored (387d). The first example of the language to be excised in this section comes from

5. See 358b with regard to the charming of Thrasymachus.

Homer's description of Achilles' inordinate grief at the loss of Patroclus (388a; *Iliad* 24.10–12, 18.23–24), followed by the powerful descriptions of Priam's grief when he learns of the loss of his son Hector (*Iliad* 22.414–15).

Poetry makes us weep over small sufferings (*smikroisin pathēmasin*) (388d), Socrates claims, sufferings such as the loss of a son or a brother or money, or anything else of this sort (387e). The individual warriors are to have no such "small sufferings," for Socrates is to take away fathers and sons and friends and money. The poet alerts us to our connection with the particular, the attachments not only between Achilles and Patroclus, but also between Hector and Andromache, between Priam and Hector. The tale of the *Iliad* traces the glory of men at the cost of their personal ties. Death is fearsome, yes, but only partly because it is a place of darkness; we also (even primarily) weep because the father will not see the son mature, because the father will need to bury the son, because the friends will no longer be able, "sitting apart from the dear companions, [to take] counsel together" (*Iliad* 23.77–78). In Callipolis there will be no fathers who weep or wives who grieve. The passages recited at length before they are removed from Callipolis remind Socrates' interlocutors of the depth of those bonds that Socrates two Books later will try to extend to the whole city and, in the process, dilute.

The philosopher Socrates in his founding of a city builds on simplicity, on one skill, one job for each individual, and thus avoids the complexity of demands on humans who love one another. He provides his citizens with a life in which they need not face the hard choices that arise from devotion to various individuals and various values and principles of behavior. The Socratic censorship of poetry destroys the tragedy of human life by presenting it as uniform, simple, and flat. There is no inability to reconcile the many roles that we all play if those many roles are turned into one; the interpretation of poetry makes the lamentation we may express for a lost son, father, or lover unnecessary. The city that he founds makes such lamentation unnecessary.

As Socrates removes grief from the poetry recited to the young he does not acknowledge the problems that this censorship would raise for him should he reflect back on those philosophic dogs of Book 2. With their dual natures, those dogs had to love the known and hate the unknown, love the close and hate the foreign. Socrates' censored poetry will enable no one among his warriors to love their own because the love of their own will bring on the banned lamentation. The flat men created in Book 3 by the poetry lack even the dual nature of the dogs. The poetry to make these warriors uniform makes them fierce towards their own as well as towards others. The censorship of poetry brings Socrates back to the confusion with which he began his storytelling, leaving us uneasy with both the principles at the base of the city and those that determine his mode of interpretation.

Narration

"Justice is the advantage of the stronger." Who says this? We all know. This is the famous challenge posed by Thrasymachus, the violent Sophist who threatens Socrates in Book 1 of the *Republic*. Of course, they are not his words. Nor does he say, "Tell me, O Socrates, do you have a wet nurse? . . . She overlooks your sniveling and does not give your nose the wiping it needs" (343a). It is Socrates speaking these words, the Socrates who is narrating this entire tale of his night at Cephalus's house to an unknown audience. It is Socrates who gives Glaucon's speech on the contractual origins of justice at the beginning of Book 2. It is he who gives Thrasymachus's speech in praise of tyranny and injustice. It is he who shows that the poets praise justice only for the advantages in reputation that it may bring.

Perhaps we would not have noticed this technicality about who is speaking at each point in the dialogue, had not the author Plato made us notice it in the middle of the third book of the *Republic*. There he has his own character Socrates explore the differences between the various kinds of narration and go, as he says, from a discussion of *logos* to a discussion of *lexis* (392c). There are those speeches that are direct, unmixed, where the poet describes all that happens in the story in his own speech, and those in which the poet imitates or mimics the speech of another between sections of narration, that is, he takes on the language, character, and tone of someone other than himself. He becomes more than one or takes on multiple personalities in the process of reciting the poem. Like the mantic seer, he speaks as if he were another. Against the principles at the foundation of the city of one man, one task, and of the interpretation of poetry, he becomes manysided.

To illustrate this point, Socrates turns to the familiar beginning of the *Iliad*, but he does not concentrate on the two heroes, Agamemnon and Achilles, in conflict over the distribution of honors; rather, he talks of the section in which a father, the priest, begs for the return of his daughter Chryseis, who has been taken as booty into the household of Agamemnon. Here the poet Homer (and those who recite his poems) must imitate the old man, weeping at the loss of his daughter as a prize of war. Homer becomes the grieving father. This has been called an "intentionally malevolent" example for Socrates to introduce at this point in the dialogue (Gadamer 1980:45). Why this curious interpretation? We can perhaps understand its malevolence for, in its portrayal of a father's attachment to a child, a relationship that runs through many of the most poignant scenes of the *Iliad,* it alerts us to the relationships that will be destroyed when Socrates, Glaucon, and Adeimantus finish founding their city with its community of wives and children in Book 5. By offering the example of a father's pleas for his daughter at the same time that he is changing it, Socrates reminds us of the power of the child-parent bonds and may also be referring us back to the early scenes of the *Republic,* where the attachment between father and son appears in the fond relationship between Cephalus and Polemarchus.

This time we are transforming the poetic tale not through excision, as had been done earlier in Book 3, but through stylistic changes. Nevertheless, the effect is the same: do not allow poetry to make us aware of our attachments to private, particular individuals, those who might turn us away from the city. The example that Socrates introduces, however, to explain his understanding of mixed and unmixed narration undermines the principles that later become the basis for the community of Callipolis. As with the excision of lamentation, we find again that an internal undermining of the Socratic narration is accomplished.

Turning the impassioned pleas of the father into Homeric narration, Socrates would have the bard say:

> The priest came and prayed that the gods give them the taking of Troy and a safe journey home and that they honoring the god receive the ransom and release his daughter. And after he said these things, the others honored him and agreed with him, but Agamemnon became angry, ordering him to leave at once and not to come back. . . . The old man hearing this was frightened and went away in silence, and while going away from the camp asked many things of Apollo . . . and prayed that the Achaians pay for his tears with the god's arrows. (393e—394a)

As Socrates drones on with this recitation, we see in the "unmixed style" the loss of passion, the loss of the immediacy of the father's suffering (a "small suffering," as Socrates might have called it a short while earlier in this dialogue). The anger and the grief of the father have been neutralized by the language of the narrator and we, the audience of Socrates' speech, in turn may feel anger and grief at the castration of Homer's poetry in the process of creating uniformity and simplicity. Yet Socrates insists: "Consider then, Adeimantus, whether it is necessary for us that the guardians be imitators (*mimētikous*) or not. Or does this not follow what was said before, that each one pursues well one task and not many, but if he tries this, laying hold of many, he will fail in all things?" (394e)

Back in Athens—that democracy resembling a many-colored coat that women and children consider "most beautiful" (557c)—Socrates recalls the speeches of the night before for his unidentified companion(s). He avoids the style of passionless narration and tells his own tale in the mixed narrative mode. Thus do we hear Socrates speaking as Thrasymachus, as Glaucon, as Polemarchus, and, indeed, even as a dishonest old man, Cephalus. We hear him frequently recite the poetry he is to censor, the poetry that alerts us to just those personal ties he wishes to destroy. We hear him quote Homeric descriptions of tables laden with sumptuous meals (390ab), while we sit awaiting our own feast that seems never to come. Socrates thus reveals to us, and to those who hear him speak, the passion of Thrasymachus, the intensity of Glaucon, the reserve of Adeimantus. While within his city of Callipolis there is to be no imitation of men who are not good and noble, honest and true, Socrates, having returned to life by going up from the Piraeus and away from the deathlike halls of Cephalus's house, can imitate those who are not noble, those who are not good, and even those who are not honest. In his own recitation of the *Republic,* Socrates becomes multisided; he becomes all the characters whom he portrays and he becomes whole and many-faceted, taking on multiple tasks rather than one.

Socrates becomes the democratic man. He is not the poet he seeks for his own city. Indeed, he is to be banished from Callipolis.

> A man, as it seems, who is able by his wisdom to be all sorts of things and to imitate everything, if such a man arrives in our city wishing to display his poems, we would adore him as someone sacred and wondrous and pleasing, but we would say that there is no such man among us in the city and that it is not lawful there be such a one, and we would send him away into another city having poured on his head and crowning him with wool. We ourselves would use a more austere and less pleasing poet and teller of tales (*mythologōi*) who would imitate for us the speech of a moderate man. (398ab)

Consistent with the theme established early on, this city will not admit individual multiplicity, even in its story tellers. The poet of mixed narration, indeed, even the Socrates of mixed narration, cannot be part of a world of unidimensionality.

The simple dismissal of mixed narration in Socrates' city continues to confirm the unidimensionality of the inhabitants of this city, a unidimensionality established initially in the city of pigs where each individual was reduced to one task, one role, one speech. The Socratic interpretation of poetry is part of a critique of democracy that runs through the entire discussion of the founding of Callipolis. Democracy demands that the citizen be multidimensional. Not only is the citizen a shoemaker, but he is also a member of the jury and the *ecclesia;* he is a father and a member of the *boulē.* No one pretends that the city that Socrates founds here is "democratic" in the Athenian (or any) sense of the term; indeed, it appears to be founded on principles that are explicitly antidemocratic. But within the structure of the dialogue that Plato writes, it is the character of Socrates who takes on for himself a multiplicity of roles. He attacks justice and then defends it; he is violent and he is humble; he does not one job, but the job of all the characters in the dialogue, giving their speeches and all their responses, their "yes's" and their "no's," as well as his own speeches and the narratives in between. As he founds the city to serve as an antidote to the openness of democracy, Socrates takes on all the qualities of a multicolored democratic man whom women and children find fair.[6]

Adeimantus, the severe brother, prefers the unmixed *mimēsis* (*mimētēn akraton*), that is, the purely dramatic poetry, but only if it is the unmixed imitation of the one who is seemly (*epieikos*) (397d). Socrates warns him that it is the mixed style that is far more pleasing to the many and to the pedagogues (397d). Adeimantus accepts and acknowledges that perhaps the pleasing does not fit into "our regime" because there is no double (*diplous*) man among us nor many-sided (*pollaplous*) men if each one fares well (397e). Does this mean that our Socrates, *pollaplous* that he is in his own narration, does not fare well? Socrates, pleasing to us as he takes on the tone and character of so many individuals, finds no place in "our regime." Socrates censors himself out of his own city. The unidimensional interpretation that leaves only one reading of the text and the unmixed imitation of the good man that leaves only one form of poetry to be recited is what neither Socrates nor Plato offers.

The section that carries the original discussion of *lexis* on to a discussion of *mimēsis* censors not only the poets of "mixed narration," but also removes tragedy and comedy. In other words, it is obvious that, in a city in which we are to find one man at one task, we cannot have some men imitate others or, specifically, have men imitate women as they would have to do in the production of tragedy and of comedy; nor can they imitate the sounds of animals or natural phenomena, horses, seas, cattle, thunder, pulleys, and so on. No comic chorus of birds or frogs or clouds could appear in Callipolis; indeed, no Socrates either, for he engages in *mimēsis* throughout the dialogue and gives pleasure for millenia to come. Socrates must eliminate tragedy from his city[7] because the actors portray those who are other than themselves, but tragedy also emerges from the multiplicity

6. Bloom (1968:360) is wrong, I believe, to describe the dialogue as simple poetry; it is the most complex of poetries, as we see the great variety of roles that the narrator Socrates (and indeed the reader of Socrates' words) must play.

7. See 394b–d and the waffling there.

of roles that one must play in life. Thus, the tragic (and epic) hero is confronted by the conflicting demands that are placed upon him or her and the choices that those demands force the hero to make. Achilles is son, friend, warrior, Achaean, and human being. The demands of such multiplicity of roles force him to make choices between these various roles. Antigone is sister, ward, woman, and fiancée; Creon is ruler, father, guardian, and uncle. When Socrates founds his city on the one man, one role principle at first, and when he introduces the equality of women and the destruction of the family later, he eliminates the potential for tragedy. The discussion of *mimēsis* in Book 3 is simply an extension of (and prelude to) the proposals that eliminate not only poetry, tragedy, and comedy, but all forms of variety from the city.

The Politics of "What Is"

In the metaphysical critique of poetry in Book 10, Socrates describes the poem or the artist's creation (including, we assume, the Platonic dialogue) as three times removed from "what is." He claims: "There are then these three sorts of couches. One which exists in nature (*en tēi phusēi ousa*) which we would say, as I think, god makes . . . the one which the craftsman makes [and] the one which the painter makes" (597b). That which exists "in nature" and is produced by god "is." All else, produced by human craft, comes into being and passes away and thus can only belong to the changeable world of what appears to be. In the moral critique of poetry in Books 2 and 3, the gods are shown to be less than divine in their immoral lives as described by the poets. "Hera bound by her son, and Hephaestus tossed out by his father when he intended to help his mother who was being struck, and the battles of the gods such as Homer composed, must not be received into the city" (378d). The gods must instead be portrayed only as the cause of what is good, never of what is bad.

Behind both the metaphysical and the moral critiques is the continued rejection of poetry because it draws us towards what is multiple and what is varied rather than towards what is uniform. In Book 10 the craftsman builds and the artist portrays many different beds or chairs or couches. They present us with a particular man or a particular bed. They make us focus in on a particular artifact or person or tree and recognize its uniqueness; thus we learn from them the great variety of chairs or of human types such as those who populate the epics of Homer. The artist does not lead us to the *idea* (or form) of the couch, that which unifies all couches whether they stand in a living room, doctor's office, or on the porch. In contrast, the god "makes that one couch in nature, so that he makes that very one alone which is a couch. Two of this sort or more were not engendered (*ephuteuthēsan*) by the god nor will they grow (*phuōsin*). . . . if he made only two, one would again come to light whose form (*to eidos*) they both would have, and the couch would be 'what is' (*ho estin*) but not the two" (597c). The god in nature creates that which is uniform, that which is whole, never in need, and that which is never multiple or capable of being divided. The artist distracts us from the simple and forces us to see variety. And, as in the Parmenidean story, the multiple we see with our senses; it is the mind alone that can perceive the chair that "is," the one form, not two, engendered by the god. The artist keeps us mired in the world of the particular, the subjective world from which the Socrates of the *Republic* says we—and especially his Callipolis—must escape.

In Book 2 we learned that the epic poets made the gods appear diverse and changing their forms over time. Socrates inquired of Adeimantus whether he supposes that the god is a wizard able treacherously to reveal himself at different times in different *ideai*, at one time actually changing himself and passing his own form into many shapes (380d). They conclude, "The god would least of all have many shapes" (381b). The god neither creates more than one form nor is himself more than one form. It is such a god existing in the world of "what is" that Socrates' Callipolis aims to emulate.

Art and the human expression of art are variable; they take on a multiplicity of forms. Poetry tells of gods who are variable, of men who are variable, who love at one moment and hate at the next, who rejoice at one moment and grieve at the next. The poets even tell of gods and men who laugh. There are to be no lovers of laughter among men or among gods or among the poets in Callipolis for "when someone lets go with powerful laughter he seeks also a powerful change (*metabolē*)" (388e). Thus, the passage from Homer where gods burst out into unquenchable laughter at the sight of Hephaestus (*Iliad* 1.599–600) disappears from the Homeric epic (389a). In Callipolis there is no changing. There is no laughter among men. All is unified and all is one. All move towards a Parmenidean "what is." There are no tragedies where Oedipus rejoices and then grieves, no comedies where gods fight and heroes laugh, that will fracture the unity of this complete city. To achieve this unified perfection of completion and wholeness, of which the treatment of poetry, its interpretation, and its narration is but one manifestation, all sorts of transformations in the current structure of human life are necessary. I shall concentrate in this section on the conflation between male and female, between polity and family, for in these proposals that form the core of Book 5 of the *Republic*, Socrates brings the critique of art and artists, poetry and poets, directly into the structure of the city.

Female into Male

The warriors molded or stamped by the myths of Books 2 and 3 blend into one another as all distinctiveness between them disappears. With their moderate souls, eschewing excess in any area, they become the perfect warriors, fearless in the face of death and desireless in the face of all pleasures. Well educated (*eu paideuomenoi*), the men become moderate, arranging things well such as—Socrates notes by-the-by—"the possession [*ktēsin*] of women and marriages and the making of children so that, according to the saying, it is necessary to make all the things of friends as much as possible common [*koina*]." "That would be most correct [*orthotata*]," responds Adeimantus, and Socrates continues that a regime so begun will go forward, "increasing as a circle" (423e–424a).[8] Half a book later, the young men from whom everything has been taken are suddenly no longer so ready to yield everything. They, including the spirited Glaucon, have given up their mistresses and their Sicilian tables, but their possessions, their wives, their fathers, and their children they seem less eager to yield—at least not before they have heard an argument explaining why they ought to accept an arrangement that will take from them their own and thrust them entirely into a community of the political whole.

Fathers such as Cephalus may leave their sons money, but fathers such as Ariston bequeath to their sons (Glaucon, Adeimantus, Plato) political power. How are they to be sure to be leaders as well as founders in Callipolis? And so they conspire, Polemarchus and Adeimantus. They shall not let it go, or so Socrates hears them whisper between themselves as they try to preserve a private space in a world becoming increasingly open. "What thing especially [*malista*] do you not let go?" "You," they reply, and then they accuse him of laziness and of robbery of a whole form (*eidos*) of the argument by speaking carelessly (*phaulōs*), "how concerning women and children it is clear to everyone that the things of friends are held in common" (449c). The conspiracy and the apprehension of Socrates gain legitimacy as Glaucon and Thrasymachus vote to "arrest" Socrates and demand that he explain why this plan for Callipolis is right (*orthōs*). And so Socrates, already arrested, yields to necessity and speaks to show why it is correct that friends hold all, including women and children, in common, that the unity of the city that "is" depends on the breaking down of all barriers between one individual and another, at least as much as is possible in a world where we are enclosed in the physical form of the human body.

8. The image is somewhat curious since a circle (*kuklos*) does not increase (and we can hardly assume Socrates is thinking in terms of snowballs), but a circle is whole and needs no more. See the discussion of the sphere in chapter 7.

The proposals that are to be set forth, though, are much more radical than Adeimantus and Polemarchus had at first feared. Polemarchus, whose father is about to leave him a great fortune, and Adeimantus, who spoke in Book 2 of what fathers tell their sons, are suspicious of the community of wives and children, the destruction of the family and its private possessions. Erotic Glaucon wondered about the making of babies and their care prior to the city's role in educating them.[9] None of the interlocutors ever imagined where Socrates would begin and that is with the equality of women and men and, as I shall suggest, with the figurative murder of the female in the quest for the city that is supposed to exist according to nature.

The previous books have prepared us for a city unified, a city unchanging, a city that "will naturally become one, but not many" (423d). Now we learn how far Socrates must go to achieve this unity "by nature" for the city; he must destroy all that has previously appeared natural and show that all we have experienced in the past is based on conventions and the failure of the human senses to comprehend nature and an underlying unity. In particular, he must take all apparent differences between the sexes and show that the mind, able to rise above the world of variable multiplicity, understands a unity that the eyes cannot see. Forced to return to what he had thought he had left behind, Socrates now admits, "It is probably right (*orthōs*) that after going through entirely the manly drama, also to go through the womanly one" (451c).[10] At least this is what Glaucon wants, he who had asked Socrates to talk about "what sort of community (*he koinōnia*) there will be for our guardians concerning the women and children and about the nurture of the children while they are still young, and in that time between being born and their education, which seems to be the most burdensome" (450c).[11] And it is this problem, the female drama of the household, the nurturing of children, the feeding and the clothing of the family, that Socrates proposes to address.

9. The noble lie had answered that question earlier, but Glaucon was not quite ready to accept such a fanciful tale, however much it may have been part of Athens's self-mythologizing. See further Benardete (1989:117–120).

10. The significant words here are *andreion* and *gunaikeion*. They are important specifically because they are *not* the words for male and female; see, e.g., Bloom's translation (1968:ad. loc.). They refer to the conventional roles for male and female—war for the man and household activities for the female. It is not simply the male and female drama, but the male and female drama as understood by the society in which Socrates engages in discourse. We may think here of the contemporary distinction between "sex" (biological) and "gender" (constructed) that characterizes research in the social sciences.

11. At the risk of imposing modern assumptions on the ancient text, could it be that Glaucon is a new father? Note that Socrates' next vocative to Glaucon is *eudaimōn*.

In fact, Socrates turns not to the female drama, to procreation and rearing of the young. He continues his focus on the manly drama of war as he turns to guarding and to who is to guard. This is when we learn that among the animals the female dogs must guard alongside the male dogs. "Or do they stay inside the house as unable, on account of the puppies and their nurture, while the males labor and have all the care about the flock?" (451d). The cloistering of female dogs seems absurd and so, by analogy, does the cloistering of women. But if the women are to engage in the same tasks as the men, then they must have the same education—and, as the process continues, become as much like the male warriors as is possible, leaving far behind the female drama. What was given to men, *gumnastikē* and *mousikē,* is now to be given to women also (452a). Whereas before the emphasis had been on *mousikē,* now, with the women added, we focus on the training of the body. Along with the men they will practice in the gymnasium, stripping like the men, old and wrinkled though their bodies may be. They are to carry arms and to ride horses. The difference between men and women that the eyes may have perceived only hides the underlying identity between the two. The one difference that remains is the strength of the body (451e). Otherwise, once women and men practice gymnastics together—naked—it will appear that "to uncover all such things is better than to shut them up" (452d). What was laughable for the eyes is snatched away by the best (*aristou*) as revealed in speeches (452d). Women traditionally hidden away in the dark recesses of the home are dragged out into the open, into the sunlight, stripped naked and trained to use their bodies for war—and no one must laugh at this radical inversion of what has in the past seemed to be according to nature. The founders of this city according to nature are searching for a deeper nature, one that unifies and leaves the city whole, unfractured by divisions introduced by a duality of sexes or a multiplicity of households.

So quickly does Socrates, through analogy and facile images, accomplish this inversion of all that had seemed natural in the past that the young men who wanted to keep their wives as wives have not been able to draw up the lines for the defence of their own. Socrates thus must act the critic to his own proposals. He must ask himself about the contradictions that may be inherent in such proposed equality, considering the principles according to which he founded his first city: one nature, one task. To respond to his self-criticism, he must show that women are no different from men *by nature.* They had agreed earlier that different natures must practice different pursuits—and that the nature of women and men is different. "But now we say that different natures (*phuseis*) must practice the same pursuits" (453e). The mistake was to rely upon their eyes to perceive nature; thus, they saw differences rather than identities, as do the "two-headed mortals" of Parmenides' poem and Heraclitus's men with "barbarian souls."

To demonstrate to his young interlocutors that men and women are no different by nature, Socrates turns to the unseen rather than the seen. We see male bodies and we see female bodies, especially when they have stripped and are practicing gymnastics naked before us. With our minds, though, we can discover the unseen, and understand that "there is no practice peculiar (*idion*) to a woman for the managing (*dioikēsis*)[12] of the polis" (455b), and that "the same nature (*hē autē phusis*) for the guarding of the city belongs to a woman and to a man," except, as Socrates takes care to add, "that the one is weaker and the other is stronger" (456a). As with Parmenides and his followers, the victory goes to the mind rather than to the eyes, to the *logos* that knows that the arrow cannot hit the target, even if the eyes watch it do so. Therefore, we must dismiss the differences perceived, the differences that divide the city and make it appear complex rather than simple, multiple rather than one. Like the autochthony myths that simplified obligations, that removed the procreative female from the foundation of the city, we must destroy the female in the process of unifying the city.

The laws concerning women, Socrates concludes, are not against nature (*para phusin*). They are not impossible dreams (e.g., dreams of spontaneous birth from the earth such as proposed in the noble lie recited but two books earlier [414c–415d]); rather, the laws he is proposing are according to nature (*kata phusin*), though they may be unlike what is done now (456c).

> If the race of men and the race of women appear to be different with regard to a particular craft or another pursuit, we shall say that it is necessary to give that to each one; but if it appears that they differ in this thing, that the female bears while the male mounts, we shall say that it has not yet been demonstrated that a woman differs from a man according to what we are saying, but that we shall still think that it is necessary that our guardians and their women engage in the same activities (454de).

In short, the conventions of society controlled by the seen rather than by "what is" according to nature have instituted differences between male and

---

12. Note the use of *dioikēsis* here, a word that according to Liddell and Scott means "properly *to manage a house*," deriving from the root *oikos* or family/household.

female. Socrates poses a nature that is unseen, and he dismisses differences so as to uncover an underlying unity.[13]

Family into City

In order to uncover the identity of the female and the male, Socrates must dismiss anything that draws our attention to the body; for the female, this means anything that relates to the processes of reproduction. The discussion of sexual equality had begun when Socrates asked Glaucon whether the female guardian dogs must stay indoors as if they were unable to guard because of the bearing and nurturing of puppies (451d). This discussion had been a prelude to the rearing and nurturing of children "before their education," as Glaucon had said. Socrates calls it "one wave" and sighs a grand sigh of relief that he has not drowned in it (457b). Nonetheless, he next turns to the larger wave (457c) that directly answers Glaucon's and the others' concerns about the rearing of children in common and the holding of wives in common. All women of the guardian class are to be *koinai* for the men; to live together in private (*idiai*) is for no one. Children likewise are held in common, Socrates explains (457cd). Here we see the true destruction of the female and her elimination from Callipolis as she dissolves into the male and family dissolves into the city. The peculiar, distinctive (*idion*) trait of the female that most vividly distinguishes her from the male, her capacity to bear children, is ignored and even dismissed to the greatest possible degree as she and the children she bears belong to no one in particular but are held communally.

Whereas previously in the Greek city procreation was the concern of the individual family, the responsibility is now transferred to the city's rulers. Even Pericles, the leader who held before the Athenians a most beautiful vision of their city for them to love, sent his bereaved citizens home to bear more children so that "in private (*idiai*) for some those born afterwards will be a forgetting of those who are no longer" (Thucydides 2.44.3). Socrates, in contrast, takes the process out of the *oikos* and makes it the direct concern of the polis. The family as a center of pious reverence for the ancestors (Fustel de Coulanges [1864] 1980: bk. 2), reproduction, maintenance of religious obligations, and inheritance of wealth (Cephalus) disappears along with private gods and private property. Moving reproduction from the family to the city obscures the boundaries between the two, just as Socrates' proposals concerning reproduction will obscure the boundaries between male and female.

13. What I am here calling unity or, more dramatically above, "the murder of the female," Benardete (1989:117) with similar concerns calls "the city's neuterization."

According to Socrates' plan, when a child is born to a woman[14] the child is to be placed in a pen (pig sty) along with other babies (460c). The mother laden with milk will nurse a child, at intervals determined by her other activities, but she will not know her own child nor will the care of the child be hers. The guardians will make provisions that these mothers "nurse a moderate time and will hand over to nurses and nurturers the sleeplessness and the rest of the burdens" (460c). It is, as Glaucon (concerned earlier with this most troublesome period in a child's life) says, "an easy way of childrearing for the women of the guardians."[15] The processes of birth and its aftermath appear as brief as and no more troublesome than the moment of conception—hardly to be noticed at all. What has appeared to the eyes as distinctive about the female, the protruding belly, the child emerging from her loins, is to be dismissed. Others care for a child thus born. Only a mind weighted down by conventions would fail to see the identity between male and female in the guardian class rather than their distinctiveness.

We must, however, think also of the obverse of this freedom from child-care that is given to women in Socrates' city. The monogamous family had offered men a certainty about paternity, but the mother knows that she is the mother with or without the family. She experiences the child within her and she endures the pains of labor. The male participates only for a brief moment. Socrates' city, where women become males and where families no longer exist as divisive forces, demands that the female work under the same uncertainty as the male. While appearances, sensations, pains may define the female as separate from the male, such experiences are to be denied in Socrates' pursuit of unity (the pain experienced by one is experienced by all), and the female comes to enjoy the males' ignorance of the child to whom she gave birth, the one who is her own.

This process of transforming the female into the male thus removes from the city, at least among the guardians, male and female (or the men's women), any particularity, any distinctiveness, any sense of what is one's own or what one contributes individually to the city, such as children. It is here that the similarities with Praxagora's proposals are most striking. Praxagora had imagined a city without private houses, private dining rooms, or private children. She had turned the city into a household where all is held in common. Socrates does this as well, eliminating any tension between *idion* and *koinon*. The most private of affairs—those bound up in family relations—are made public as the family as any sort of distinctive

14. Though autochthony is part of the mythic background for this city, Socrates does not propose birth from the earth as a continuing mode of asexual reproduction.

15. We might comment here that Glaucon still uses the possessive, i.e., these are not women guardians, but they are the women "owned by" the male guardians.

unit, whether for piety or for wealth, disappears. After he describes the careful monitoring of sexual relations necessary to produce the finest off-spring, Socrates asks: "Do we have any greater evil for the city than that which splits it and makes it many rather than one? Or a greater good than what both binds and makes it one?" (462ab). It is privacy (*idiōsis*) that loosens (*dialuei*) the city—and so privacy must disappear, along with the women who in the past may have appeared to be different from the men and who, most importantly, had symbolized the private life in Greek lit-erature ever since the Homeric epics.

Phrases such as "my own" and "not my own" divide the city and so are removed from the speech of the inhabitants—or at least they must say "my own" and "not my own" about the same things (462c). Such a city will be governed best (*hautē arista dioikeitai*), Socrates asserts. (One can wonder whether it will need to be governed at all.) Or in language that will be attacked by Aristotle: "Whichever city is closest to one human being [is it not governed best]? Such that whenever the finger of any of us is harmed, the whole community (*pasa hē koinōnia*) suffers the pain as a whole while the part is suffering" (462c–d). No private pains, no private pleasures, no private wives, no private children, no private labor, and no private nurs-ing. As Glaucon realizes this unity does more than simply eliminate the family, it transforms the city into a family as well: "Everyone whom he might chance upon, he will think to be either a brother or a sister or a father or a mother or a son or daughter or offspring or ancestors" (463c). Socrates expands the image because not only in name but in action will they be like brothers and fathers and sons, sisters and mothers and daugh-ters. The city will indeed be one and not many, and as one they shall thus share in the community of pains and pleasures, the greatest good for the city, "as we agreed upon" (464a–b).

No opposition between male and female, between family and city, or between private and public means the unity of this city. To create this unity, Socrates has had to eliminate the family, the female, and the body from his city. The family dissolves into the city as no one has his or her own mother, father, daughter, or son. The female dissolves into the male, a weaker version, to be sure, as childbirth is virtually taken away from her and she takes on all the qualities of the male warrior (while he takes on none of the qualities of the female). The body disappears as its satisfactions are denied; it, the body, had defined boundaries between individuals, but now the pain in my finger is not mine alone. My neighbor feels it too. Even my body, my pain, is not my own. Any tensions raised in the tragic actions considered in chapter 3 thus disappear. They do so only because Socrates has eliminated opposition, an otherness based on the diversity that comes from sexual differences and the physical bodies of human beings and from the families that are part of, but not the same as, the city. As a result, though, he has created a city that can exist only at a moment in time—or for an unmoving eternity. Like the gods he sought to create with the poetry of Book 2, this city has no motion, no capacity for change and, thus, as a city of speech, of mind, created through dialogue, it is unable to regenerate itself. It has no relation to human bodies that grow, change, give birth, and die apart from one another.[16]

According to Parmenides, "what is" neither comes into being nor dies, but always "is." Thus, reproduction becomes a contradiction for "what is"—and yet Socrates, unable to separate completely bodies from his Callipolis with its warriors, confronts with his companions in speech the political problem of the city's reproducing itself. If the city did exist only as a moment in time in the speech of men or as an unchanging eternity in the world of "what is," then such concerns would be unnecessary. But this city is grounded in more than speech, more than memory, more than *nous*. Similarly, Thucydides has the plague and the death of bodies follow the funeral oration that had created the historian's city of speech. Plato recognizes the same tension, only he has his Socrates go to the creation of new bodies rather than their destruction. Socrates thus encounters a series of problems and contradictions. Having eliminated "my own" and "not my own" from the individual vocabulary of the citizens, having made his city a model of "what is," he then relies on the citizens' eroticism, desire of "what is not," for the sexuality necessary to repopulate the city. He now assumes a sexual drive—a drive to possess another's body—that he earlier wished to deny. Thus, women who were just a short time ago equal to men, indeed transformed into males, become prizes for the man who has performed well in battle. Socrates imagines a sexuality without particular bodies, or with bodies that have been trained to desire nothing. It is Glaucon who recalls that there will remain "erotic necessities" (485d), though it is unclear whence they come.

Socrates, furthermore, tries to make prohibitions against incest—calculating that children born in the "tenth month" after a "marriage" are to be children of all the parents "married" at that time, and their children are to be grandchildren of all, but brothers and sisters are to be allowed to procreate "if the lot should fall that way and the Pythia answers that way in addition" (461e). He does not at first appear to populate the city with Oedipuses and Jocastas, as Praxagora had done, though he clearly allows incest between siblings. But, as Glaucon says shortly, everyone will judge

---

16. As dramatic counterpoint to the speech of the dialogue, we might remember the supper promised, but never brought. As Socrates discourses on his city in speech, the stomachs of his interlocutors are, no doubt, growling.

each person he meets as a father, mother, brother, son, and so on. The city-become-family demands it and so the city will not be able to sustain any prohibitions against incest. Once the city is so transformed into a family, incest becomes inevitable (Nichols 1987:109; Bloom 1968:386) and, indeed, even desirable if "there can be no rational ground to forbid any kind of incest if the offspring promise to be good" (Benardete 1989:119).

Callipolis's need to reproduce itself begins to show its distance from the perfection of "what is." In the Way of Truth there was no need for regeneration, no need to get embroiled in these complications. "What is" cannot become "what is not" and so always "is," never diminished nor augmented. By contrast, the city does exist in the material world, and Glaucon, Adeimantus, and Thrasymachus (perhaps) care naught for leadership in a world they can neither see nor experience. Thus, Socrates explores the processes of procreation. During this exploration (this preface to the third wave of the philosopher kings, we might add), we begin to see the inadequacy of a city that tries to eliminate the seen in favor of the unseen, the coming-into-being in favor of the "what is," the female in favor of the male, and the family itself in favor of the community.

In Books 8 and 9 Socrates traces the downfall of the monistic ideal he has envisioned through speech. Callipolis's demise occurs precisely because of the inability of men to use their reason to control the physical world of which this city is now a part. Having established the corporeality of the city by worrying about its reproduction over time, the body now comes to control the city and gains its own victory over the mind. All the mathematical calculations of the philosophers fail to control the movements of the seasons and the ways of sex, and so the guardian rulers arrange for births not propitious for the preservation of the city. It is thus that Callipolis decays as "what is" never could.

The process of decay clarifies for us what Callipolis has tried to accomplish, for as we descend from the city of speech to tyranny we watch the city become, at first, more divided within itself: the female divorces herself from the male and the family from the city; it then rolls back upon itself and the conflation between male and female, between city and family, reappears in the discourse about tyranny. As a preface for the ensuing transition of regimes, Socrates has his companions agree that these things are required in a city well organized (*oikein*): "women in common, children in common and all the education, and so too the activities for war and for peace in common . . . no private thing for anyone, but in common for all" (543ab). But the community is disrupted by faction (*stasin*) (547a); divisions set in rather than the comprehensive unity desired. At first, the struggling against one another leads only to private possession of houses and land. With the house and the land belonging to one and not another, we find the reappearance of families distinct from one another and, more importantly, distinct from the city. Boundaries appear (*periboloi oikēseōn*), and private nests (*neottiai idiai*) are set up where the men hide the money that they then squander on their women, women who are no longer in the gymnasia practicing with the men, hardly aware of their reproductive capacities.

This regime, Glaucon remarks, is "mixed (*memeigmenēn*)" (548c). No longer does the pure Callipolis dominate the discourse. It is mixed in that it incorporates good and bad features, but also in that the inhabitants now differ from one another. In particular, the female differs from the male. It is she who, Pandora-like, brings evils to the city by emphasizing that which is her own, that which is private rather than common. As the new regime is founded on honors and glory, it is inherently competitive, and the female inhabitants of this regime compete. They observe the differential levels of esteem that their own husbands have and they complain to their own sons, who, since they live in families, they now recognize as their own. The women complain that they are not married to a ruler because their husbands lack ambition—a trait they hope that their sons will develop. The fracturing of the pristine unity of Callipolis arises from the reintroduction of privacy, of distinctiveness, and the comparisons that such a sense of privacy allow between the self and others. The *koinōnia* of Callipolis fades. The son urged on by his mother develops the soul of the oligarch and therewith is born the oligarchic regime. The men themselves now compete, now perceive themselves as individuals rather than as parts of a whole, and in turn inspire the many with the same attitudes, as the best of cities deteriorates further towards democracy. Apart from their love of money, these oligarchs violate the one person, one tasks principle: they are busybodies (*polupragmones*), making money and fighting wars at the same time (551e–552a).

Nevertheless, the point of complete deterioration is not the oligarchy nor the democracy (which is so far from the uniformity and unity of Callipolis that it resembles a many-colored cloak [557c]), but rather the tyranny that curiously resembles Callipolis. Here, in the world of the tyrant, we find the conflation of the male and the female, of the family and the city. But instead of the female becoming the male, the male ruler becomes a female. He is confined by fear in his house where he "lives for the most part like a woman (*hōs gunē*)" (579b). Instead of the city becoming the family, the family becomes a city. "Out of each one of the private men (*tōn idiotōn*) whoever are wealthy in the city possess many servants/slaves. For these men are like tyrants in this way: they rule over men, but the tyrant's number [of men] differs" (578d). The similarity in these respects between the supposed best, Callipolis, and the worst, tyranny, is striking, perhaps suggesting the inadequacies of both—the one attempting to impose the male view as the totality of the existence, the other representing the dominance of the female view, the one seeing only the *koinōnia*, the other only the *idion*. Both lack the capacity of regeneration and both die ignoble deaths.

Tyranny is for Socrates the end of the descending regimes. Callipolis is the beginning. The sterility of both comes from an excessive desire to make what is many one, to escape the tragedies as well as the comedies that plague a world where men and women must interact in the processes of birth and generation, where privacy must contend with community, where poets sing and where laughter is on occasion heard. Socrates may not openly laugh in the *Republic*, but Glaucon does, and even within the *Republic* Socrates recites poetry that was banished from his Callipolis. Socrates also welcomes the foreigner as he praises the festival of the Thessalians (327a); he lives as a public person and as a private man; he is a busybody interfering unwelcomed in everyone else's affairs (*Apology* 31c); and he is a philosopher like the philosophers mentioned in the *Republic*, who cannot communicate what he sees in his trances.[17]

Conclusion

Socrates' city fails because men do not have the ability to abstract from a physical nature and make all simple, to discover a nature that lives only in the mind. The desire on Socrates' part to create in speech what is abstracted from the physical is captured by his attempts to destroy the boundaries between male and female and to escape the tragedy of the playwrights by obliterating the boundary between family and city that brings on tragedy, but he errs in speech as the tragic heroes did by over-emphasizing the efficacy of the *logos*. The human body calls him back to the petty issues of reproduction. The heroic city Socrates has created has a deathlike quality. There is no creativity within it, no art, no birth; it is a world in which neither male nor female exists, in which the masculine model of rational omnipotence has reigned to create a vision of monistic simplicity, from which variable poetry, mixed narration, gods who change form, and humans who laugh or practice more than one craft are all to be excluded. Such a city, in a sense, calls forth its own tragedy, for it is a denial of itself. Callipolis becomes a wasteland—a beautiful city that can survive only in the speech of its creator. In Plato's dialogue about *erōs*, the *Symposium*, the critique that is internal to the *Republic* is more openly articulated and the escape from tragedy less tangible.

17. *Symposium* 175cd. For a fine discussion of the difference between the philosophers of the *Republic* and Socrates, see further Nichols (1984).

7 Plato's *Symposium:* A Reassessment of Callipolis

Out of two to become one.

Symposium

The *Symposium* concludes with a Socratic victory. Socrates is forcing Agathon (the tragedian) and Aristophanes (the comic poet) to agree that the same man can write both comedy and tragedy. The victory is over those who fail to see the underlying unity of the creativity of the dramatic author. It is not so much that one man performs more than one task in contradiction to the founding principles of Callipolis, but that the two endeavors are really the same once we go beyond surface differences that appear on stage. Indeed, in the text of the dialogue itself we find a conflation of comedy and tragedy as the characters explore the passions that drive individuals to seek unity with another—and the limits and dangers of such a unity.[1] Yet Socrates, arguing for this underlying unity, gains control of the discourse not by the force of his reason, but because of the strength of his body, in particular, his ability to withstand the effects of too much wine (176c, 214a, 220a); his two interlocutors nod off into a drunken slumber as he rises to go to the Lyceum and spend the rest of the day as he spends all others.

The tension in the final scene of the dialogue between discourse and body captures an ambiguity that permeates the speeches offered in praise of love. Reason goes behind what is seen to discover what unifies our experiences in this world; meanwhile, particular bodies call us back to the divisions within human experience—our separate-

1. For similar concerns, but from a slightly different perspective, see Clay (1983).

ness from others, our particularity. The speeches offered wander back and forth between these two perspectives, finding diversity in the bodies that we see, which comprise the political world, and unity in the unseen, which goes beyond bodies and takes us as well beyond the political world. As with the debate at the end of the dialogue, any final resolution of the role of *erōs* in the conflict between body and reason, seen and unseen, the many and the one eludes all the speakers, not least of all Socrates. The *Republic*, abstracting from *erōs* and thus from the private and peculiar (*idion*), had built a city that was unified by eliminating difference and diversity. The *Symposium* enables us to reassess Callipolis as we are led to question the perfection of a city so unified, so internally complete, so immobile as Callipolis. In this chapter, I shall focus primarily on the speech offered by Aristophanes; I will then consider the Socratic response, for that is in part how we must read his speech; and finally, I will turn briefly to Alcibiades' subsequent undermining of the fantasy that permeates Socrates' words.[2]

Plato gives to Aristophanes in this dialogue a speech full of wondrous and fanciful images worthy of the art of the comic poet. Aristophanes speaks of our ancestors, creatures spherical in shape, with eight limbs, rolling about, rebelling against the gods, and procreating autochthonously. In these strange creatures in which we find our original shape, our *eidos*, our nature, we see the comedian's analogue to Callipolis, that city of words, undivided, internally complete, and whole in itself. Of the perfection that Socrates tried to create in Callipolis, Aristophanes says it existed in the bodies of men only in the distant past—or as the result of access to the net of Hephaestus that can bind together eternally the bodies and souls of lovers. Callipolis and those individuals reclaiming their past with Hephaestus's net reach a state of completion and attain their "nature," or their *eidos*, but in the process they become immobile and sterile.[3]

Socrates' speech introduces generation through the feminine voice of the seer Diotima, but she ultimately leads him and us beyond the dual and the many to conclude by imagining a world of perfection unmarked by the messy diversity of two sexes and multiple forms of beauty. It is the voice of the political man, Alcibiades, that reminds us of the complexity

2. The first part of the chapter draws heavily on Saxonhouse (1985a); the latter part draws, not quite so heavily, on Saxonhouse (1984b). I have been greatly influenced by Nussbaum's (1979a; 1986) arguments suggesting that we must understand Alcibiades' speech as a modification of Socrates' speech. By focusing attention primarily on these three speeches, I recognize that this means I look only at a fragment of the work. For a richer and more complete, though often questionable, reading of the dialogue, see especially Rosen (1987), whose insights frequently find their way into this chapter.

3. I am using here the concept of *eidos* explored by Benardete (1973) in his discussion of the *Statesman* but which is applicable to the *Symposium* as well.

of human existence, the uneasy relationship between the seen and the unseen, and the awkward presence of a Socrates—whole and complete in himself—in that world. The Socrates of Alcibiades' speech is similar to the spherical creatures inhabiting Aristophanes' ancient history as well as the Callipolis of the *Republic*. All appear immune to the longings, the *erōs* of men, and they stand deathlike, needing nothing, wanting nothing, in their immobility.

Thrasymachus had scornfully warned the guests at Cephalus's house that if they accepted the leadership of Socrates, all they could expect would be a feast of words. That, indeed, was all they got during their long night in the Piraeus. In the *Symposium*, the setting is reversed; dinner is served. The body does not disappear. Aristophanes' speech, the central one (albeit by chance) of the seven speeches, focuses our attention most vividly on our bodies—as is proper for the comic poet. But Plato gives to Aristophanes' speech a serious switch, moving it away from the body at the end and giving the whole discourse a troublesome, tragic air that will be recalled in the Socratic version of the tale of human longing. In the end, both Aristophanes and Socrates portray humans who, having satisfied their *erōs*, having attained their desired perfection, care nought for food. Alcibiades shows us in the person of Socrates a unique example of such closure, one who disdains the food others crave,[4] but who also poses for us the question of what role such an individual can play in human affairs. The analogies between Aristophanes' spherical creatures, Diotima's "beautiful itself," Alcibiades' Socrates, and Socrates' Callipolis leave us open for the reconsideration of the meaning of political unity that Aristotle will later present.

Aristophanes' Speech and the Net of Hephaestus

In his *Politics*, Aristotle links for us Socrates' Callipolis and Aristophanes' speech in the *Symposium*.

> Socrates especially praises that the city be one, a unity which both appears to be and which he says to be the work of love (*tēs philias*) just as in the speeches about love (*erotikois logois*) we know that Aristophanes says that on account of their strong love lovers are eager to grow together and both become one instead of two. In such a case it is necessary that both or one be destroyed, but in a city it is necessary that love (*tēn philian*)

---

4. Apart from the actual words of Alcibiades, we must recall that Socrates, standing immobile and unresponsive on a neighbor's porch, missed the dinner that was served by the servants of Agathon.

become watery on account of the community and one will least
of all say "mine" whether it be a son for a father or a father for
a son.[5]

Socrates' mistake, according to Aristotle, is that he fails to distinguish between lovers and cities. For us, as for Aristotle, the distinction is obvious.
Lovers are two people devoted to each other, ready to say, "Yes, we want
it," if offered the net of Hephaestus, a finely spun web that would bind
them together for an eternity. The city encompasses many people and its
expanse must "water down" the intensity of the passion that is felt by
lovers.[6] Love is the desire to appropriate someone else, make him or her
your own, to obliterate the distinctions between you. The city as we know
it evokes no such intensity, no such specificity. Our feelings of patriotism
may be strong, but only in the imagery of a Pericles can we become *erastai*
of the city. We cannot visualize a unity with and appropriation of the city
in the way that we can visualize a unity with a lover. Sexuality is not part
of our relationship with the city. Nevertheless, for the Socrates and Aristophanes of Plato the passion is the same. It is the passion for a unity, the
creation of one out of two or one out of many. It is the drive to overcome
our individual inadequacies, our needs and incompletion through a union
with another or with many others. It is the search for a unity that can
overcome the diversity we see with our eyes. While sexuality may not be
part of the relationship with the city, it arises from the same source: our
needfulness of others. The intensity of the desire for unity that both Aristophanes and Socrates appear to encourage is, however, self-destructive in
its abstractions from the limits of the body—that which defines our separation from others. Aristotle in his turn encourages moderation and the
wise rejection of the net of Hephaestus should it be offered, for he knows
that complete unity is not possible without death.

Why does Plato give to both Socrates describing the city and Aristophanes describing lovers the same drive, the same need to obliterate the
boundaries that divide them? While Aristotle in his moderation is clearly
correct to espy the differences between lovers desiring eternal unity and
the watered-down love of citizens for their cities, for Plato these differences appear to be less significant than the similarities. Both reveal the
needfulness of the human species, the inability of the individual to be
divinely self-sufficient, independent of all others. *Erōs* is the acknowledge-
ment of that inadequacy; at the same time it is the drive to complete

5. *Politics* 1262b9–17. The terms *erōs* and *philia* appear to be interchangeable in this
passage. According to Dover (1978:50 n. 20), they are not distinct in the classical period.

6. Aristotle, as we shall see in the next chapter, is not so much worried about "watering
down" love as opening up the door for impieties.

oneself, to find one's form, one's *eidos,* a state in which there is no need-fulness. The city of Callipolis that has become "what is," complete in and of itself, can claim to eliminate *erōs;* all has been unified and is self-sufficient. The lovers who have been offered and accept the net of Hephaestus become like Socrates' Callipolis; they are whole, unchanging, and free from the suffering *erōs* causes.

The story of the net of Hephaestus is told in the *Odyssey* by the singer Demodocus to entertain Odysseus, a guest in the house of Alcinoos. He sings of the secret love affair of Ares and Aphrodite, the wife of Hephaestus. Alerted to this affair, Hephaestus goes to his smithy and hammers out a net "thin like spider webs, which not even one of the blessed gods could see" (8.279–80),[7] which he then hangs over the bed to catch the two lovers in their act of love. They are trapped "so neither of them could stir a limb or get up" (8.298), unable to escape their pleasure or their shame. All the gods, though not the goddesses, come to observe and laugh uncontrollably. All laugh, that is, except Hermes. When asked by Apollo whether he, "caught in the strong fastenings," would "be willing to sleep in bed by the side of Aphrodite the golden," Hermes responds that he only wishes it could be he with "thrice the number of endless fastenings and even with all the gods and goddesses looking on" (8.336–41). Shame cannot limit his desire to be unified with the beautiful. Our existence as incomplete beings leads towards this desire for union with others and, more specifically, with others who are beautiful, as Aphrodite is, in body if not in character. The net of Hephaestus would ensure the permanence of that union, the cessation of all desire, and we would care not at all about food or shelter or sleep. We would all want the net—or would we? While Aristophanes ends his speech with the story of the net, the content of the speech raises questions about whether we would eagerly accept the net were it offered.

The lame Hephaestus understands more than the swift Hermes, for Hephaestus says to Zeus and the other gods: "I think they will not go on lying thus even for a little, / much though they are in love, I think they will have no wish / for sleeping, but then my fastenings and my snare will contain them" (8.315–17). Sexual intercourse assuages the longing for completion that haunts those who are incomplete, but only momentarily; the pleasure passes with the act itself. Sexuality, so often ignored by modern theorists, announces vividly our dependence on others, but it is only one sign of that characteristic human incompletion, and its transitory resolution is not the final answer. The vision of a human *eidos* or completion carries with it the tragic knowledge that it can never be achieved by mor-

---

7. The translation here and those that follow from the *Odyssey* are by Lattimore (1967).

tals limited by the boundaries of their bodies. Sexuality illustrates sharply the inadequacies of a union dependent on bodies. It is the comic poet who most vividly portrays us as bodily creatures and thereby shows us the limited unity between bodies and the limits of a city, founded in speech, that abstracts from the body for the sake of an unseen wholeness.

Aristophanes has made us laugh often. He has shown us fantastical images and feats on the Attic stage, images of men as they could never be—transformed into birds, sailing to heaven on dung beetles, defending their poetry in Hades. Along with these fantastical images, he shows us ourselves as we do not like to see ourselves. With a focus on our bodies, he reveals how ugly we really are at the same time that he makes us laugh at our own ugliness. As we watch (or read) an Aristophanic comedy, we become vividly aware of our bodily functions, which transform our amazing potential on the comic stage into grotesque expressions of our dependence. Our physical bodies, bent and crooked bodies, bodies in need of being filled and in need of being purged, bodies needing to be scratched or to be soothed, show us our distance from the beauty of the divine forms.

Plato, as the author of the *Symposium,* transforms Aristophanes into one of his own comic characters, one who is stuffed (185c) and then emptied. Plato goes even further: he turns Aristophanes' comedy into tragedy and thus turns Aristophanes' speech into the work of an ugly tragedian. The final question of the dialogue is answered in part by the portrayal within the dialogue of Aristophanes. The tragic poet on the Attic stage shows to the Athenians their mortality, their distance from the divine. But in so doing, he makes mortals beautiful as they struggle against the net of necessity. Agathon, in the speech following Aristophanes', makes cruel gods appear beautiful. Even destructive *atē* walks softly and delicately as she topples men and cities (195d). The piety of the tragedian is evident in his respect for a divine power that we cannot conquer. Aristophanes, under the control of the Platonic literary art, becomes a tragedian who evokes fear and pity with his praise of love, not by beautifying the fearful, but by depicting the ugly. The tale he tells is grotesque, filled with absurd images that offend the decorum maintained by the earlier speakers even in their descriptions of indecorous actions. Unlike other dramatists, Aristophanes does not uplift us with the beauty of our necessary tragedy. Plato plays the ultimate trick on Aristophanes: he leaves him without the beauty and gentleness of the prizewinning Agathon, and yet makes his speech a tragic portrayal of the human condition. Eryximachus the doctor, the technician, applauds Aristophanes' speech, saying he has spoken sweetly (*hēdeōs*) (193e). The unpoetic doctor fails to recognize the tragedy that Plato's Aristophanes reveals and that Aristotle understands when he describes the

Aristophanic lovers: death alone can assuage the longing that arises from the incompletion of our bodies.

Aristophanes appears briefly at the beginning of the dialogue to admit to his drowning, as he phrases it, in the drink of the night before (176b). His true entrance, though, comes when it is his turn to speak. Apollodorus, reciting Aristodemus's report of the evening's events, says, "Aristodemus said that it was necessary that Aristophanes speak, but there chanced (*tuchein*) to come upon him a certain hiccup from fullness (*hupo plēsmonēs*) or some other cause and he was not able to speak" (185c). These hiccups have caused many a commentator to reflect on the significance of the change in the order of speeches. We need merely note that they indicate Aristophanes' bondage to his body; even in this setting of lofty discourse, the body limits what he can or cannot do. Most of the others at Agathon's house are similarly limited; such bondage has turned them to discourse. Like Cephalus, they are not true lovers of speech; they engage in speech making because the avenues of bodily satisfaction have been closed to them by their earlier excesses.

Despite Eryximachus's claims that the world is orderly, it is chance, *tuchē*, that places Eryximachus and Aristophanes in direct counterpoint. Their speeches become a pair—offering opposing views of reality and the place of humanity, *technē* and politics in our world. Eryximachus goes beyond the limits of the polis that characterized the first two speeches and talks of the beauty and the harmony of the cosmos. When Eryximachus looks at the natural world he, like his Presocratic predecessors, observes diversity, opposites, and the difficulty of integrating that which is not all alike. The city builds itself up with citizens who are similar to one another, similar in origins, and similar in birth, sex, and wealth, whereas the natural world accommodates and integrates opposing forces that are (as he quotes from Heraclitus) "brought apart and carried back together" (187a). The ancient city was not a melting pot; it excluded, as we have seen in our discussion of *Ion*, those who were different. Eryximachus, the scientist in the company, cannot accept the citizen's avoidance of diversity; indeed, he understands his world by establishing dichotomies and then asserting that an excess on either side of the dichotomy leads to disorder. What exists, according to the doctor, is a careful balancing of parts, of opposites, of hot and cold, of dry and moist. Nature composed of variety and diversity on occasion becomes disharmonious, but the doctor's *technē*—the understanding of those opposites—can quickly reestablish the natural order of things.

The hiccups of Aristophanes had come by chance, disrupting the order of the speeches. They need to be treated by creating yet more disharmony, the tickling and the sneezing to which Aristophanes must subject himself as the doctor discourses on the harmony of the universe. Eryximachus, with his vision of a natural harmony and a benevolent nature, is the sugar coating for the harsh reality that Aristophanes has to teach us about love and ourselves, about the tyranny of nature. While Eryximachus talks of order, Aristophanes reveals human suffering—*pathos*—and shows that love must be a doctor (189d; 191d; 193d), easing the pain that nature has assigned to us. Eryximachus could never do this because he begins with a harmonious nature of complementary opposites. Politics and cities have no role in his world, and nature provides the order that politics tries to create. Aristophanes' nature embodies none of this harmony. His own body is not harmonious, and the nature he describes demands a political world to work against the chaotic existence that comes from our own incompletion and disharmony.

At the beginning of his own speech, Eryximachus suggests that he himself will complete the insufficiently complete (*ouk hikanōs apetelese*) (185d–186a) speech offered by Pausanias. Eryximachus initially has a vision of the world in which such completion is possible; it is necessary that he try to put an end (*telos*) to the speech. At the conclusion of his speech, Eryximachus no longer pretends completion. The order he has posited, the possible comprehension of the whole, is placed in question as he now suggests that Aristophanes fill in (*anaplēroun*) what he, the doctor, has omitted (188e). Aristophanes abhors a vacuum; any emptiness offends. His comedies portray men and women eager to fill up the holes in their bodies. But as he fills in the holes in Eryximachus's speech, he makes more apparent the incompletion of the human form and thus the impossibility of ever achieving the harmony and filling in that Eryximachus's reflections assume. Aristophanes' destruction of this vision will set the scene for Socrates' more elaborate account of the harmony that comes only from the transcendence of the bodily disharmony Aristophanes describes.[8]

Let us begin to look directly at the speech of Aristophanes. The task that he sets up for himself is to discover the "power" of love. Aristophanes describes love as most friendly to mankind (*philanthrōpotatos*) (189cd). According to traditional Greek mythology, Prometheus held this honor. His story, told twice by Hesiod as well as by Aeschylus, highlights the conflict between gods and men. Though he helps men, Prometheus can do nothing to mitigate the gods' hostility to mortals. Through the gift of fire, however, he helps men survive on their own and become civilized, taming the natural forces of the gods. Aristophanes proclaims that love,

---

8. Edelstein (1945) makes a valiant effort to resurrect Eryximachus before generations of readers who have scoffed at this pompous doctor. The argument from the persepctive of dramatic role is persuasive—but it falls short when considered in conjunction with what exactly Eryximachus says.

philanthrōpotatos, should have the sacrifices, the temples, the altars that men reserve for the gods. He replaces the Olympians with a power that eases pain rather than exacerbates it.

To explain the philanthropy of love and its power, Aristophanes turns to our "ancient nature," our bodies as they once were—or could have been only in the imaginings of Aristophanes. Our nature has changed, and may change again if we are not pious. It is not our own. A changing human form raises questions about the nature, the *phusis,* of the human being. The underlying unity of men is not what is unseen, hidden behind the veil of physical forms. Rather, it lies in our past. What is ontological in Parmenides and the *Republic* is historical in Aristophanes. Socrates, as he brought women into the city of the *Republic,* had questioned the naturalness of the customs we observe. Customs change: men now strip for gymnastic exercises. Customs thus cannot be used as the basis for comprehending nature. According to Aristophanes' story, neither can the bodies that we now have be so considered, as, for example, we consider the place of women in political society. To be in accord with nature is to recover that ancient form of which we learn only through the poetic speech of the comic artist. *Erōs* directs us towards our former perfection, makes us aware of the inadequacy of our bodies, and leads us beyond the currently observed world.[9] The bodies in which we now find ourselves are not our "natural" shapes. In the past, in what I shall here call Time A, there were three sexes, according to Aristophanes' story: the double male, the double female, and hermaphrodite.[10] Our present bodies suffer and endure pain (*pathos*) and longing (*pothos*), that is, *erōs.* This *erōs* alerts us to our true form and how we ourselves are only halves of what we once were; love makes us long to be whole, to uncover this truth (191a).

What was this ancient form for which we now long? It was a form without *erōs,* for it was self-complete. It needed no one and nothing. Its spherical shape suggested the absence of a beginning or an end.[11] There was no interdependence among these spherical bodies, not even for the sake of procreation. "They gave birth (*etikton*) not in each other (*eis allēlous*), but in the earth, just like the crickets" (191c). The absence of need made them divine. Gods that we now honor, who need sacrifices, need

9. Socrates as the *object* of *erōs* shall perform this role in Alcibiades' speech; see below pp. 179–83.

10. As Neumann (1966a:421) points out, there are problems with using the phrase "double male" since the original beings were not double anything; "double" implies divisibility. These ancient creatures were unities.

11. Cf. Nussbaum (1979a:139, 171 n. 13; 1986:172 n. 20) for her discussion of the spherical creatures and their relationship to Xenophanes' and Aristotle's conceptions of divinity.

honors, need sexual relations (at least some of them), are inferior divinities, lacking the perfection once found in those ancient human forms. Those eight-limbed beings, our ancestors, are our true gods. Among those autochthonous, spherical creatures there was no political life, there were no families. Cities, households, lovers, even—or especially—philosophy, all reveal our distance from the perfection of self-completion, showing humans to be needful creatures, unable to survive or procreate on their own. They arise from those feelings of incompletion that are unknown to those spherical creatures.

The sense of completion, though, arouses in those ancient forms terrible thoughts and proud looks, such thoughts and looks that they rebel against the gods. They do not need gods as do mortals of a later time. Callipolis could dispense with the old gods, overthrowing them and creating new gods fashioned after the wholeness and immobility of the city itself. When men or cities are incomplete, piety enters, confirming our inadequacy and dependence on others. Pride (*hubris*) is the product of completion and independence. The spherical creatures do not rebel because they want what the gods have. They want nothing. Arrogance alone incites rebellion.[12]

Aristophanes compares this rebellion with the deeds of Ephialtes and Otus as told in the *Odyssey:* these two giants "made great threats / against the immortal gods on Olympus, that they would carry / the turmoil of battle with all its many sorrows against them" (11.313–14). In the *Iliad,* Dione, comforting Aphrodite, who was injured by the mortal Diomedes, remarks on the pains that the Olympian gods must suffer from mortals: "Ares had to endure it when strong Ephialtes and Otus / sons of Aloeus, chained him in bonds that were too strong for him / and three months and ten he lay chained in the brazen cauldron; / and how might Ares, insatiable of fighting, have perished," had he not been rescued at the last moment by Hermes.[13] The three and ten months with Ares chained are three and ten months when war is stilled. His release unleashes the pains and sufferings of war. These are not the immortal gods of Callipolitean poetry. They cause much hardship. Had the assault of Otus and Ephialtes been successful, they would have accomplished great things. Had the assault of the high-minded spherical men been successful, they

12. As we read this section of Aristophanes' speech, we must keep in mind Socrates' role in this dialogue and especially Alcibiades' speech "praising" Socrates, which I shall discuss below. Socrates is hubristic (175e; 215b; 219c); he feels the lack of nothing even in the cold of a winter camp. He earns the scorn and hatred of his fellow soldiers who harshly feel their wants, and he is impervious to the sexual appeals that Alcibiades makes. He is the closest modern equivalent of the ancient, spherical creatures.

13. *Iliad* 5. 385–91. Lattimore (1951) translation.

too would have accomplished great things, in particular, eternal happiness and the absence of pain for mortals.

The spherical humans of ancient times, however, were not victorious. The gods take counsel. They are like humans, with political institutions, in need of others, depending on men for honors and sacrifices. Human gods, through their politics, are able to defend themselves against divine mortals. Zeus, in a most human and ungodly fashion, thus "devises a plan" to make humans weaker and more numerous. It is a plan that will force men into families and into political life. The first step leading to what I shall call "Time B" is the famous splitting of the round human beings in half. This makes humans as needful and incomplete, that is, dependent on others, as Zeus and the other gods are. No longer will humans have proud thoughts; they will attend only to their lack of their other half.

While spherical, these beings corresponded to the heavenly bodies, the double men to the sun, hermaphrodites to the moon, double women to the earth. When cut in half, they are transformed into lowly objects such as one might find on the table of a poor peasant. Aristophanes compares them to apples, to eggs, and to flat fish. The division removes mortals from the perfection of heavenly bodies and puts them in the mundane world of food. Apollo refashions them, working like a shoemaker with his last, leaving a few wrinkles around the naval to remind them of their "ancient suffering," as Aristophanes puts it (191a). But the language here is not precise. The suffering is not ancient; it is present, what we feel now and have felt ever since the slicing. Our heads have been turned around so that we can see those ugly wrinkles and be reminded constantly of what has been, of the unity we have lost—and of the gods' power to destroy the human perfection that once, long ago, we enjoyed.

Aristophanes thus tells of conflict between men and gods. Throughout his speech Aristophanes urges piety, but he himself is not pious. He mocks and belittles the gods at the same time that he invokes a piety based on fear. The humans viewing their split forms accept the order of Zeus, but they do so because of terror. The tickling of Aristophanes' nose and his consequent sneezing created order; order comes at a price that it is often not pleasant to pay (189a). Zeus is a tyrant controlling others for the sake of the honors and the sacrifices he craves. Navels and the wrinkles around them are like the men hanged in the city square or heads on stakes at the city's gates. They remind us of the tyrant's power to destroy those who threaten him. Our simple navel, which enters human history at the same times as *erōs,* reveals our dependence on the divine authority of the gods. *Erōs,* as the drive to escape that dependence, is born of the tyranny of Zeus. To honor love, to strive to recreate that ancient unity, is the only form of rebellion against the gods that we have left, at least in Aristophanes' version.

As often happens, though, the tyrannical exercise of power misfires. The suffering Zeus causes is too great. Instead of doubling the number of his servants as he had anticipated, Zeus now has none. Humans, so busy pursuing their mates, ignore the gods as well as the demands of their own bodies for food and rest. Humans in Time B are dying. So again Zeus devises a *mechanē*: sexual reproduction. The *pathos* and *pothos* that had controlled the half-beings in their search for their mates up to this point had been asexual. When they did encounter their other half—or one that they hoped was their other half—they would stand with their arms around one another, ignoring any need for food, clothing, and shelter. The desire to remain together overcame all else. Procreation during Time B was still in the earth, asexual, as though they cared not at all about the continuation of the species. It is to the humans at this stage that Aristotle refers in his discussion of unity from diversity (*Politics* 1262b9–17)—the halves for whom the discovery of the appropriate mate is of such importance that they destroy themselves and each other in their discovery. It is not only the lack of clothing and shelter that kills them off; the unity that they achieve transforms them into beings who no longer have any potential. They are whatever they might be. At such a point they no longer need others; they become asocial and apolitical. In Aristotle's later model, they become either gods or beasts. They are "what is," satisfying the needs neither of Zeus nor of other men. They are Callipolis writ small.

Rebellious humans no longer threaten Zeus; in Time B he must face the prospect of their disappearance. By giving them sexuality, in what I shall call "Time C," he gives them back life. He places the genitals in front and "through these he made generation in one another through the male in the female" (191c). Through sexuality, *erōs* becomes a source of life rather than death. Now the unity is no longer the clasping of arms around the other but includes penetration, which in turn can lead to the creation of a new individual. Generation, though, is not the only consequence. There is also the satiety achieved when copulation takes place. Instead of striving to be unified always, unity can be achieved and then relaxed. The term used to express this satiety is fullness (*plēsmonē*) (191c), the same fullness that caused Aristophanes' hiccups (185c). Once satisfied, men are able—and want—to turn to other activities. Hephaestus well understood that the lovemaking of Ares and Aphrodite could not last forever. With sexuality the desire for unity ceases at the moment fullness is achieved. Zeus's *mechanē* works: humans survive. They now have time to honor the gods and to offer them sacrifices.

During Time B there was no art, no philosophy, no family, no city; the human race was driven only by *erōs* for one's ancient form. Once that form was found, there was no need for further activity or motion. In Time C, released from the unrelenting power of *erōs*, we build other realms of satisfaction. Satiety allows for activities that enable us to survive despite our incompletion. *Erōs* draws us back to our original nature, but our sexuality and the potential for sexual satisfaction prevents us from returning completely to that ancient form. We become ignorant of the chains that the gods have placed over us. By soothing our pain through sexual fulfilment, by making us disregard our original form, we become the servants of the gods. The sexual *erōs* occurring during Time C is thus portrayed by Aristophanes as a trick of the gods to keep the human race alive. It is not, as Aristophanes had at first suggested, the result of any pity Zeus may have felt for the human species. Zeus acts out of self-interest. Aristophanes does not sing an encomium for *erōs* such as Phaedrus had requested. Instead, he damns the gods. His plea to honor love with temples and sacrifices is part of his own arrogant rebellion against the Olympians, matched by Socrates' own rebellion through the reform of poetry in the *Republic*.

Aristophanes offers considerable detail about our lives in Time C and especially about those who originally were the double men. They receive the greatest praise; they are the bravest, the most manly by nature (192a). They find satiety in each other and turn to politics, not to the family or sexual generation as do the original hermaphrodites. "Upon becoming mature, such men alone go into *ta politika* . . . they love young boys and naturally pay no attention to marriage and children" (192ab). In contrast to Aristotle, Aristophanes does not view the family as natural. It is not the aim of *erōs*, certainly not in Time B where there is no sexuality and where it is only by the by in Time C. Genesis had no part of the life we led in Time A. If there was any birth, it was autochthonous; autochthony required neither female nor the family. Heterosexual genesis is a response to and evidence of our subordination to the gods, of our weakness in Time C. If nature is what is old, what existed in Time A, then marriage cannot be based in nature. The males in Aristophanes' story are "forced (*anagkazontai*)" to marry by custom (192b). Marriage is sanctified by the gods to keep men from becoming too powerful. The family prevents men from uniting and threatening the gods again, from finding the power and arrogance in unity such as their ancestors experienced.

Whereas in the first part of his speech Aristophanes distinguishes clearly between Time B and Time C, towards the end he conflates the two, slyly moving from a focus on the body to the psyche. He no longer distinguishes between the three original sexes. He talks about all and describes the meetings of those "made" for each other. The encounter with our true mate occurs by chance as we go running around, unsystematically searching for that elusive individual, mostly in vain. The naturally ordered universe of Eryximachus's speech does not exist in Aristophanes' model. The world is as chaotic and as governed by chance as are the hiccups that interrupted the order of this most orderly of symposia. If and when one does chance on one's mate, one is wonderously struck by the *oikeiotēs* (192c), the family feeling, the sense that the other one is one's own. This "familiar" person will end all the searching, all the chaos one may sense.

Aristophanes does not propose the random, promiscuous coupling of bodies. There is one body, one specific other to which we can attach ourselves.[14] This other body upon which we may chance has no specific qualities of goodness or evil, beauty or ugliness, brown or red hair that arouses our sense of awe. We do not desire union with the other because he or she is beautiful; we do so simply because there is this underlying, unseen "kindred sense." Love is not love of beauty; it is of ourselves, or rather ourselves as we used to be. It is thus neither orderly nor necessarily directed towards that which is good. The description of Apollo's surgery has shown us how ugly are the bodies of those we desire—covered with wrinkles, paunchy, full of holes—quite unlike the divine perfection of the spherical shapes. Yet we overlook all that is ugly and grotesque and perceive only the underlying, invisible *oikeiotēs*.

At this point in the speech, bodies—round ones, cut and sewn-up ones, ugly ones—yield to that which has no shape and is incapable of being cut or sewn (or seen), namely the soul. We can love those with wrinkled, paunchy bodies because Aristophanes, under Plato's control, begins to abstract from the body and to attend to an unseen present force, not only a distant past. The pain felt by other than the body cannot be satisfied by the physical, sexual union of Time C. Those made for each other come to want more than sexual satisfaction. They wish to end out their lives living with one another (*diatelountes met'allēlōn dia biou*) (192c).[15] This love, Aristophanes now tells us, is not simply sexual coupling. Once the soul appears, the sexuality that had freed men for other tasks no longer provides an adequate release from pain. With the movement from the body to the soul, from physical union to psychic union, desires become ineffable. Twice Aristophanes repeats that lovers are unable to express what it is they want: *oud' an echoien eipein* (192c) and *ho ou dunatai eipein* (192d). We can articulate what the body needs when we talk about sexual union but now, with reference to the soul, simple descriptions of sexual couplings, heterosexual or homosexual, are inadequate. The human being split as a body also has a double soul. Zeus placated the body's longing when he moved the genitals, but he could not do this for the longing of the unseen soul.

14. Nussbaum (1979a) describes the importance of this "specific other" in Alcibiades' speech.
15. Pausanias expresses the same thought (181d) but leaves out *diatelein,* thus ignoring the undercurrent of death that Aristophanes introduces at this point in his speech.

It is here that Aristophanes introduces the parable of Hephaestus's net to help us express that ineffable longing felt by the soul. He does not tell the whole story of the adulterous lovers caught by the shrewd Hephaestus. Rather, he has Hephaestus appear before Aristophanic lovers with the tools of his trade to say:

> Are you eager for this, to become as much as possible joined with each other, so as not to leave one another, day nor night? If you are eager for this, I am willing to fuse and weld you together so that being two you will become one; and as long as you live, being one, you will both live in common with one another and when you die, there again in Hades, having died, you will be one in common instead of two. But think if you long for (*erate*) this, if it is sufficient should you chance upon it. (192d–e)

Hephaestus's offer, Aristophanes claims, would be rejected by no one. The god offers lovers a chance for revenge on the gods, for he allows mortals to make light of their mortality. Bodies having been once split cannot be joined permanently, as the humans of Time B discovered, without death. Hephaestus, though, provides not for the body, but for the soul, as he talks of a life in common after death. The mortality of the body becomes irrelevant and the joining he proposes ignores the limits that bodies might create. Aristotle is right. Unity of bodies alone is impossible without death, while the unity of the souls is possible only after death.

If love is so strong for another, if out of two we become one, life itself ceases to be important. Human life characterized by potential is eclipsed by the net of Hephaestus. It becomes an escape from the potential to be other, to be many, to grow or diminish, to change from "what is." The net, though, can only be offered to us in the speech or the comedies of Aristophanes. Hephaestus does not stand before us; the souls of two cannot be bound together by the tools of the smithy. The search for our ancient nature when we were whole (*holoi*) (192e) must be carried on within the realm of the mortal life of our bodies. Aristotle's predictions hold: the complete melding of those bodies would mean death. We must struggle with the tragic acknowledgment that the net—even if it were available—could never help us overcome our sense of incompletion without destroying us. Thus, Plato transforms the comic artist into a tragedian.

Aristophanes ends his speech with a plea for piety. The gods retain their power over us precisely because the net of Hephaestus is unavailable, because we cannot ensure our own completion and immortality by making death irrelevant. Because of an earlier injustice we were dispersed (*diōikis-thēmen*) (193a) by the god. Aristophanes anachronistically compares the

gods' first splitting of the human race to the Spartans' more recent disper-
sal of the Arcadians, who in their disloyalty to the Spartans acted as the
original spherical beings had acted towards the Olympian gods. The Lacedaemonians destroyed the unity of the city. Isolated from one another,
the Arcadians became weakened. The current desire of the Arcadians to
become a city again parallels the *erōs* that motivates men to seek their
mates by nature. Here the analogy between the individual and the polis
works as it does not in the *Republic*. Not to live in the city is the consequence of a hostile power (Sparta, in this case) intent on preserving its
own dominance. Not to be part of the city is to endure pain and longing,
such as that experienced by the divided beings of Time B. The power to
cause such pain in others is divine. Callipolis was founded by Socrates to
eliminate that pain, to rebel against the power of the gods, to be self-
sufficient in its unity. That unity, though, which goes beyond the bodies
of men and women, has the same consequences as the acceptance of the
net of Hephaestus.

Socrates' Speech and the Unity of Male and Female

Socrates' speech is, on the surface, an optimistic retelling of the Aristophanic myth of a lost unity to be regained only at the pleasure of the gods.
In the Socratic version, told in the voice of the mantic seer Diotima, we
can move from the love of beautiful objects to the beautiful itself by climb-
ing the ladder of love, by "begetting (*tokos*) on the beautiful" (260b)—
whatever that may mean; thereby, we ease the pain of this longing that is
love and enjoy everlasting happiness without depending on the gifts of a
niggardly god or on random searches through the mass of humanity for
our special mate. We become complete simply by contemplation—free
from any net spun by the smithy of the gods. Whether we continue to
exist as human beings once we have attained that state, however, remains
as problematic as the consequences of accepting the net of Hephaestus or
of inhabiting a city called Callipolis.

For both Aristophanes and Socrates, *erōs* is the desire to be complete in
oneself. For both, though, that completion depends on others: for Aristophanes there is the specific other for whom we search; for Socrates there
is a more generalized other—a beautiful other—that may or may not be a
person. But while Aristophanes emphasizes likeness (*oikeiotēs*), Socrates,
at least at the beginning of his speech, emphasizes the imaginative and
creative interplay of opposites. Socrates himself enacts this interplay by
taking on for himself male and female voices. In the language of Callipolis,
he is more than one. Himself double, he maintains his interest in the in-
termingling of opposites by telling the tale of the birth of love through

sexual generation and making heterosexuality the central metaphor for the ascent up the ladder of love. Heterosexual generation is not hidden away as in the *Republic* (or in tragedies such as *Seven Against Thebes, Eumenides,* or *Ion*). Socrates had dealt with the "female drama" in the *Republic* only under compulsion and with the hesitation of a man about to commit involuntary man(woman?)slaughter. In the earlier speeches of the *Symposium* there had been, for the most part, the same resistence to heterosexuality. Phaedrus had established the mood initially by denying love any birth: as the oldest (and therefore most deserving of honor) of the gods, Eros could have no parents. Pausanias in his turn had insisted that the heavenly love had no mother (*amētōr*) (180d); only vulgar, popular love was born of the female.

Yet, it is precisely the heterosexual generation of love as the intermediary point between opposites that engages Socrates in his discourse with Diotima.[16] Socrates' tale—for like Aristophanes' address, it is more of a story than a speech—begins as he recalls a conversation between himself and Diotima that parallels the conversation that he has just had with Agathon. As a young man, Socrates, like Agathon, had thought of love as beautiful, as shining, and so forth. Diotima needed to teach him that love was "of the beautiful" and therefore could not be beautiful itself, for it would not desire what it did not lack. Does this mean that love is ugly? The young Socrates, as Agathon after him, had seen the world in terms of dichotomies—male and female, friend and enemy, beauty and ugliness. Socrates, a man speaking in a woman's voice and Diotima, a mortal offering the speech of the gods, both illustrate the inadequacies of such dichotomies. Diotima urges Socrates to look at that which is in-between rather than at the oppositions. "Have you not observed that there is something half-way between wisdom and ignorance?" she asks a befuddled Socrates (202a). From here she moves to the daemon, one who is neither human nor god, but both. Eros is such a daemon, an intermediary between humans and gods, just like the prophetess herself.

Socrates pushes Diotima, inquiring about the generation of love. Pointedly, he rejects the stories of Phaedrus and Pausanias and asks, "Of what father and mother [is love]?" (203a). Diotima responds: "That is a rather long tale to tell. All the same I will tell you (*erō*)" (203b). There follows Diotima's charming tale of Need (*Penia*) the mother plotting to become pregnant by Way (*Poros*). Penia is like Socrates, or a Socrates in a feminine dress. She hangs around doorways—as had Socrates earlier in the evening. Resourceless, without a way, she must seduce, scheme, devise plans to take

16. One might also want to think about the possible relationship of Diotima to the goddess who educates the *Kouros* of Parmenides' poem about "what is."

advantage of the drunken, sleeping Poros, he who has a way and is in need of nothing.[17] He is full and satisfied, simply lying in a drunken stupor. Sufficient unto himself and satisfied in his fullness, he creates nothing before his union with wily Penia.[18] Only through the activities of Penia does he become a partner (of some sort) in the creation of the passion that will move men out of their own self-satisfied stupor to search, to scheme, to acquire the completion that they themselves lack. Penia in a sense "begets upon" Poros and is the model for the later ascent up a ladder of unresponsive beauty.

Eros, born from this union, incorporates qualities from both the mother and the father. The female Penia, though, gives to Eros those qualities that make him most similar to Socrates. From his mother, Eros is always shoeless and homeless, sleeping on the ground without bedding, resting on porches, always in need. Though Diotima claims that from his father he inherits his scheming nature (*epiboulos*), it is precisely this quality that characterizes Penia in the story of Eros's birth (203b, 203d). Like Eros, though, Socrates is neither female nor male; he is both, just as in the speech that he offers to praise love he is both male and female.[19] Instead of being one, as would be required in Callipolis, he becomes more than one and defies any sharp dichotomization—so much for tales of generation that exclude the female, or that present her as the mere flowerpot in which the male sows his seed. Plato via Socrates via Diotima brings the female fully into the process of generation. Rather than excluding that which is other, this encomium on love incorporates many, not one, and welcomes rather than dismisses the multiple.

Once Diotima has described the generation of Eros, Socrates pauses, unsatisfied, always wanting more than he has: "Well then, O stranger. You speak well. Love being of this sort, what use does he have for human beings?" (204c). The answer offered is enmeshed in a process of appropriation—the appropriation forever of the beauty we lack for ourselves. With the hindsight of modern liberalism, we might at first think of a Hobbesian state of nature inhabited by Macpherson's possessive individuals, but Diotima, introducing the language of procreation, escapes any

17. Can we think of Poros as the sleeping Athens of the *Apology*, which Socrates in the guise of an insect rather than a woman stirs out of its slumber?

18. One can wonder what is the character of Penia's union with Poros. Perhaps we must understand this generation according to the language of "begetting upon" as used later in Diotima's speech. It remains unclear whether the object of one's *erōs* needs to respond in order to be "begot upon." See below the discussion of Alcibiades' speech and especially the arguments of Nussbaum (1979; 1986).

19. Rosen (1987:202) comments as well on Socrates' androgyny, particularly in contrast to the androgyny of Agathon.

such conclusions. We appropriate through a creativity modeled on the processes of procreation. In a startling phrase, Diotima suggests that all humans, male and female, are pregnant (*kuousin . . . pantes anthropoi*) (260c). There is no distinction between male as begetter and female as bearer.[20] Indeed, the male here is transformed into a female, capable of pregnancy and of bringing forth another.[21] Socrates in the *Republic,* as we have seen in chapter 6, had destroyed the female; he had chosen to deny as much as possible her involvement in procreation and had made her pregnancy and labor a brief moment in time. Here, in the feminized speech of the male, pregnancy is elevated, granted to the male as well as to the female. The virility, strength, and courage of the father pales before the pregnant body and then the pregnant soul. We must emulate the female body with its capacity to reproduce as we ascend the ladder of love. The processes of male impregnation yield to the priority of the language of female pregnancy. Begetting on the beautiful, as the language that follows phrases it, is not male fertilization of the female, but the giving birth to what is in oneself, stimulated, shall we say, by the presence of one who is or that which is beautiful.[22]

The earlier speeches had tried to eliminate the female and procreation from the discourse about love, ignoring the hermaphroditic aspect of human nature and the necessary interaction between male and female, just as Callipolis and Eteocles had done in their dreams of autochthony. The earlier speeches saw only a male world, one flawed by its unidimensionality and by its focus on death. The incorporation of the female into the male form makes it creative rather than unmoving. She offers pregnancy to the sterile male. The feminine principle here moves us beyond the homosexual

20. Cf. *Republic* 454d–e.

21. The editor of the Loeb edition of the *Symposium* finds this confusing and notes, concerning 206c, "The argument requires the application of 'begetting' and such terms indifferently to either sex." Or see the more recent Price (1989:15): "Bearing is indicated by the recurrent description of the lover as 'pregnant.' . . . Yet it is inescapable that begetting, and indeed impregnating, is man's role in sexual procreation; Plato will touch on that as quickly and vaguely as he can . . . blurring the distinction by effectively subsuming begetting under bearing, as if sperm were a kind of foetus."

22. It has been tempting to criticize Plato for appropriating pregnancy for the male. O'Brien (1981:129) comments, "This is quite a stunning inversion of the real process of reproduction in which the sex-act is all that *men* actually contribute to biological life." Hartsock (1985:97) writes, "The real activity of reproduction is thus replaced by the mental activity of achieving wisdom and immortality." Brown (1988a:606–07) says, "One kind of feminist reading might cast it as simply another instance of men seeking to appropriate for themselves the one distinctive thing women have." I see the process here more as an inversion of the model used in the *Republic,* where the female was turned into a male. Here the male becomes a female, just as Socrates giving speech to the female Diotima himself becomes female according to the principles of the *Republic* as he speaks Diotima's words.

armies of Phaedrus's speech, beyond a wife seeking death as the expression of love for her husband. Eryximachus's speech described the balance joining opposites within all of nature and yet he does not deal with male and female couplings. The harmony Eryximachus envisions is static. Socratic love finds its worth in creativity, not in its capacity to destroy or merely preserve. What does it create? A vast array of objects from human children to laws to poems to images of virtue. Love always maintains its role as a daemon, as an intermediary. As such, it does not limit that which is other, but "being in-between it fills both [*aphoteron sumpleroi*] so that it binds together the all to itself" (202e).

As Diotima educates Socrates to see a world comprised of female as well as male, she also leads him to an understanding of the underlying unity of experience. Thus, the latter part of Socrates' speech moves from love as an intermediary to love as the pursuer of immortality, paralleling the movement we saw in Aristophanes' speech. Immortality for humans, though, can only make sense if we look beyond the visible. On the most basic level, Diotima reminds him that a living creature "is said to be the same from childhood until old age. This one, however, while never having within him the same things, nevertheless is called the same, but he is always becoming new, part being destroyed, with respect to his hair, his flesh, his bones, and everything else about his body" (207d). This is true also about the soul we don't see, for "habits, character, opinions, desires, pleasures, griefs, fears, everything of this sort" do not remain the same in each person, but "some come into being and others are destroyed" (207e). Despite these changes, visible and invisible, the person is said to be the same. Thus, mortal creatures possess immortality not by becoming an unchanging being but by replacing themselves through regeneration. "In this way (*tautēi tēi mechanēi*) [cf. 191b], O Socrates, mortal nature partakes of immortality" (208b). And so she commands Socrates: "Do not wonder (*mē thaumaze*) if everything honors its offshoot (*apoblastēma*) by nature" (208b).

But Socrates does wonder; *ethaumasa*, he says (208b), as well he might considering the treatment of his own "offshoots" (*Apology* 31b; *Crito* 45d). Diotima leads him beyond the body and physical offspring that enable us to conquer mortality to the less tangible forms. Rather than looking for the specific mate one may chance upon (*entuchein*), it is by having a beautiful soul and being well provisioned (*euporein*) with speech about virtue (209b) that one becomes pregnant, bears, and gives birth—but not to bodies. Indeed, this common nurturing itself gives birth to a greater community (*meizōn koinōnia*) than human children create; it generates a deathless community, a *koinōnia* that itself can give birth without bodies. If only Callipolis could have attained such perfection!

Diotima speaks of fame, of laws, of virtue. She takes Socrates beyond beautiful bodies to souls where offspring take the form of discourse (*gennan logous kalous* 210a; *tiktein logous* 210c). As the lover makes this ascent, he looks less and less at the particular body or form of the beautiful, at the individual object upon which he begets, and, once he perceives the beautiful (*to kalon*) abstracted from the particular and sees the whole in kinship with itself, he no longer lives as a female servant (*oiketēs*) or a lowly slave (*douleurōs phaulos*) to a specific child or practice. Instead, the lover now turns to the vast sea of the beautiful and gives birth (*tiktei*) to beautiful speech and magnificent thoughts (210d). By turning to this sea of beauty, humans transcend the body just as they would do should they accept the net of Hephaestus. Both comic poet and Socratic seer move beyond the confines of the body to end the suffering entailed in human longing. Callipolis, building its polity free from the constraints of body, could eliminate—or at least try to eliminate—the female body and, indeed, the bodies of all, as Socrates proclaimed a city so unified that bodily boundaries could not separate the inhabitants.

Socrates, via Diotima, pursuing immortality through generation up the ladder of love, escapes the body and thus the city as well. Socrates introduced Diotima to his companions as the seer who had delayed the plague in Athens by ten years. We cannot accept this praise uncritically, though. Had the plague occurred ten years earlier, it would not have affected Athens during the first year of the Peloponnesian War, that is, it would not have been so destructive of human life. The Athenians would not yet have been crowded into the city and the plague would not have spread so quickly through a vast proportion of the population. Diotima's control of natural forces through her mantic arts is such that she could hold off a divinely sent disease (for such were diseases at that time), but this power was not informed by an understanding of the cities of men; she did not foresee the political conflicts that Thucydides said were moving the Greek cities inexorably towards war. Neither Diotima nor Socrates, who praises her wisdom, acknowledges the political forces of the world within which we live. Procreation achieved on the beautiful, unlike that achieved in the cities or in families, is unmixed (*amikton*), untouched by the flesh of men and color and all the other lowly mortal elements.

Although a vision of the beautiful such as Diotima describes will leave the viewer with true virtue and not just *eidōla* of virtue (212a), the ending of this speech recalls the ending of Aristophanes' speech. The net Hephaestus offered his lovers with the promise of eternal unity is replaced with the vision of the beautiful: "When once you see it . . . if it were possible, you are ready, no longer to eat nor to drink but only to look on and have intercourse (*suneinai*) with it" (211d). Seeing the beautiful makes one behave as do those men and women of Time B who, having found their mates, no longer care about food or shelter; to Zeus's dismay, the human species dies off, a theme carried on by the net of Hephaestus that binds souls together for an eternity in Hades. Diotima teaches Socrates how to move beyond a particular love to an unseen beauty with which one joins oneself as if in sexual union. But the perfection of that condition means death for Socrates' men, caring nought for food and drink, just as it did for Aristophanes' creatures.

It is Alcibiades whose entrance takes us down from these heights and returns us to the particular bodies that make up the city. He reminds us of the trial that awaits Socrates even as he may turn to beauty unalloyed, of the statues of the Hermae lying shattered at the crossroads, of the appeal of praise coming from the many. It is Alcibiades, accompanied by the flute girl, who reminds the group, as Diotima the seer could not, that the female and sexuality, music, passions, and gluttony are all of the human experience. It is Alcibiades who causes the party to deteriorate into an orgy of excessive drink, but it is also Alcibiades who has the last speech of the evening.

Alcibiades' Speech: Marsyas, the Sirens, and the Allure of Socrates

Alcibiades' arrival is announced by the tumultuous noise outside the closed door. Earlier in the evening the door had been wide open. No one questioned Aristodemus's entrance. As the evening focused more and more within, it excluded the outside world of the city. That world now demands admittance. Amidst the noise, the encomiasts hear the sound of the flute. Earlier in the evening the flute girl had been dismissed: "I say that the flute girl . . . be allowed to go away, playing to herself or to the women within," Eryximachus had proposed (176e). Alcibiades now appears at the doors of Agathon's house supported by the flute girl; her flute will provide the metaphor for the speech of Socrates in Alcibiades' own encomium, not of love, but of Socrates. Alcibiades thus demotes the Socratic voice from that of a mantic seer transmitting the speech of the gods to the frivolity of the flute girl.

Alcibiades' speech is at best ambivalent, if not downright nasty. Curiously, though, it becomes nasty by changing Socrates from that in-between creature he had been in his own speech, the daemon "love," to the object of love in Alcibiades' speech. Already early in the dialogue Socrates appears unaccustomedly "beautiful." Aristodemus had told Apollodorus that he had met Socrates coming from the baths and that Socrates had put on sandals. "Where are you going having become so beautiful (*houtō kalos gegenēmenos*)?" (174a), Aristodemus had asked. Socrates with sloping forehead and bulging eyes beautiful? Yet, Aristodemus is one of several *erastai* of Socrates (173b) and Apollodorus admits to making it his concern to know each day whatever Socrates does or says (172e). Showing his characteristic hubris, Socrates even portrays himself before the company as one who is desired: he pleads for protection from Alcibiades' jealousy. "From that time when I have been beloved of this one, it is no longer possible for me to look at or discourse with anyone handsome" (213cd). Alcibiades takes this Socrates, as the object of men's desires (perhaps the "beautiful upon which pregnant men beget"), and shows him to have no place in the world that he, Alcibiades, the hero and beloved of many, traverses. Competitive with Socrates, who needs neither beauty of form nor military honors to allure, Alcibiades, eager to "pay Socrates back" (213d), removes Socrates from this world of men, leaving himself alone, one enmeshed in the political world of the many, as the object of desire.

Alcibiades begins his "praise"[23] of Socrates with an analogy between Socrates and those ugly Sileni that sit in the statuary shop, ugly figures on the outside but which, when opened up, contain certain statues of the gods (215b). He compares Socrates as well to the satyr Marsyas whose pride in his own ability to play the flute led him to challenge the beautiful Apollo to a musical contest. The contest, as would be expected, ended with Apollo's victory and the flaying alive of the proud Marsyas. "Are you not *hubristēs*. . . . Are you not a flute player?" Alcibiades asks Socrates (215b). Further, Socrates is like those destructive women, the Sirens, "enchanters of all mankind whoever comes their way" (*Odyssey* 12.39–40). Those who hear the Sirens during their travels have no chance of returning home, drawn instead to the destructive reefs surrounding their island. Men must either fill their ears with wax so that they cannot hear the Sirens' song, or tie themselves to the masts of their ships so that they are not able to approach the seductive singers and thus destroy themselves. Alcibiades hears Socrates' song and is enchanted, but like Odysseus, he escapes the death awaiting him on the treacherous reefs of philosophy and returns home to the political world.

The tunes Socrates sings upon his invisible flute and the Siren-like songs he chants cause, in Alcibiades' version, pain, *pathos,* suffering. Aristophanes had spoken of our longing for a nature lost somewhere in our distant past. Alcibiades now speaks of a Socrates who stings us with the recognition of our distance from any natural perfection. So powerful is the pain that Socrates arouses that "it seemed to me that it was not worthwhile

23. The quotation marks used here are implied in the subsequent references to Alcibiades' speech as the praise he offers is constantly undermined by the details that he offers. Socrates is not the only character in the Platonic dialogues who uses irony.

living as I did" (216a). In particular, Socrates makes Alcibiades and the others who hear him recognize that he and they are not whole, that they lack much (*pollou endeēs*), "since I do not attend to my own affairs, but am involved in the things of Athens (*ta d'Athenaion*)" (216a). In other words, Socrates' songs, like those of the Sirens, enchant his listener and throw him off course into such confusion that he turns away from Athens, from the established route to fame and fortune, from the community of many. Alcibiades must cover his ears and run away lest "I become old sitting beside him" (216a).

Returning to the political world, Alcibiades enjoys the honors that the many bestow, the many who esteem the beauty that is visible, the wealth, and the charisma of the vibrant young Alcibiades. They make Alcibiades feel whole and desired, the object of love, not the lover. Then he approaches Socrates again, and the feelings of completion fade and the inadequacies become apparent. Socrates, scorning what other men value, scorns the beauty and popularity that give Alcibiades pleasure. He shows him beauties that go beyond the gifts that the city can bestow. He makes attention to the "things of the Athenians" appear worthless. "Know that if someone is beautiful it is of no concern to him at all, but he scorns such a person to such a degree that no one would believe it, nor [does he care] if someone is wealthy or has some other great honor among those esteemed by the many" (216de). Having the "statues of the gods within," Socrates does not need what other men need. Complete in himself, Socrates does not belong where other men belong. In an act that Alcibiades can only understand as arrogant (217e; 219c), Socrates scorns, in particular, the body of Alcibiades. In the famous but perverse scene, the beautiful young man suffering from the most painful of "snake bites" (217e) and drawn towards the destructive song of this male version of the Sirens tries to seduce the ugly, Silenus-like old man.[24] Thus, in contrast to what would be expected according to nature or custom (see Pausanias's speech), from a night spent alone with Socrates, under a cloak with his arms around this wondrous man, Alcibiades rises as if he had slept beside his father or his older brother (219d).

To Alcibiades' dismay, Socrates values the unseen within himself over the observable beauty of form. The eight-limbed creatures of Aristophanes displayed a similar contempt for the divine creatures who were supposed to rule over them. They saw the gods' inadequacies, denied them honors, and rose against them. In response, the gods split them in half; in a sense, Alcibiades does the same, opening up Socrates and showing us what is

---

24. Moments before, he himself had been eager to seduce "the most wise and beautiful [*sophōtatou kai kallistou*]," Agathon (212e).

within, making him weak by revealing a disharmony between the external and internal. Unlike the gods of the earlier speech, however, Alcibiades does not achieve an automatic victory, for in opening up Socrates he has shown us why Socrates has no needs; he has the golden statues that live within his soul. Socrates reminds Alcibiades that all he, Alcibiades, has to offer is bronze. Whereas the gods of Aristophanes' speech got their revenge by making men needy, governed by the pain of *erōs*, Alcibiades gets his revenge on Socrates by showing those assembled in Agathon's house that Socrates is not needful, that he has no *erōs*. We may be drawn to him by his songs, but only to our own destruction. We would do well to avoid his speech, cover our ears lest we find ourselves shipwrecked forever on the shores of philosophy.

Alcibiades' revenge takes the form of apparent praise as he describes the inability of Socrates to be part of the community of men. He shows us Socrates in settings where Alcibiades shines, namely, on the battlefield and in the city. While he may sing well in the confines of Agathon's house, in the city, and in war, he moves here as if he is a comic character in an Aristophanic comedy. First Alcibiades tells of Potideia, where Socrates is oblivious to all that the other men in the camp require. He surpassed all, including Alcibiades, in enduring the hardships that they encountered there. Others suffered when there was no food (220a). Socrates did not. Others yielded to the powers of drink. Socrates did not. "Most marvelous of all, no one of humans has ever seen Socrates drunk" (220a). Others, when the cold of winter came, stayed within their tents or wrapped themselves up prodigiously. Socrates did not; "easily, he journeyed shoeless over the ice" (220b). And then there is the trance. There, Socrates stands motionless while others eat their meals and sleep at night. Socrates, like the beautiful itself, or like a Parmenidean "what is," is unchanging and unresponsive. The men gaze in wonderment, but he does not acknowledge their gazes.[25] The next day dawn comes, the sun rises, and Socrates goes away.

We learn also of his performance in military actions when he saved Alcibiades' life. Alcibiades begins this part of the story alerting us to the presentation of the award for military valor to himself. He tells us that he had urged the generals not to give the award to him, as they intended to do, presumably because of the valor of his own performance in battle, but to Socrates. Socrates, though, would have none of this generosity, scorning what was sought most eagerly by most men. The generals thus awarded the prize to Alcibiades as planned. There was also the retreat at Delium, with Alcibiades upon on his horse looking down at the foot sol-

---

25. Compare Alcibiades' constant need for public approbation.

diers. From this lofty position he sees Socrates on foot, hardly acknowledging that he was in the midst of a military campaign, but "swaggering like a water bird and turning his eyes sideways" (221b; *Clouds* 362), to borrow a phrase from Aristophanes. Thus, Alcibiades concludes that his Socrates is not similar to anyone. Great Athenian leaders can look for their analogues in the ancient heroes of the Homeric epics, the Achilles, and the Nestors. Alcibiades finds the analogue for Socrates in the ugly Sileni, the lusty satyrs and the destructive, seductive songstresses.

Alcibiades' speech is mixed. I have emphasized the attack against Socrates that is implicit in it, for too often only the words of praise are acknowledged. But Socrates is complex—a man worthy of adoration for the beauty within, despite the ugliness of form, and a man who cannot fit into a city comprised of individuals who are incomplete, who are in need of one another and of the physical goods that sustain their lives. When Aristophanes' lovers found each other and became whole, they cared nothing for food nor for life itself. When Diotima's philosophers gazed on beauty, they cared nothing for food nor for life itself. Socrates in Alcibiades' speech cares nothing for food nor for honors nor for life itself. When Alcibiades gazes on Socrates, he too cares not at all for food or drink or the pleasures of political office. But he, along with Plato, perceives complexity, both attraction and repulsion, both beauty and deformity, virtue and arrogance. The political man, drunk and supported by the body of the flute girl, exists in a world that is complex and multiple. The Socrates of Alcibiades' speech makes him feel uncomfortable in that world, but once he escapes from the spell of Socrates, he can stay in the world—and report to and warn others about the dangerous and obscure beauty of his satyr.

Alcibiades may have had the last speech, but Socrates in a sense has the last word. As reported by Aristodemus, Socrates, no longer reciting Diotima's speech, finds an underlying unity not in a realm accessible only to the few who can follow Diotima up her ladder to the undifferentiated sea of beauty, but in the very activities of the men gathered in Agathon's house. As Aristodemus reports, "Socrates forces them to agree that it belongs to the same man (*tou autou andros*) to have the knowledge to make comedy and tragedy and that the writer of tragedy is also the writer of comedy" (223d). The speeches of the participants, some more elegantly, others less so, all incorporated the tragedies of human limitations and the comedy of human aspirations. Plato's dialogues, complex in their structure, incorporate this diversity even as Socrates appears unwilling to do so in politics and even as Diotima teaches of a pure and unmixed beauty. The *Symposium* with its nested speeches, with its complexity of structure, with its beautiful but ugly Socrates (174a; 215b), with its comedy and its tragedies, with its lovers and beloveds gives us a dialogue that makes us question the Plato who unambiguously moves us beyond our senses, our experience of the multiple, to a unified, Parmenidean "what is." Diotima's speech with its ladder of love leads us in that direction, but Plato's dialogues with their many parts and their multifaceted characters remind us of the dangers of such a view. The epistemological demand for unity and uniformity does not necessarily translate easily or well to the political need for multiplicity. Diotima expresses the drive to the former. The Socrates of Alcibiades' speech portrays the consequences of bringing such a vision into the city—and Plato as the author of this dialogue leaves us acknowledging the ambiguity of the pursuit of unity.

The turn to Aristotle in part 3 will explore whether Aristotle moves us beyond the dialogue to the city itself in the continuing exploration of the relationship of unity to diversity. Aristotle does not give into Alcibiades completely; he will not run away with his ears filled with wax from the Siren song of Socrates. But he will suggest that the completion of the human form can be found in political life as a Socrates or Diotima urging us to look upon a beauty unalloyed could not. He will give us cities whole and multiple that lead to life rather than to death. He will prepare us for the study of political science as the earlier political theorists of the Greek world feared to do.

Part Three
Aristotle: Diversity and the Birth of Political Science

> A child begins by calling all men father and all women mother, but later distinguishes each of them.
>
> *Physics*

> The greatest part of the ancient things are less articulated than the newer ones.
>
> *Politics*

Though Aristotle begins his *Physics* with the epistemological exhortation for us, the knowers of nature, to proceed from the obscure whole to the clearer, more knowable nature of particulars, the analogy he offers of a child learning to distinguish his father and his mother from other men and women draws us back to the themes of the *Republic* and suggests especially Aristotle's critique of that regime in the second book of the *Politics*. Socrates' Callipolis is a world of children unable to discriminate, unable to recognize, acknowledge, or value the difference between one man who is one's father and one woman who is one's mother from all other men and all other women. The process of maturation—and of learning to comprehend the natural world—is the process of recognizing the diversity of that which exists in nature and acknowledging a multiplicity of forms, rather than trying to unify that world into an all encompassing whole. "To investigate whether what exists is one and motionless is not a contribution to the science of nature" (184b25–185a1). Thus dismissing Parmenides, Aristotle sets us off into a political world that builds on multiplicity and diversity.

In the third book of the *Politics*, Aristotle grapples with the problem of majority rule and inquires about the justifications that can be given for accepting the wisdom of the many rather than that of the excellent few. He extols the collective wisdom of the many by calling forth a series of analogies from potluck dinners to sculptures, all of which draw on the excellences of the many, but he stops himself short suddenly when he asks, The majority of *what* multitude? "By Zeus, it is clear that this is impossible about certain ones. For the same speech would be fit for wild beasts. For what difference applies to some [multitude] and wild beasts, so to speak?" (1281b18–20). If we are to talk about the many and the few, how are we going to separate off "our many" from the other "manys"? How do we distinguish the population that is "ours" and the one that includes wild beasts? As the child who learns to recognize her mother, so too must the city learn to recognize its citizens—especially as they are distinct from others within and without the city. The problem of the herd of wild animals startles Aristotle precisely because it forces him to confront what is for him the most profound political challenge: the definition of what distinguishes and what unites, what can both separate out one group, one species, one family, from all others, and yet at the same time unite that group for the sake of the sharing on which the political community is based. When the Ukrainians of the Soviet Union claim independence, when the nation of Yugoslavia divides into Croats and Slavs and perhaps even more ethnic groups, when universities and colleges provide centers for Asian-Americans, Black Americans, and Hispanics, they are all reenacting the Aristotelian confrontation with boundaries and the difficulties that all communities must face in any attempt to identify the members of any group.

The pre-Socratics had granted to the mind the chore of distinguishing and discovering the underlying unity in that which appeared diverse. Aristotle grants this task to the mind as well, but it is a mind that acts through the creative art of politics, a human craft that divides and unites, that creates, without Platonic *erōs*, the unity of the one out of the many. The question with which we conclude this exploration of Greek thought is, Does Aristotle fear those parts so that he argues for their destruction or exclusion as do some of the characters of the tragedies we discussed earlier, or does he welcome them as he welcomes the child now able to perceive her mother standing out, identified and particularized among the mass of women she may experience?[1]

---

1. We must beware lest the romanticized version of the Aristotelian community that has become the touchstone of the current communitarian imagination obscure Aristotle's understanding of the *politeia* and transform him into an advocate of Callipolis rather than its critic. See on this, especially, the criticism by Yack (1985) of such misguided readings. The subsequent discussion will focus on the *Politics*. Others have well illustrated the interdependence of Aristotle's biology, teleology, and nature; see especially Salkever (1990). My concern here

It is in the acknowledgment of that diversity, in the articulation of the view that new things have more parts than ancient ones, that Aristotle gives birth to political science, the study of politics, or *politikē*, as a multiplicity of regimes composed of a multiplicity of parts. To view the political world as a whole, or to try to make it such a comprehensive body so unarticulated in its parts that in its uniformity it can escape conflict, is to deny the study of politics. The balancing of different claims, the order built on compromise and conflict over the meaning of the good life, the just and the unjust—these are the elements of the political world. *Politikē* is born with the intrusion of the many, with the overthrow of Parmenides, with the open readmission, rather than the banishment, of what the eyes perceive. Aristotle observes the world around him in its great multiplicty of forms, and from that observation, political science emerges.[2]

---

is not the etiology of Aristotle's thought, but how that thought responds to the issues that we have been discussing so far in this book.

2. Salkever (1990:chap. 2) develops Aristotle as the social scientist, translating *politikē* as "the equivalent of modern social science" (59). In this volume, it means to take politics seriously, not to attempt to transform or transcend it. The missionary zeal is not missing from Aristotle, as Salkever's book so vividly illustrates, but the evaluations and judgments come from a delight in the many-colored cloak of political life that Socrates appeared to scorn in the *Republic*. Salkever explores Aristotle's "practice" of social science in which "descriptions of observed phenomena" are only the preface to "four separate kinds of judgments" (57–58). My concern in the following chapters is to draw out the significance of Aristotle's willingness to base his judgments on "observed phenomena"—or the multiple world accessible to the eyes. Salkever's text carries this point further by illustrating how Aristotle's observed phenomena become the basis for a social science from which its modern practitioners could learn much and, in particular, how it can "inform practical deliberation . . . that invites further discussion and revision" (58). The story that this volume tells requires only that we recognize the significance of Aristotle's willingness to accept a world comprised of parts in constant motion which the eyes observe. Salkever's argument draws out the implications for theoretical and evaluative analysis of the development present here. Aristotle's moral theory has experienced a significant revival in recent years, especially in the quite distinctive works of MacIntyre (1981) and Nussbaum (1986). The focus of the subsequent chapters, though, is on the structure of the political community as composite and yet unified and not on questions of individual or communal choice.

8 The Challenge of the Family

The *Politics* begins, "Since every polis we see is some sort of sharing (*koinōnia*) . . ."[1] The questions for the rest of the book, then, are: Who shares, what is it that they share, and what does this sharing tell us about the aims and limits of politics? How do we recognize those who share as distinct from those who do not and how is sharing to be effected? Or, to phrase it in slightly different form, is the unity that is created by the sharing according to nature or is it the construction of human craft, both epistemological and political? To study politics is to study a process of sharing. There are many forms of sharing: we share a journey, a class, a meal, but that does not mean that we each have the same reasons for heading towards the same destination or that we gain the same knowledge or that we eat the same food. We can share ancestors or lawnmowers or enemies, and that sharing will establish a set of relationships between us that may or may not be of our own choosing. Or we can share qualities: hair color, gender, bipededness. In a fashion

1. *Koinōnia* is often translated as partnership (Lord 1984) or association (Barker 1948; Euben 1990:9 calls this a "tepid translation"). See also the Sinclair translation in which Saunders keeps "association" in his revision (1981). St. Thomas Aquinas, drawing on Aristotle, refers regularly to the *communio* when writing about the *koinōnia*. See, e.g., *Summa Theologica* I–II: Question 96. For this discussion of Aristotle I prefer "sharing" since that manages to capture, as well as I believe English can, the notion that a community is not one organic whole (though those analogies have plagued and will plague us as we proceed), but a bringing together of discrete parts that have in common some trait or possession.

similar to the Eleatic Stranger in the *Statesman,* Aristotle sets himself the task of discovering that particular form of sharing that is uniquely political, that sets the polis apart from the block association that protects a neighborhood and from the dinner party where all gather around one table. To do this, he begins with a reverse of the procedure in the *Republic,* in which the larger by analogy illuminated the smaller. Here the smaller, the household, will illuminate the profound differences between it and the larger realm of sharing entailed in the city. It is to this structure of the family that Aristotle turns first and so shall we, always remembering Aristotle's caveat that the city is not simply a large family (1252a12–13). We must understand how the family differs from the city in order to understand what each one is—and, more particularly for our purposes, how each one responds to and incorporates the diversity of its parts.

While the nature of a thing is its *telos,* Aristotle tells us, and the city reaches its *telos* with the self-sufficiency that allows those (some) within it to live well, rather than just to live, he has little patience with an elaboration of this point in his work on politics. Here (as opposed to the *Nicomachean Ethics,* for instance) he is eager to move his discussion to the parts rather than to the whole. After the very brief passage in Book 1, chapter 2, 1253a1–39, on which too many discussions of Aristotle's *Politics* are based, he proceeds: "Since it is clear out of what parts (*ex hōn moriōn*) the city is erected, it is necessary first (*prōton*) to speak about the management of the household. For every city is composed out of households" (1253b1–3).[2] The household out of which the city is composed remains the topic for the rest of this book and lies at the heart of the next book as well. To understand the city we must understand the parts out of which it is constructed, and to understand the parts we must further divide them into their constituent parts. Thus, the first in-depth discussion in the *Politics* turns our attention to the slave and the master.

Looking at the relationship in which there are the most profound differences between one human being and another, Aristotle nevertheless uncovers the equally profound difficulty of articulating and discovering those differences. Having posited a world of differences, how do our eyes enable us—indeed, can they?—to discover those differences? As he tells us frequently, the world is composite, it is not one. Parmenides, dismissing his senses, ignored too much. But having asserted that there are these parts, that the world is multiple, that we observe a variety of forms, how do we distinguish those parts and set them into an order that is constructive and

---

2. Curiously, by making this claim at the very beginning of the book, he already dismisses Socrates' Callipolis—and Praxagora's reformed Athens.

not explosive of the life lived well? Aristotle deals with observed diversity in the world, not through denial, as so many of the others we have discussed have done, but through typologies and hierarchy. He tries valiantly to resolve the problem of diversity by imposing hierarchy rather than by ignoring or conflating differences. He is too careful an observer of the world around us, however, to let his desire for order obscure the difficulties his hierarchical model creates. He is not a prisoner of his assumptions, and part of the excitement of reading Aristotle lies in his willingness to grapple with what he sees when it does not accord with the postulates he has asserted.[3] Thus, if he is to embrace the diversity he uncovers through his observations of the natural world, he must move beyond the hierarchical model to which he turns first. It is at that point that the polity becomes the political scientist's solution to the question of diversity—and Aristotle becomes the hero of this book. But let us turn in this chapter to the problem before we look to Aristotle's solution in the next.

Book 1: The Family Is Not an Individual

"Straightaway from birth it is established that certain things (*enia*) are for being ruled and others for ruling [1254a23–24]. . . . whatever is established out of many things and becomes one kind of sharing [*hen ti koinon*] . . . there appears in every case that which rules and that which is ruled" (1254a28–31). The natural world is a composite world, one that brings together many things in all sorts of arrangements. But in that bringing together—whether it be within the human person him- or herself—or within the family or the city, there will be hierarchy, the principle according to which the parts are organized. No family or city or person[4] is a random conglomeration of parts. There is an order affirmed by nature that demands the hierarchical relation of ruler and ruled, of better and

3. It is the straightforward acceptance of Aristotle as a theorist of hierarchy that undermines some of the feminist attacks against Aristotle. See, e.g., Okin (1979:80), who, by emphasizing Aristotle's functionalism and hierarchical world, concludes that he has "established a philosophic framework by which he can legitimize the status quo." Rather, Aristotle's willingness to observe enables him to raise questions that can work to delegitimize the staus quo. See especially Salkever (1990:chap. 4). Brown's analysis (1988b:chap. 3), by attending to Aristotle's struggle to deal with the tension between the part and the whole, offers a more powerful critique of Aristotle from a feminist perspective, though I find that in her attempt to dichotomize mind and body she fails to take adequate account of Aristotle's powers of observation. See further Saxonhouse (1989).

4. We should notice here that Aristotle immediately uses the animal as an example of that which is composite: "It is possible first to see in an animal (*zōiōi*) both despotic and political rule" (1254b3–4). The difficulty that organic images raise for a study of Aristotle as a theorist of diversity and multiplicity will need to be addressed, but he clearly sees the animal as a being composed of multiple parts that are often at war with one another.

inferior. Hierarchy gives meaning and a means of survival to the individual. So the soul rules over the body, the mind over the passion (1254b4–6), and the master over the slave.[5]

Parmenides had avoided such a set of relationships because he had denied all differences—no body distinct from soul, no master distinct from slave, only "what is." Within "what is" there is no differentiation, so there could be no hierarchy. In contrast, Heraclitus's *logos* was able to admit the high and the low, to bind together opposites by exploring their subjective rather than objective diversity. Aristotle replaces the Heraclitean *logos* with the principle of hierarchy. It is through that principle that opposites, masters and slaves, males and females, body and soul, parents and children, share and become part of a whole. Multiplicity does not lead to the political and epistemological chaos that Parmenides had feared. The principle of hierarchy can preclude such an eventuality—that is, it can do so if it is clear who is the ruler and who is the ruled, who is higher and who is lower, as in the case of the body and the soul. The challenge that Aristotle faces, then, having asserted that the city is a form of sharing and that all cities are composites, like families and living creatures, is to analyze these composites and discover the underlying order that informs and relates the parts. The fear of diversity is a fear of disorder; if that diversity leads by nature into order, there is nothing to fear. A hierarchy by nature alleviates that fear—but can we find that hierarchy with ease?

Aristotle begins his analysis with the discussion of the most profound inequality, and thus most hierarchical relationship, among humans: that between master and slave. He opens with the question of whether it is according to nature or whether it is unjust and therefore based only on the force of the stronger. If it is the latter, as in fact most slavery will turn out to be, then there is not the hierarchy in nature that he originally sought. If this is the case, then order must emerge from elsewhere. Slavery is based on the analogy of the human being as a composite being and the relationship between the master and the slave. The master is like the soul, the slave like the body. One must be careful, though; we must only look to the human being who is well ordered for our analogy, not to the individual where the body rules over the soul, where the hierarchy by nature does not obtain. Beyond this caveat, the analogy wavers further, for no human being can be just soul and just body. As Aristotle makes clear, although he has defined the slave as an animate possession for production rather than action, we still must ask whether anyone of this sort actually exists "and whether it is better and just for someone to be a slave or not, or if all slavery is opposed to nature" (1254a17–19). This is the problem he con-

5. See further Zuckert (1983).

fronts, and despite the claim that it is not difficult to calculate this by reason or to learn from what has happened, the exploration of the problem leaves us confounded as to whether there can be differences between human beings that can justify slavery "according to nature (*phusei*)" (1254a18).

The problem arises because of the ungraciousness of nature, which fails to clarify for us who is master and who is slave. Having found *in* nature the hierarchical principles that are to organize our existence, we then need to ask how we are to discover the boundaries between those who rule and those who are to be subjects. Enslavement as the result of wars that may be unjust cannot justify slavery, nor can slaves as parents justify the enslavement of the child of the slaves (1255a4ff). Postulating a world that can incorporate opposites into a unified whole (the master-slave relation), we are left with the task of finding the ruler and the ruled. The corrupt societies in which we live are based on force and not on nature; birth from slaves and conquest as criteria for deciding who is slave and who is master leave Aristotle dissatisfied. Aristotle is no Callicles; in the relation of higher and lower, force or physical strength is not to be the determinant. We must look elsewhere—but where? "Nature also wishes to make the bodies of free individuals and of slaves different, the latter strong for necessary things, the former straight and useless for such endeavors, but useful for the political life[6] . . . but it often turns out the opposite way, some having the bodies of free individuals while others have the souls" (1254b27–34). Because of this, it is impossible to distinguish between the slave by nature and the ruler by nature, as we could if the bodies of the free individuals were as different as the images of gods. As with the pre-Socratics, Aristotle—the great observer of nature, the detailer, for example, of morning sickness in pregnant women (*History of Animals* 7.4) or the eating patterns of cows (ibid. 8.7)—is aware of the limits of observation and the failure of our eyes to tell us about the proper order of human beings in their relationships with one another. Humans do not have the bodies of gods—and even if they did, those bodies would say nothing about their souls. And yet Aristotle concludes this exploration: "That certain individuals are free by nature and certain ones slaves is evident and for the latter slavery is beneficial and it is just" (1255a1–3). The principle holds—even though the limits of human observation make the accurate application of that principle virtually impossible.

6. We may well ask what the body of a free man is to look like in contrast to that of a slave; Newman (1887:II.147) suggests that the body of a slave should be stooped like that of an animal, while that of the citizen should be upright. But there are many physical tasks that require upright posture that slaves presumably would have to perform. It seems, for example, that debates in the assembly hardly require particularly good posture.

There is, of course, one criterion that we can perhaps use to distinguish between human beings, where sight *may* be adequate to establish in practice principles of hierarchy: this is sex. Nature has not deserted us here. We can distinguish between the male and the female even if we cannot easily distinguish by sight between the master and the slave. As Aristotle repeats descriptively, and presumably prescriptively as well, several times in his work the male has authority over the female,[7] at least according to nature. But this does not happen invariably. Though it would be in opposition to what is natural (*para phusin*), there are occasions when the female soul is superior to the male soul. Just as nature does not always arrange that the child of a slave is slavish, it does not assure that the soul of the female is always inferior to the soul of the male.[8] The household in which we might be able to find a model of the hierarchical arrangement of parts thus also leaves us somewhat confused about the possibility of creating a justly founded unity.

Instead of a hierarchy of one human being over another, as in the case of slaves and women, where ambiguity seems on occasion to reign, Aristotle turns to a more accessible hierarchy over a world external to the household, namely, the natural world that must be gathered, brought back to the household, and guarded. In this hierarchy over the external world the family can share; it becomes one through the process of sharing goods rather than through the process of ruling over one another. Within the household there is the sharing of all things and no place for the exchange of goods, whether through barter or coin (1257a17–21). The latter are only necessary when those participating in the sharing have become "more numerous" and households become separate and distinct (*kechōrismenoi*) from one another (as in the village) (1257a22). At this point of development, when the households do separate, exchange can enter because what was whole and belonged to all is now divided and belongs only to a part that can transfer (i.e., exchange) the goods it has.

This section of the *Politics* may seem surprising, coming as it does immediately after his discussion of the parts of the *oikos*. Suddenly we see the *oikos* as whole instead of as a composite unit, as undifferentiated, whereas

---

7. See previous discussions of the translation of *kurios* as having authority over, rather than being superior to, in Saxonhouse (1985b: 74). See that work also for a more extensive discussion of the issues raised in this paragraph.

8. As has been noted before by Nichols (1983: 181–82) and myself (1985b: 73), a classic case is the Tecmessa story. It is to her that Ajax utters the famous or notorious words: "Silence is beautiful in a woman," the same phrase that Aristotle cites as he discusses the varieties of virtues rather than their unity. The citation, though, is peculiarly inappropriate since in the case of Tecmessa and Ajax it is the wife speaking who offers sage advice and the mad husband who orders her to be silent.

moments earlier it had been a series relations between opposites, husband and wife, child and father, master and slave. The focus has shifted from an analysis of the parts of the *oikos,* an analysis that had left us in something of a quandary about who should rule over whom when we have difficulty defining who is better and who is inferior, to a concern with what makes the *oikos* a whole, a distinct part separated off from the larger sphere of numerous other households. That unity arises from the common sharing of the goods acquired; the sharing raises us above the divisions of masters and slaves, as the sharing of the city will raise us above the divisions that plague the city.

What, then, is the lesson by the end of Book 1? The articulation of parts within the family leads to the problem of assessment; the limits of observation preclude any assurance that when we set the master over the slave we are indeed granting authority to the one who is superior in virtue. What may be true within the individual with regard to the relationship between soul and body does not necessarily translate easily by analogy to master and slave. A unity based on the arbitrary rule over the better by the worse is contrary to nature, a perversion. The unity of the family comes from its sharing, not from hierarchy; and sharing, not hierarchy, preserves the family. Nevertheless, as the model of the individual does not translate well to the family, we must next question whether the model of sharing within the family translates to the city. Book 2 explores this problem.

Book 2: The City Is Not a Family

Book 2 begins by studying regimes founded in speech, creations of the intellect that, like Zeno's paradoxes, refuse to acknowledge the world we see and the world we experience—the arrow hitting the target and the mother looking at her own child. Each of the regimes studied tries to abstract from differences of one form or another in order to create a conflict-free political whole, but it is, in Aristotle's assessment, precisely in the process of abstraction from differences that the regimes of the mind fail. It is in this context that we encounter first Aristotle's critique of Callipolis, followed by a series of rather negative evaluations of other regimes in speech and deed (Nichols 1987: pt. 3).

Callipolis under Attack

In the pursuit of political unity for his city, Socrates had tried to suppress differences between families and between male and female.[9] As Praxagora had done in her Athens on the comic stage, Socrates had also broken down walls and transformed the female into the male warrior or

---

9. This section draws heavily on Saxonhouse (1982).

male *ecclesiast,* this time through the art of speech rather than through disguise. Thus, the family in the *Republic* was destroyed and with it the female as distinct from the male, the philosopher as distinct from the political leader (Saxonhouse 1976:195–212). After the first two chapters of Book 1, Aristotle had asserted that it is clear (*phaneron*) out of what parts the city is established and so had launched into the arrangements of the household for, as we have noted, "every city is established out of households and there are parts of *oikonomia* from which again the household is established" (1253b2–3). In Book 2 he considers (and rejects) the possibility of a city that is not "established out of households," that may try to eliminate parts in order to unify the many into one through the obliteration of boundaries. By repudiating Socrates' destruction of the family and his equation of the female and male, Aristotle allows the female an existence not defined by the male's militaristic or political activities. That existence may not offer much more than the satisfaction of physical needs, but it does not transform the female into an inferior male, who may be assigned to fight with the men but is perhaps relegated to the rear lines during battles (471d).

Socrates had been able to argue for sexual equality because he abstracted the soul from the body; early in Book 5 of the *Republic* he had tried to make the body of the female irrelevant (460d). He posited no more difference between male and female than between long-haired and bald men (454c), as if what we are can be separated from what our bodies define. With the unifying power of the mind ascendant over the lowly sight of physical things, male and female are almost indistinguishable. Aristotle, in contrast, observes that "for the most part there seems to be no case in which the soul can act or be acted upon without involving the body."[10] We cannot transcend the body through an act of intellectual abstraction. The excellence of the male must relate to the male body, that of the female to her body—and that of the slave to his or hers. The focus on bodies does not, as it does for Socrates, create boundaries between individuals that must be overcome through training and institutions before there can be a political unity. Bodies, in fact, rather than serving as dividers among individuals, reveal the necessary interdependence that the processes of sharing satisfy. Bodies on the most basic level will lead us into social interactions. Assumptions of natural gregariousness are not necessary; we are needful and while we may need the goods of nature, we need others even more (Nichols 1983). The regeneration of the city does not depend on any residue of erotic necessities among desexed citizens; the natural drives of male and female bodies remain a part of Aristotle's political

---

10. *De Anima* 403a5–7; cf. the subsequent discussion in 412b10ff.

world. He need not eliminate diversity in the search for unity; diversity instead becomes the very source of unity.

To understand the basis of Aristotle's critique of Callipolis we must first understand what he does not consider worthy of direct criticism, namely, the proposals for equality of the sexes and for the philosopher kings. In his biological works, especially *The Generation of Animals,* Aristotle describes sexual differentiation as "a necessity required by nature." He assumes that we can never abstract from these differences in our considerations of social life, for "the race of creatures . . . has got to be kept in being" (767b8–10; Peck translation 1953). It is our differences that unite us in the common goal of procreation; it is the concern with the shared endeavor that brings those who are different together—it is not the exclusion of one nor the transformation of the other that is necessary to draw what is disparate into a unity.[11] In all of his analysis of women and household relations throughout Books 1 and 2, Aristotle never indicates that his disagreement with Socrates is based on a rejection of Socrates' claim that women can be the equals of men. Nor does he openly reject the notion of the philosopher-ruler; indeed, in later sections of the treatise he will present arguments that can be construed as demanding the acceptance of such a ruler should such an individual of outstanding ability appear within the city.[12]

Had Aristotle attacked Socrates' city on the grounds that philosopher-kings and the equality of the male and the female were absurd, he would have had to deal with questions of hierarchy that he posits inheres in all of nature; of who rules over whom; of whether the philosopher by nature is the ruler over the many; and of whether the male by nature has authority over the female. Book 1 had left us unsettled about those questions. In fact, the exploration of the regimes in speech and in deed in Book 2 focuses not at all on hierarchy, but on questions of sharing, of what is and what can be common, of what role that which is private plays in a world where something must be shared. The city, he asserts, cannot become a family—for in doing so the family would disappear. We can read Book 2, in large part, as a defense of the female whom Callipolis in its pursuit of unity sought to destroy through communism. The challenge that Aristotle faces is to show that the parts, especially the household composed of both

11. We do not find in Aristotle patriarchal arguments. Despite his biology, which gives women less *dunamis,* power or energy, than the male, there is no claim that the weak female *needs* the male's superior leadership; cf. here the discussion of patriarchal theories of the sixteenth and seventeenth centuries in Schochet (1975: 183, 151n.48, 202).

12. See Dobbs (1985), who argues that the rejection of Socrates' proposals for communism within the guardian class is based on Aristotle's contention that such a regime would preclude the emergence of a philosopher-ruler; that, according to Dobbs, is the basis for his fundamental opposition to Callipolis. See also Nichols (1987: 225 n. 18).

male and female, support the existence of the whole rather than destroy it. To focus on the equality of the sexes would have diverted Aristotle from attention to the broader question of the diversity of parts.

It is important to keep in mind as well that the defense of the family has nothing to do with the question of reproduction. Socrates had faced the difficulty of regenerating the city through his curious eugenics scheme. Aristotle, at the end of Book 1 of the *Politics*, after detailing the relation between masters and slaves and the acquisition of sustenance for the family, turns to the family as an organization of those who are free and have the potential for virtue. Concerns about the possession of virtue, he suggests, should dominate questions about the possession of lifeless objects (*apsuchon*) and the mastery over slaves to which the previous discussion had been devoted. Neither the acquisition of material goods or slaves nor the rule over slaves entails virtue. The more critical question is whether those ruled have virtues. Again turning to the most extreme case, slavery, Aristotle presents us with a confusion: if slaves do have virtue, then how do they differ from free men? and, if they do not have virtue, they must still be human since they must be sharers (*koinōnountes*) in reason and it would be strange or absurd (*atopon*) if they were not human (1259a26–28). In this case, as in so many of his attempts to puzzle through a problem, Aristotle does not arrive at an easy solution. Rather, he suggests that both the master and the slave must be virtuous, only in different ways. This analysis leads him to the further argument that the soul must be related to the function (*to ergon*) and the determinant of function is nature. The nature of a child is to grow, the nature of the slave is to perform menial tasks. Curiously, Aristotle fails to mention here the "function" of the wife or woman. It is clearly neither to grow nor to perform menial tasks, but he does not define the female *ergon* as reproduction.

The argument against Socrates' destruction of the family will not rest on the view of the female as simply a baby-producing machine. The existence of the family gives more than new citizens to the city. Indeed, Aristotle makes it clear that the virtues that concern the male and the female, the child and the father, must be addressed in any discussion of political regimes. "Since every household is a part (*meros*) of the city, and these things [parts] of the household, it is necessary to look at the virtue of the part with regard to the virtue of the whole" (1260b12–15). That the "part" has to do with women and children makes no difference to Aristotle for "women are a half part of the free individuals and out of the children come the sharers (*koinōnoi*) of the regime" (1260b18–20). The parts—the household, the women, and the children—are acknowledged; they are not blended into an indiscriminate whole. None is to be eliminated for the sake of a whole without discrete, articulated parts. By not contesting

Socrates on the issue of feminine function at this point and by not focusing on the issue of sexual equality that introduced Socrates' best city,
Aristotle underscores the real grounds for his disagreement with Socrates,
grounds that do not come from questions of function or the assumption of
a natural hierarchy; rather, they emerge from a concern with the true source
of a political unity that must rise above diversity and yet not destroy it.

Book 2 serves as a transition between the discussion of the parts of the
family and the parts of the city. It reveals where the family fits into the city
as a constitutive part, as the link between the private world composed of
a set of hierarchical relations (albeit, perhaps, unnaturally so) and the public world where the constituent parts relate to one another as equals. Aristotle's analysis of Socrates' city suggests that the goals of the city (unity,
the absence of faction, and devotion to the whole rather than the part) are
misguided and misapplied. The pursuit of unity ignores the *telos* of the
city and in so doing makes impossible, indeed impious, demands on its
members. Aristotle does not, in his turn, praise the city riven by strife,
but the goal of unity must acknowledge the limits of unity as well.

Book 2 begins with a discussion of those things that citizens hold in
common, and Aristotle himself first creates a community of observers:
"Since we choose to study (*thēorēsai*) concerning sharing of political
life . . ." (1260b27–28). Those who share in this community of study are
not engaged in some form of political sharing, but they do share the
search, the text, the questions, and the criticism of existing regimes as well
as imagined ones, just as the household shares the goods that enable it to
survive. We understand what the family shares and we even understand
what a community of investigators exploring the nature of the city shares,
but the city, what in the world does it share? The answer to this question
is not at all evident, and the thrust of Book 2 is the preliminary exploration
of this problem.

Aristotle begins by noting that it is necessary that all citizens share
(*koinōnein*) all things or nothing, or some things and not others. It is immediately clear that it is impossible to share nothing (1260b37–40), for
then there would be no city. "For the regime (*politeia*) is some sort of
sharing (*koinōnia tis*)" (1260b40). What, then, does it share and how
much? At a minimum, citizens share a geographical location, but they do
not share all the land; they share a specific parcel of land. There must be
some boundaries that define an area as distinct (*idion*) from that area outside it, but common (*koinon*) for those within. This is the minimal condition and seems patently obvious. Can this be why we read Aristotle? We
should note, however, the development of Aristotle's argument. It is not
the boundaries that define the city, as he will make clear later when he
dismisses the idea that a wall around the Peloponnese could create a polis.

It is the *sharing* of the place that defines the city, but the sharing does not mean that each one owns the whole, as would be the case in a Socratic model. Rather, we can perhaps think of Aristotle's vision in terms of a patchwork quilt where each part owns a patch, but there is still a quilt. They share in the whole by possessing a part. This, as we subsequently learn, will not be enough to argue that the city exists; it is only the starting point from which the city may arise. The question is how much more than owning the patch of the quilt is necessary to make one a citizen of a city.

Aristotle sees the problem as a continuum. Is it better to share all things, as in Socrates' Callipolis, or not to share some, that is, is it better to have all in common or to retain a sphere that is private and separate from what is held in common, to continue to hold on to one's private patch, to let others have their patch and yet all share in the quilt? The opposition between the two ends of the continuum is starkly presented at one end by Socrates, who says that it is necessary that children and women and possessions be shared and, at the other end, there is that which is done "now," presumably in fourth century Athens where households, property, and wives continue to be private and assemblies, courts, and the gods of the city are *koina*. The challenge Aristotle sets for himself in Book 2 is, Where on the continuum does the polis rest and how do we find that spot? Do we discover it in nature or do we create it ourselves? The attempt to answer this problem leads to a direct attack on Plato's *Republic* because the "sharing of women involves many other difficulties and especially Socrates does not make clear in this argument the advantage, for what reason it is necessary to set down this sort of law" (1261a10–12).

The attack on Callipolis is twofold: (a) the supposed end or *to telos* of the city and (b) its feasibility.[13] It is the *telos* that Aristotle attacks first: "I mean that the whole (*pasan*) city that is the best possible city is to be entirely one" (1261a15–16). This, he says is the *hupothesis* Socrates establishes. From this hypothesis that Socrates neither develops as a goal nor justifies in the *Republic*, Callipolis is born. Near the beginning of Book 5 Socrates simply observed: "I do not think that there would be debate concerning the benefit of a community of women and a community of children, that it would not be the greatest good, if it would be possible" (457d). While Glaucon allows Socrates to get away with this statement, Aristotle demurs; the city cannot become one without being transformed into a family and then an individual without articulated parts. He accepts neither that the community of women and children is "the greatest good for the city" nor that unity is the true end of the polis.

13. Nussbaum (1981) interprets this section with reference to the discussions in the *Nicomachean Ethics;* the criticism of Plato comes down to issues of autonomy of choice for the individual citizens. This takes the passage out of its context in the *Politics* and thus abstracts from its role as a critique of the *political* consequences of Socrates' city.

In contrast, Aristotle asserts, "being one," denying differences in form, is what destroys the cities. To support this, he turns first to etymology, then to what we might call psychology, and finally to nature itself. He begins by playing on the linguistic ambiguity of the Greek word *panta,* which leaves open the possibility of all sharing together or each one sharing individually a thing. The former, he says, is impossible because human beings cannot simply become one and altogether hold an object as if the boundaries between our bodies might melt (or, in the image of the *Republic,* as if we all would say "ouch" when one person hurts her finger). The latter meaning of the word, though, is possible as all individually can possess one object—only, we must recognize and acknowledge, this common possession will lead to conflict (1261b30–32). Thus, what is possible, that everyone can claim to own a pot, a child, a wife as one's own, arouses controversy rather than unity, and Socrates' claims about what is best for the city, the common ownership of goods and children and wives, fails.

Aristotle's attack does not rest here: even if each one owns the same thing and somehow conflict over that possession is avoided, then the object owned, be it pot, wife, or child, will be least cared for "just as in household chores many attendants sometimes take care [of affairs] in a worse fashion than the few" (1261b36–38). They assume that others will take on those responsibilities. In his treatment of friendship in the *Nicomachean Ethics,* Aristotle discusses the relationship between caring for something and loving it. It is in the nature of things that we love what we create. We exist through our activity, and since we love our existence, we love what that existence has brought into being, whether it be our handiwork (*ergon*) or our children. "On account of these things mothers love their offspring more [than fathers]. Childbirth is more painful and they know with greater certainty that the [children] are their own" (1168a24–26). By destroying the attachment to what is one's own, one's creation, Socrates destroys the possibility of love as caring for another.[14] Since in Socrates' Callipolis there will not be the love of what one has created, the city will be inhabited by a body of unattached and apathetic citizens who will not even love that which is their own. Thus, mutual ownership leads either to conflict or apathy—but not to unity. It is families within the city that serve as bulwarks against conflict and indifference.

Aristotle elaborates on the argument from the *Ethics* when he suggests that the community of wives and children would make more sense among the workers of Socrates' city than among its rulers. Any attachment to what is their own would be destroyed and the workers would be less likely

---

14. That Plato, on the other hand, recognizes this problem is clear from the very beginning scenes of the *Republic,* where family ties play a profound role and the discussion turns to the love of what one has created, whether that be a child or wealth (330a–c;331d).

to bring about the feared revolution and change. The city, which does not protect what is theirs (since they have nothing), would be irrelevant to their lives. The identity of the self gives strength to the city; but that identity is lost when all share all things. Diversity enables and empowers; it does not take power away. Losing oneself in the whole or the "what is" obliterates the city that comes from what is not similar. Aristotle does describe love (*philia*) as the greatest good for the city (1262b7–8), for then there will be the least *stasis,* conflict, and division; that is, unity comes from *philia* and so the inquiry must be what brings about *philia*—and the answer is not unity. It is, rather, a love for the specific other (Vlastos 1981; Lord 1978). Far from diluting the care for what is public, as Socrates feared if the divisions are allowed to enter the city, such a love of what is one's own within the context of the family is essential for the support of the public realm. The destruction of *philia* through Socrates' reforms brings on apathy.

Indifference appears to be the real threat to Socrates' city. How do those who have no love for anything private develop a love for the city or even a concern for its welfare? Aristotle uses two images to make his argument: first, he goes back to Aristophanes' speech in the *Symposium* and the net of Hephaestus, observing the underlying implication that excessive love, regardless of its object, leads to the destruction of both lover and beloved; and second, he asks us to reflect on the dilution of sugar in a great amount of water so that its taste is lost. Either extreme must be avoided. The destruction of the family in Callipolis entails both extremes. The mean is the family where passion does not lead to destruction but to procreation and where love can still be "tasted" within the limited and particular attachments there. Aristotle concludes that there are two things that cause people to care (*kēdesthai*) and to love: the private, (*to idion*), that which is distinctly one's own, and contentment (*to agapēton*) (1262b22–23). Both find their place in the family. In Socrates' city where there is no family, there is no *idion* and thus none of the friendly feeling that is necessary to hold a city of multiple parts together. The destruction of the family and assimilation of parts to one another within the city of Callipolis feed on one another and in so doing destroy the city.

From etymology and psychology, Aristotle turns to his observations of nature and the fact that we readily note that children look like their parents physically, externally, in ways that are obvious to the senses. Nature itself supports the relationship between parent and child by making children resemble those who bore them. Thus, Socrates' city, supposedly founded on principles of nature, appears to be a perversion of that which is natural (Strauss 1964: chap. 2). The resemblance noted between parents and their children occurs not only among humans, but holds across all species of animals—including cows and mares whose offspring likewise take on the characteristics of their parents. (1262a21–24).[15] Socrates' references to Glaucon's birds and dogs in Book 5 of the *Republic* do not support only, as Socrates supposed, his eugenics scheme, but they also reveal its limitations, for the very principle of eugenics entails assumptions according to which members of the city will indeed be able to recognize their own through the display of inherited traits.

The proposals not only threaten the stability of the community by rejecting the love of one's own, but they pervert the bond imposed by nature between parent and child. Because these bonds are natural, to ignore them, according to Aristotle, will lead to unholy acts. He draws forth our horror at the unnatural, indeed monstrous,[16] deeds of violence against parents, acts that are more horrid since they are against those who are closest rather than against strangers and nonrelatives. Oedipus has killed his father and slept with his mother; the unholiness of these acts is not diminished by his ignorance of the deed, as Oedipus' self-blinding affirms. Still more offensive to nature is the fact that Socrates allows sexual intercourse between fathers and sons and even between brothers, which Aristotle considers "most unseemly" (*aprepestaton*). Precautions against incest in Socrates' city are neither satisfactory nor taken seriously. In order to destroy the family and to unify the city by so doing, Socrates is willing to repudiate the piety and holiness that the family had in Greek life. He is denying the naturalness of the customs, while Aristotle finds the natural in what has been practiced.

Behind the Platonic search for wholeness within the city is the fear of faction, of bringing epistemological and political conflicts into the arena of communal action. Though Plato makes conflict the crux of his dialogues, Socrates in the *Republic* also appears to treat it as the bane of the political community. For Aristotle, as we will see below, faction may be threatening in the context of the city, but it is in the nature of the city for citizens to debate about the good and the bad, the advantageous and the disadvantageous—or else not be citizens. To have factions is to be a polis, so to speak.

The city, Aristotle insists at the beginning of his discussion of Callipolis, is composed of a certain multitude (*plēthos gar ti*) (1261a18), a notion that will be repeated throughout the work, but it is not just any multitude; it must be composed of a multitude that is different in form, *eidos,* "for the city does not come into being out of those who are similar" (1261a24). Aristotle, never one to resist repeating himself, adds again that

15. See further Saxonhouse (1985b: 82, esp. n. 28).
16. The word *atopon* is used twice in this section; see 1262a32, 1262a37.

it is necessary that the polis come into being out of those who differ in form (*eidei diapherei*) (1261a30). On these grounds, he distinguishes between an alliance and a polis; the alliance can be comprised of identical parts, each attending to its own affairs. To add more simply adds weight to the alliance; the analogy here is of a scale where it does not matter if the added parts are all identical or not. It is only the collective weight that matters. The city is not such a conglomeration; there must be parts that relate more profoundly than the simple adding of units suggests. The parts must satisfy the needs of each other, must meet the insufficiencies of one another. Without the language of *erōs* that dominated the speeches of Aristophanes and Socrates in the *Symposium,* insufficiency leads to a unity with others who are different without the destruction of the self. We can see this model of interdependence in the realm of the family and human sexuality and, thus, observe that which distinguishes an alliance of possibly identical parts from a sharing that builds on the differences in form of its members.[17] From Aristotle's critique we begin to see that Callipolis was not even a family, for the family, like the city, must be built up from parts that depend upon one another, that cannot exist in splendid isolation; through their needfulness they can survive only through cooperation with those who are different.

Aristotle's attack on Socrates' city confronts directly the issue of unity as based on an identity of form such as Socrates decrees for his men and women in Callipolis. Aristotle begins with an emphasis on the importance of diversity within the city. In a famous analogy he compares the Socratic city to an individual; the more unity the city has, the more like an individual the city becomes. Emphasis on unity mutes differentiation: in Socrates' city, the male must equal the female since differentiation would generate disunity and any recognition of bodily distinctions would emphasize the physical boundaries that isolate one individual from another. For Aristotle, it is precisely the differences in form (*eidos*) that are crucial to the existence of the polis. These differences in form entail differences in function. Socrates ignored differences of function based on differences of visible form; male and female, though they may appear different when we view them with our eyes, can be, when we go beyond the visible, the same and therefore need not differ in function. Aristotle prefers the conceptual framework that he developed in the *Nicomachean Ethics,* namely, propor-

---

17. Some of the difficulties of reading this passage are captured, for instance, by Jowett (1885:II, pt. 1:44), who in commenting on Book 2, chapter 3 claims, "The state like the nation is not a mere aggregate, but has an organic unity of higher and lower elements." There is nothing in Aristotle's language to suggest "organic unity." The language of Jowett is medieval rather than ancient Greek. See, however, *Phaedrus* 264c, where Socrates uses organic imagery to describe the structure of discourse.

tional justice (5.3). Those who are to be treated justly do not need to be identical. Justice does not depend on equality. The whole process of proportional justice is to identify that area in which individuals are *not* the same and according to which they may be treated differently. Introducing principles of mathematics, Aristotle suggests how differences between units must be acknowledged and how distributions must take account of those differences (1131a1–b18). The conflict, as he is well aware, arises over defining which differences in form matter when one distributes any sort of good. But justice itself hardly depends on identity of form. The identity that Socrates develops in Callipolis precludes or makes unnecessary proportional justice.[18] Aristotle, in contrast, places proportional justice at the heart of political life.

Later in Book 3 Aristotle further specifies that political equality need not assume equality in *eidos,* form or shape, and thereby function. It need only assume a sharing, and those who are different in form, in what we observe, are as capable of sharing as those who are the same in form. The polis need not depend on making the male the same as the female, nor the shoemaker the same as the carpenter, for they can share despite their difference.[19] If we conceptualize the city as a realm of sharing rather than as a community, we feel far more comfortable with the diversity of the inhabitants. Though I travel to Washington and my husband Mr. Y travels to Washington on the same plane, I go to visit our daughter and he goes to visit a museum. Still, we share the journey. Or if I travel with my husband to visit our daughter together, he travels to visit his daughter and I to visit mine, though she may be the very same person. When we share in the polis, we do so in order to attain our independent ends, though the ends may be the same. A herd of animals, though, does not share.

As Aristotle develops his critique of Socrates, he contrasts the roles of the shoemaker and the carpenter and the role of each as citizen. As craftsmen they cannot exchange roles; the farmer cannot, for the sake of argument, learn the skills of the shoemaker, nor, for the sake of argument, can the female become a male. Within the context of reproduction, the male and the female cannot exchange roles, even less so than the farmer and the shoemaker. But shoemaker, carpenter, male, and female function beyond

18. Here, we must remember that we are only speaking about the group for whom Socrates decrees a communistic way of life.

19. That Aristotle uses the shoemaker and the carpenter as examples of his point is intriguing since the city of pigs is founded precisely on the principle of the differentiation of form. In what Socrates calls "the true city" (372e), it is the differentiation of form, the farmer and the shoemaker (369d), that enables the city to come into being. It is only when we have reached the third city, the city of our dreams, that such differentiation must be muted, and a unity based identity prevails.

the role defined by their form and can be citizens as well. The human being is portrayed by Aristotle not only as a composite being, having both a body and a soul, and within the soul both passion and reason, but also as having a variety of roles. He had begun the *Politics* by claiming that "nature does not make such a thing as the metal workers make the Delphian knife, in an economizing fashion,[20] but one for one, for each of the tools would perform most beautifully not serving many tasks but one" (1252b1–5). Echoes of the city of pigs and the justice of Book 4 of the *Republic* resound. As Aristotle proceeds, that claim gets moderated with regard to humans, and we watch individuals in an "economizing fashion" playing more than just one role. The individual is not only a shoemaker/artisan or a female/mother. We cannot perform only one role in our lives and split citizenship off from our being productive and reproductive creatures.[21] We are, at the very least, both, though Socrates had tried his hardest to escape such necessities in his city. Aristotle's acceptance of the multiplicity of human roles plays havoc with the one person, one job principle of the *Republic*. The one person, one job principle, as we saw above in chapter 6, is part of the Socratic effort to simplify, to transform a messy world into one that we can easily order. The identity of parts and the destruction of boundaries that characterizes the city of Book 5 is a further expression of this goal of simplification.

Aristotle develops his argument against Socrates by claiming that, even if we were all equal in form with every difference obliterated, the political community would have to act against such identity and make us unequal. Within the city, all cannot rule at the same time: some must be ruled and others must be rulers. By definition, the polis composed of citizens is a community of rulers and ruled; the hierarchical attaches to the city but not as in Callipolis, where it depended on the noble lie. The differences in hierarchical structure depend on a profoundly different conception of rule, a difference that again captures the epistemological choice between the many and the one. Socrates' philosopher-ruler turns to the scientific knowledge that he or she then applies to the political realm. It is abstract knowledge that is universal, but accessible only to the one who has ascended to a vision of the good. There are no turns to be taken in ruling since the one who rules "knows"; there is no ambiguity in making choices for the city. Political science in Plato's *Republic* takes the knower outside of the city. The lessons the knower was to learn could be acquired

20. I take this translation of *penichrōs* from Lord's (1984) translation.
21. How much time we devote to being productive and how much to being reproductive, though, is another question.

by the contemplation of spheres in motion, of musical harmonics. Political truths existed beyond the particular, beyond anything that had to do with political life.

According to Aristotle's view of politics as practiced in the world that we experience and about which he writes, there is no precise knowledge available to political rulers. Practical knowledge admits of no precise answers (*Nicomachean Ethics* I.3). Since the rulers have no special or unique (*idion* is the perfect word here) access to universal knowledge, they can exchange places with the ruled, not because there will be no difference between Tweedledee and Tweedledum, but rather because there will be those differences. The knowledge that one has will not be identical to that of the other. In Socrates' city, exchange of rule does not matter since the object is uniform and whoever "sees" that object knows the same things as all others. Denying the uniformity of an unchanging object of political science, Aristotle again denies the uniformity of the participants in the activity of politics. The regular change in rulers will have beneficial consequences for the city precisely because different rulers will have different responses to the practical problems that confront all political actors.

The exchange of roles, then, depends not on the similarity of citizens but on their differences. In this way, the city is unlike the family where roles are permanent, where the male rules, and the wife and children are subjects. Their permanence may come from the differences of precise knowledge that belongs to each: the male is the wealth gatherer, who practices the art of *chrēsmatistikē*, whereas the female guards what has been acquired. What does "getting" have to do with being male and what does "guarding" have to do with being female? Well might one ask, but such a question distracts from the differences between the family and the science of acquisition, where knowledge of hierarchy is possible (if one chooses to rely on observable differences of gender) and diversity among rulers is not necessary, and the political community, where knowledge is contingent and therefore diversity becomes the central feature. The family that is able to differentiate ruler from ruled on the basis of form enjoys a more precise model of justice than is possible in political life. Because differences in *eidos* within the family are observable, the family can openly display a unity in diversity that perhaps becomes impossible in political life. In the polis, obvious differences in *eidos* may be present, but they tell us nothing about the quality of mind and what that mind has discovered. Rulers may possess bodies that are stooped and similar to those of slaves. The family may offer an ideal model of social organization (though even this is questionable) that is unavailable to the city. When Socrates builds his Callipolis on the model of the family, he ignores the profoundly differing epistemological principles that distinguish the family from the city. Aristotle, who has accepted sight while acknowledging its limits, makes us aware of those differences.

Other Misguided Dreams of the Unified Polity

The other regimes in speech and deed that comprise the subject matter of the remainder of Book 2 are not as extreme as Callipolis in their efforts to achieve a unity, but each one is still challenged by the threat of division; various proposals offered by *idiōtai*, private individuals, and by lawgivers, all try to meet those threats. All come under critical scrutiny by Aristotle for failing to recognize the place of diversity within the context of the political community. Behind all these discussions remains the place of the family within the context of the city. A large number of the proposals and practices considered by Aristotle seek to unify the city by, in some way, eliminating the pull or importance of the family. The family divides the city and that divisiveness is attacked by others through an attack on the status of the family.

Phaleas, for instance, is among those who worry that all conflicts (*staseis*) come from the disproportionate wealth of some and the consequent divisions between rich and poor. He tries to equalize wealth—or, as the Greek suggests, "to make level" or "to make uniform" (*homalisthēnai*) (1266b2)—by entering into the relationships between families and manipulating the giving and receiving of dowries so that wealthy give and the poor receive. Since such a proposal ignores the serious practical absurdities of so trying to equalize or level wealth (e.g., the problem of inheritance if one does not also equalize the number of children in each family), Aristotle contends that it cannot be the solution to problems within the city precisely because humans (and the families in which they marry and give birth) are not identical, neither in worth nor in passions nor in numbers. Musing on this point, Aristotle reflects that it is more important to make uniform the desires (*tas epithumias homalizein*) (1266b29–30) than wealth; this uniformity of desire can only come from a sufficient education by the *nomoi*. He admits that Phaleas alludes to such an education that is uniform for all, but again Aristotle has problems with this since Phaleas does not clarify the goal for which this education aims. It could be, for instance, for the domination of others. Furthermore, identical education for different individuals will not "level the passions."

As Aristotle understands it, internal upheavals do not originate in the inequality of wealth only, but more significantly, they come from the equality of honors. "The many [may be angered] by an inequality of possessions, but the men of accomplishment (*charientes*) will be angered about honors, if they [the honors] are equal" (1266b40–1267a1). Or, as

Aristotle says a few lines later, one does not become a tyrant so as not to be cold (1267a14). Equality of wealth does not lead to the end of conflicts, for men desire more than wealth. They desire the distinction that comes with honors, what sets them apart from others. Socrates' regime took that distinction away from the individual; so does Phaleas's. The latter's mistake was to consider only one dimension of human interaction and conflict, namely, wealth, but there are, Aristotle reminds us, many levels on which conflict will take place. The legislator who presumes to create the unified whole by eliminating conflict in one realm alone must fail, just as, as in the case of Callipolis, the one who eliminates conflict in all creates a monster, not a city.

With the language of *ison* and *anison*, Aristotle again reminds us of the discussions of distributive justice in the fifth book of the *Ethics*. Proportional justice must depend on the diversity of skills, of values, of claims. The city comprised of that diversity must confront the claims of proportional justice; to center the constitution on the equalization of private property is to ignore those claims of difference and thus is to draw the city into further divisions rather than unity. The task for the political leader, as Aristotle suggests, has nothing to do with equalizing external possessions or honors or even children, but rather with limiting desires in general so that the good individuals (*epieikeis*) have no desire to take advantage of their wealth and acquire more, and the less worthy (*phauloi*) are not able to seek more (1267b5–8). Equalizing is a policy decision that will lead to stasis or disunity, but not unity for the city. The political leader is the one who observes differences, who works with those differences and makes them compatible through distributive justice. He does not make them identical, destroying them in order to make them equal. A unity derived from equality gives birth to its own dissolution quite simply because the young of one household will not equal the young of another, but more basically because of the profound differences that we find among human beings. To ignore those differences is to be unjust. Looking for the underlying, unifying characteristic as had the pre-Socratics, for example, accomplishes little when applied to the political world. It is the diversity with which the legislator must deal.

Hippodamus, yet another speculator on the "good regime," whose style of dressing hardly encompasses any uniform principle with his cheap clothing and expensive jewelry (Nichols 1987:165), provides yet another example of one who tries to rise above the messy particulars of the city to suggest a unity founded on mathematical principles accessible only to the mind and not to eyes. As Strauss (1964:19) observes, Hippodamus "arrived at great confusion because he did not pay attention to the peculiar character of political things." He did not ask, for example, "if they do not share in the regime, how they might have any friendly feelings towards the regime" (1268a24–25). Instead, Hippodamus, with calculations and a reliance on the number three, thought to encompass the whole of nature within mathematical concepts. Like Socrates, he proposed the principle of one person, one task for his city so that the farmers would farm and the warriors would war and would be fed off a land that was "common." But to preclude the transformation of warriors into farmers, warriors could not farm that common land. In such a situation there would have to be those who farm the common land but share not at all in the city and therefore would become its enemies. Hippodamus's plans would have required a large number of slaves, thus building in unstable divisions rather than unity and stability.

In the one area that Hippodamus does not ask for an artificial unity, he again miscalculates, for he has each juror condemn, acquit, or come up with his own distinctions in cases brought to trial. Here, according to Aristotle's analysis, he goes to the other extreme, allowing for too much individuality. The jurors do not "share in thinking (*koinologōntai*) with one another" (1268b10–11). Thus they will wander in so many directions that judgments or decisions will become impossible to arrive at.

In the case of the city of Sparta, the problem is just the opposite from what we saw in Phaleas's proposals. Rather than trying to equalize the parts, the regime eliminates or rather ignores one-half of the population. "Just as man and woman are a part of a household, it is clear that it is necessary to think that the city is nearly divided into two parts into both a number of men and a number of women, so that in such regimes, there is foolish thinking about the women—to think that half of the polis is to be uncontrolled by the *nomoi*" (1269b14–19). The lawgiver wished the whole city to be strong, but arranged it only with a view towards the men, completely ignoring the women, as if they were not there to be considered. Such disregard can only work to the detriment of the city as a whole: the women become luxurious and make the men care about wealth, they become licentious, and they are unable to defend the city when a foreign army attacks. The inability on the legislator's part to integrate the two halves will bring about the decline of the whole regime, no matter how well-structured the one half may be.

When the Lacedaemonians do try to integrate members of the city with a view to the community of the whole, they do so badly. Instead of recognizing differences in wealth between individuals, the Spartans treat all as of equal wealth. They ask all citizens to contribute, "though some are especially poor and not able to pay the fee so that the opposite turns out to what the legislator had planned" (1271a29–31). While the plan was to develop a democracy, this equalization in fact destroys any democracy by excluding those who cannot pay the assessment. Once again, a refusal to acknowledge that differences must be accounted for leads to the perversion of what may be positive aims. Aristotle here expresses no hostility to the concept of common meals as a unifying device for the city; what he objects to is the attempt to equalize that which cannot be equalized, to treat as the same that which is not. The Cretans, in contrast, take a portion of what is produced rather than a set amount. "That the affairs concerning the common messes have been arranged better for the Cretans than for the Lacedaemonians is clear" (1272a26–27). Further, the Cretans understand the importance of sharing so that none feel excluded from involvement in the city. Unlike the Spartans, "they do not share in the rule of those outside." Thus, there are no helots to revolt (1272b19–20).

The survey of regimes dreamed of, planned and in practice, has not yielded a uniform model of political organization. Rather, it has revealed a variety of organizational styles. Discussions concerning the family did not lead to varieties, but rather to parts. Discussion of regimes leads to both variety and parts. By the conclusion of Book 2, from our study of the many, we know well that diversity is not the destroyer of the polis. Attempts to "level," to make identical, to exclude that which is other, to ignore that which is other, all are flawed. All have identified a goal, namely unity, and then searched for the means to achieve that goal; but in so doing, all abstract from the goal of politics or, more particularly, have failed to identify what that goal is. Aristotle knows now that that goal can be neither unity nor identity. The subsequent books develop what the goals must be and where diversity fits into those goals.

We know that the polis is a form of sharing—as is the family. In the family, the sharing does not lead to conflict because the hierarchies at least are well established by sight. The question of proportional justice does not surface, at least openly, in the family of ancient Greece. This will not be the case with the polis. There the hierarchy is not established by nature, however much we may wish for the sort of stability that such natural hierarchies might provide. Questions concerning proportional justice do surface and we must be willing to accept the conflict about justice that comes from diversity. It is on that diversity that the city's unity depends. It is the admission of diversity into the study of things political, the willingness to face and not escape from diversity, that makes Aristotle the originator of the scientific study of politics.

9 The Study of Politics: Unity Out of Diversity

> If any person thinks the examination of the rest of the animal kingdom an unworthy task, he must hold in like disesteem the study of men. For no one can look at the elements of the human frame—blood, flesh, bone, vessels, and the like— without much repugnance. . . . Similarly, the true object of architecture is not bricks, mortar, or timber, but the house.
>
> *Parts of Animals*[1]

To write the *Politics,* tradition has it, Aristotle studied 150 constitutions and their histories. As is obvious, this did not entail poring over dusty documents in a badly lit basement of a university library. Aristotle had first to identify the polis, what sort of institution it was that he intended to study, and then assess what it might mean to study it. He gives us the conceptualization of the polis as an object of study, not as an object of devotion such as we might find in the funeral orations, nor as a participant in a war such as Thucydides may have offered us, but as composed of parts, a collection of individuals, out of which emerges something that we can call a polis, just as out of bricks, mortar, and timber emerges something we can call a house.

Plato may have asked who the statesman is who actively leads the citizens of a polis and he may have asked what would be the best regime that we might find in our dreams, and out of what does a polis come to be, but he had not asked what a polis is. The question as Aristotle phrases it at the beginning of the third book of the *Politics*—What in the world is the polis? (*ti pote estin hē polis*) (1274b33–34)—evokes the frustration he must have felt as he embarked on this study. If we look at an animal, a cow or a pig or a human, or at a house, we know what it

---

1. See translation by W. Ogle of *Parts of Animals* 645a26–34 in Barnes (1984).

is we are studying;[2] we do not enjoy such a luxury with the polis for, as with all social constructions, it is not something that we can observe with our eyes—though we know that there is such a thing as a polis. Thus, people disagree (*amphisbētousin*) about what a city is, "some saying that it is the city that has taken an action, others that it is not the city, but the oligarchy or the tyranny [that has done so]" (1274b34–35). We speak as if the city were one, and yet it is not. We speak as if we could observe the city, and yet we cannot.[3]

It is in the third book of the *Politics* that Aristotle confronts this problem and raises for us the difficulties of talking as if the city were one when we know that it is not. The questions that he raises make us recognize the inescapable diversity within a city that we often pretend is a unified entity. Aristotle's queries make us reconsider language that claims that the polis acts, *peprachenai tēn praxin,* when of course it is only parts of the city that can act. In so doing, he makes us explore the way in which the regime unifies the diversity of the city—but never overcomes it.

Those regimes that Aristotle and his students collected revealed a world that was not composed of an orderly series of wholes; rather, the study of regimes found a world often convulsed by revolutions and political conflicts, by a multiplicity of options, as Book 5 of the *Politics* so vividly illustrates. The parts did not settle comfortably next to one another, as do the blood and bones of a human being. In a house well built, the mortar will not conflict with the bricks, and the house stands. The whole remains. This is not so in the life of a city, for the parts will always be in conflict and the stability of the city is always threatened. The study of politics becomes the study of parts in potential conflict, parts that must be organized in the creation of a whole dependent on human choice.

These conflicts arise because the criteria for determining the hierarchy of better and worse have never been carefully articulated and because the eyes, as we saw in chapter 8, are inadequate; thus, men disagree, not only about what is the city in the first place, but about who should have power within that indeterminate city. The criteria for making that determination, as Aristotle understands them, must refer to what is unseen, what is in the soul. To place those who are better in positions of authority over those who are worse, we must know who is better and who is worse. How can

2. Much work has been done recently on the issue of perception in Aristotle's writing, but always from the perspective of perceiving an object, a *phantasm,* that which appears. Unfortunately, a city does not "appear." See especially Modrak (1987).

3. About the transformation of the city into an object of intellection, see Euben (1990) and Loraux (1986).

we do this? Does the polis and the *politeia* or regime give us special insight into this problem? Regimes, the *politeiai*, do establish such external criteria through speech, criteria such as wealth, birth from citizen parents, education at certain universities or colleges, membership in certain religious groups. But these criteria are external and subject themselves to debate, if not the cause of war itself. Nor do they derive from Aristotle's concept of a natural hierarchy of better and worse of which we learned so much in Book 1 of the *Politics*. The lessons of Plato that made us look within are not forgotten and bring to Aristotle's understanding of politics a sense of tragedy, a sense that the best is unattainable and that the unity sought through the political art must be limited by our recognition of the fallibility of human observation.[4]

The *politeia* becomes the artificial mechanism for uniting parts into a whole because once again nature has deserted us, just as it had done with the slave. Nature does not give us a ruler who is so outstanding that he (or she) stands forth as a god among men. The study of politics reveals what and from where unity can emerge in a community that does not exist simply by nature, but which we must create through the exercise of our natural capacity to debate and make choices. And, most particularly, it reveals the fragility of that unity that does not come from nature but from human choice.

The science of politics as Aristotle bequeaths it to us is the observation of institutions that we can see only in the actions of human beings. He teaches us how that study can give us insight into what often appear to be impenetrable questions, for example, what is the city that we do not see? In so educating us, he also shows us how our study cannot only search for what is one and whole, what is the city. Rather, we must learn of the varieties of cities, precisely because there cannot be one as the city remains a composite of a multiplicity of parts. The unity of Callipolis goes beyond politics to a world that we will never experience and probably would never want to experience. The pre-Socratics had raised questions concerning the reality of what we see; Aristotle, while deeply aware of the limits of observation, affirms our dependence on what we see in order to understand what we cannot see, what we construct through our minds. Thus, he moves us back to a world of diversity from which the earliest philosophers and characters in the tragedies of the playwrights had tried to rescue us. In so doing, we begin the study of politics.

4. The inadequacy of reliance on external criteria for judging who should have authority within a political community is certainly not original with Aristotle; one need only reflect for a moment on the tension-laden first book of the *Iliad*. See further Saxonhouse (1988b).

The Unity of Parts

> We agree that every city has not one part but more [than one].
>
> *Politics*

Aristotle, the master of logic, the inventor of the syllogism, relies heavily in his *Politics* on analogies to help us understand the composite nature of the city. Bodies, winds, choruses on the Attic stage, ships full of sailors, and meals that we eat together all impinge on our senses and perhaps enable us to conceptualize the unity of parts that make up the city. It is to such images that Aristotle turns our attention as he urges us to "see" the polis as a composite that becomes one. Let us turn to these analogies and explore to what degree they may help, or sometimes hinder, our understanding of a composite whole.[5]

Within the first few pages of the *Politics*, we learn from Aristotle that "it is necessary that the whole be prior to (*proteron*) the part" (1253a20). Unfortunately for us, who are interpreting and trying to learn from Aristotle, he explains this priority with an analogy that can be confusing and distorting of what he seems to mean elsewhere. "When the whole is destroyed, there is no longer a foot or a hand . . . for everything is defined by its work and its capacity, so that such sorts of things no longer being should not be said to be the same, but to have the same name" (1253a20–25). A hand that is not part of a body—or part of a body that is alive—may look like a hand and we may even call it a hand, but it is not a hand because it cannot perform the tasks for which it exists; it cannot fulfill its potential. Similarly with a human being: if that person is not part of the city, then he or she may still be human and we may even call that person a human, but he or she is not fully human because that individual

---

5. Barker (1948:95–96) has an extensive note (Note 0) in his edition of the *Politics* on the issue of compounds, aggregates, and wholes: "The terms 'compound' (*syntheton*) [the actual word that Aristotle uses is *sugkeimenon*] and 'whole' (*holon*) are both technical terms of Aristotle's philosophy. The 'compound' is the genus: the 'whole' is a species of that genus. 'Compounds,' as defined by Grote . . . 'are of two sorts—aggregates like a heap (mechanical) and aggregates like a syllable (organic).' 'Wholes' are aggregates of the second or organic kind; they have a Form which gives them an organic unity, and an End or Final Cause which gives them a single purpose. The polis is such a 'whole.' " It is precisely with this conclusion that I disagree. To consider the city an organic whole is (a) to ignore the conflict that is a central part of the life of the city; and (b) to ignore the degree to which the city is a construct of human craft. Barker continues his note: "There is a further point to be noted in regard to the idea of 'compound.' . . . The idea involves a distinction between the ruling element or elements and those which are subject to rule: in other words it involves a hierarchy of rule and subordination." With this claim I have no disagreement.

is not performing the tasks for which the individual exists. The hand of a dead person cannot function as a hand.

Early in the first book Aristotle had made clear that to be human was to be part of such a whole—that to exist independently of the polis "by nature and not on account of chance" was to be less than human, to be either like Homer's Cyclops, "without tribe (or clan), without custom and without ancestral hearth," or like a checker piece that has no game (1253a2–7). The insistence that the city is "by nature" does not mean its temporal—or its ethical—priority. Rather, we must understand it as its theoretical priority. In order to understand who the human being is, we must understand that creature as a part of the whole that is the polis. We can only comprehend the hand insofar as we have observed and acknowledged the existence of the live human body. To have seen a corpse or a hand severed from a body gives us little comprehension of what in the world a hand may be. Thus, the analogy of the city with the body need not necessarily suggest the prior importance of the body over the hand; the issues are rather those of the conditions under which one can fulfill oneself and the prerequisites of any sort of knowledge. A hand can only be a hand as part of a body and it can only be known within such a context. A human can only be fully human as part of a city and likewise can only be understood within the context of the city.

Despite the organicism of the image, this is clear, but what that organicism obfuscates is the obvious difference between a city that is the artificial creation of the human intellect and craft through the mechanism of the *politeia* and the natural existence of an animal whose existence is independent of the creative intellect of the human being. That is why the question of what in the world is the city arises in the first place. If it simply came into being as a cow does, we would not question what it is, where its boundaries are. If we ask what a cow is, we can observe a cow and our eyes will tell us certain things about that cow.[6] Our eyes cannot pick out a city as it can a body. While the analogy can help us understand what the place of the human being is with regard to the city, it does not resolve for us the problem: What in the world is the city?

Taxis

In Book 3 Aristotle leads us away from problems of sexual differentiation and natural hierarchies that had been central in the first two books. Instead, we are to search for the unity of parts that are similar rather than different, the city as made up of citizens. Within the first few lines of Book

6. Cf. Nussbaum (1978) on how limited is the level of knowledge available to the eyes, but this does not disturb the point I am making about what is seen and what is unseen. The problem of the limits has already come up in chapter 8 and will come up again in this chapter.

3, Aristotle reiterates that the polis is of those things that are *sugkeimenoi* and, "just as any other [aspect] of the whole put together comes from many parts, it is clear that first the *politēs* must be sought" (1274b39–41). Again, we learn that there is dispute not only about what a city is, but who its citizens are, that is, not only do we not know what the whole is, we do not even know what its parts are. It is as if we were looking to discover a cow but did not even know how to define a hoof, or looking for a checkers game and did not know what a checker piece looks like. Before we can find the citizen we must understand that the citizen and the city depend upon a *taxis*, an arrangement of parts. "We see . . . that the *politeia* of those inhabiting a city is a sort of ordering [*taxis tis*]" (1274b37–38). The language is that of a general putting warriors in order, preparing for battle. Without the efforts of the general, each warrior exists as an individual, moving independently of one another. The Homeric heroes striding the battlefield before the Trojan walls fought as individuals, one on one; this was not a *taxis*. Once a general imposes an "arrangement," the warriors lose that independence; they become, through the command of their general, a unified body ready for unified action. But that unity comes not from the natural inclinations of men to fight together in well-organized units. It comes from the skill of the general whose art can unite those radically independent men so that they act in unison. It is the same with the city. There could never be a city were there not imposed an order, a regime that organizes the parts.[7]

The military analogy here is far more applicable than the body analogy of Book 1; nevertheless, there are a variety of problems that attend this analogy as well. Aristotle is explicit about not wanting to understand war as the goal of the city (Book 7). When the general orders his troops, he does so to win battles—the unity of warriors brings together the strength of many into one great force and the enemy can be faced. With the goal defined, the basis of unity is understood. Though "living well" equals the goal of the city, it is unclear how unity of parts will achieve that end. While the *taxis* helps us understand the unity of distinct parts as the body and hand do not, it also makes us wonder about the sources and the end of that unity. Beyond raising the question of what in the world the city is, we also wonder *why* in the world is the city?

The general arranges his soldiers as the regime arranges its citizens. But the regime goes further; it makes its citizens. First, we understand that, in terms of the ironic quip of Gorgias of Leontini, that, just as *holmoi* are

7. As Nichols (1987) points out in her discussion of Book II, underlying the critique of many of those regimes is the rejection of "city planning," so to speak, the rejection of the ability of a single law giver, whether it be Minos or Lycurgus or the fantasies of Phaleus and Hippodamus to impose order on what is multiple and varied.

made by *holmopoioi*, so too are Larisaians made by craftsmen for there are certain "lariso-makers" (1275b26–30).[8] Through the mere act of defining who is and who is not a citizen, the regime or a founder like Cleisthenes brings into being citizens who comprise the city. Choice, not nature, makes the citizen, and precisely for this reason we find debates (*amphisbē-tēma*) arising not only over who is a citizen, but over who is "justly" (*di-kaios*) a citizen. It is a debate that Aristotle declares moot, for just as we have unjust rulers, so we have citizens who, by performing the offices of citizens, by definition are citizens. A hand is a hand is a hand, whether we so define it or not.

The River and the Chorus

It is this unnaturalness of the city that creates the next problem for Aristotle as he acknowledges further confusion: if the definitions of citizen change, is the city still the same city? Is a democracy-become-oligarchy, as had happened in Athens, still Athens? It is to Heraclitus's fragment that Aristotle appears to turn as he considers this problem: "Must it be said that the city is the same although always with some dying and some being born, just as we are accustomed to say that the rivers and springs are the same although there is always some water coming and some flowing away" (1276a35–39). For Heraclitus, the river was indeed one and the same despite the apparent changes. The flowing stream that we see with our eyes only bewilders those who do not know and understand the underlying unity accessible to those with *logos*. It is the same for Aristotle. The changing bodies of citizens do not destroy the unity of the city that itself depends on the form or *politeia* given it by those who have constructed it. Heraclitus's *logos*, in this case, is replaced by the *politeia*. If the *politeia* changes, though, then the city changes as well. Repeating himself, Aristotle asserts, "The city is a certain sort of sharing (*koinōnia tis*)," but he adds this time: "It is a sharing of the citizens of the *politeia* and when the *politeia* becomes other in form (*tōi eidei*) and different it would seem that it is necessary that the polis also is not the same" (1276b1–4). It is not the citizens who make the city, but the sharing of the *politeia*—or so it seems necessary to think.

The next analogy, he claims, supports this apparent necessity as he turns from flowing water and rivers to a chorus comprised of discrete individuals: "We say that the chorus which is at one point a comic chorus, at another tragic is different, although the humans are frequently the same. Likewise with every other sharing and compound (*sunthesin*) should there be another form (*eidos heteron*) of the compound" (1276b4–8). From

8. See further Winthrop (1975:408–10).

here we move on to Dorian and Phrygian harmonies that come from the
same notes, but in different arrangements. The formal cause of any compound here seems to take priority over any material cause. The bodies that
comprise the city—and without which the city cannot be—do not give us
the city. It is the organization of those bodies. By defining the city, along
with the rivers and the chorus and the harmonies of musical notes, Aristotle is asserting a unity of the parts that emerges not from the parts themselves, their identity or their melding, but from the manner in which they
are arranged, be it by art as in the city or the chorus, or by nature as in the
stream. Understanding unity from this perspective as sharing in a structure
allows for vast varieties of parts. We need not send the women from the
city in order to have a whole, nor need we transform them into men. We
need not deny that which we see as Parmenides had urged us to do; rather,
we can observe variety and yet, by accepting the priority of form over
matter, we can see the unity of "that above and that below," of the stream
that always flows, of the regime that survives over generations.

As almost a footnote to this discussion, Aristotle muses whether "it is
just" to dissolve debts or not to dissolve debts whenever the city changes
(*metabalē*) into another regime. That, he tells us, is "another story" (*logos
heteros*)" (1276b13–15). The issue of justice is here removed from the
discussion of politics, inaccessible in a world in which there are such transformations, where the same individual becomes a different one because he
or she shares in a different political structure. The world of politics is a
world of flux, one in which unity is not permanent and where what is
shared will change and, as that happens, so do the parts. Thus, while we
may now think of the chorus to help us understand that the democracy is
not an oligarchy, that conclusion tells us nothing about justice.

The Ship

Aristotle, however, is not yet ready to abandon the concern with justice,
however distant it may be from what he has discussed so far—and so he
next challenges himself with the problem of whether the virtue of the
good man and the enthusiastic citizen are the same or different. Leaving
aside the issue of who is the good man, perhaps because he had already
given his lectures on *Ethics,* he insists that the virtue of the citizen must be
grasped in some sort of stamp (*tupōi*) (1276b19), and from chorus and
musical harmonies he turns to sailors on a ship. "Just as the sailor is a
certain one of those who share (*tōn koinōnōn*), so too do we say the citizen is one who shares" (1276b20–21). They share in some common activity—not in rights or in property or even in characteristics. "While the
sailors are not equal in capacity, for one is a rower, another a captain,
another the look-out man . . . it is clear that the most precise *logos* of

the excellence of each one is individual (*idios*), at the same time that some sharing (*koinos tis*) fits each one" (1276b20–26). What the sailors share—despite their varied roles in the process—is the pursuit of the safety of the ship. They share a goal or an end. The unity of the diverse parts is achieved by a focus on what is to be accomplished. No organicism is necessary in this image; no sameness is necessary. The *idion* survives within the context of the *koinon*. It is the same, Aristotle tells us here, for the citizen: "Although they are unequal (*anomoiōn*) the safety of that which they share is their task, and what they share is the regime (*politeia*)" (1276b28–29). From this Aristotle concludes that the virtue of the citizen must relate to the city—presumably just as the virtue of a sailor must relate to the particular ship in which he sails. The bulging biceps necessary for the rower of a trireme would not be a requirement for the captain of a nuclear-powered submarine.

Beyond and more important than different or partial virtues for the different regimes is that even *within* the regime there will be different virtues. A ship cannot sail if everyone is captain or everyone is rower. And while it is necessary for all to possess the virtue of the eager (*spoudaios*) citizen, this does not mean that all citizens are alike (*homoious*) (1276b40). Again the analogies fly fast and free: the city is out of that which is dissimilar (*ex anomoiōn*), just as an animal is made up of *psuchē* and body, just as a soul has *logos* and desire, just as a household has a man and a female, and possession a despot and a slave (1277a5–8). The excellence of each differs from the other—just as, again, the leader of the chorus differs from the others in the chorus.

This discussion about the various virtues is not intended to demonstrate that the city is composed of parts. This is obvious; we see sailors on a ship and need not assume they are "one," nor in the carefully choreographed movements of the chorus does that group of individual singers on stage appear as "one." The issue that set Aristotle's discussion in motion was that of virtue, the excellence of the human being and the excellence of the citizen. The lack of identity between them reveals the status of the city in the world of multiplicity and variability. The man of absolute virtue has no place in Aristotle's city. By its very nature, the polity requires a diversity of parts. The challenge nevertheless remains: how much diversity? Just as the chorus includes the leader and the respondents, but not everyone on stage, the city has to define who is in and who is out, who is part of the city and who is not. If similarity or identity is *not* the criterion, then where do we find the boundaries?

We move with Aristotle from parts back to citizens who rule and the distinction now made between those who rule over those who are inferior, the rule of the master over the slave, or slavish (*andrapodōdes*) rule over servile activities. But there is another kind of rule according to which one rules over those who are similar in race (*tōi genei*) and free. "This we call political rule" (1277b8–9). After emphasizing the diversity of the parts of the city, Aristotle now tells us that a city is based on what is similar. This issue arises precisely because, as a composite unit incorporating diverse parts, the city must also specify what makes it whole—or a unit distinct from all others. As an artificial construction, the city may try to find a natural unity in a similarity of parts, but Aristotle does not at this point develop this suggestion or linger over this point; instead, he moves the reader quickly back to the differences and the distinct virtues that are necessary whether one rules or is ruled, "just as moderation and courage of a male and a female are not the same" (1277b20–21). The parts retain their different qualities, and the issue of race and of freedom is left behind in a single phrase.

In the beginning of Book 3, then, Aristotle, struggling with the definition of what in the world is the city, ends up emphasizing the diversity of parts and the multiplicities of virtues. Any natural unity based on similarities enjoys a brief phrase that fails to sustain the argument or even Aristotle's attention here. The exploration of the problem he has set for himself turns his own study of politics, as it had turned his study of those who wrote about politics, to parts joined by the artificial unity of the *politeia*. To claim a unity in nature is to go beyond Aristotle.

While the unity may not come from nature, this does not stifle the quest for what defines the city. Aristotle first alerts us to the multiplicity of regimes according to those who rule in them: those who care about the welfare of the whole as does the ruler in the house or a pilot on a ship; those who care only about the welfare of the ruler as does a master over a slave; those where the ruling body includes one or a few; and those where it includes many. The multiplicity of regimes derives from a multiplicity of claims, from the political dependence on partial rather than complete justice. Precisely because the city is not composed of units that are identical, debates arise about which criteria are to be identified as establishing the boundaries that separate rulers from ruled. It is in the process of exploring the possible locus of these boundaries that Aristotle expounds most forcefully on what does *not* make a city, on what similarities or dissimilarities are to be dismissed.

The primary contest is between those who say similarity in goods (*chrēmata*) and those who say similarity in free birth identify equality. By disputing the claims of both sides, Aristotle clarifies what the city is by describing what it is not and where its unity comes from by asserting whence it does not come. Those who claim equality based on possessions forget that the city comes into being "not only for the sake of living but rather for the sake of living well" (1280a31). Were it otherwise, we could call any group of slaves or other living creatures a city. Such a conclusion is unsatisfying for Aristotle since such creatures "do not share in happiness nor in a life according to choice" (1280a33–34). The minimum criterion for participation in the city is established. The variations of regimes may establish a multiplicity of criteria for membership, but they become additions to the fundamental concern with the capacity for happiness and for choice. This is required in order to be part of a whole that is a polis. All other criteria will serve to exclude.

Thus, to study what in the world the city is, we also must understand what it is not. Recognizing the inadequacy of wealth as a criterion enables us to see that a city is not an alliance between trading partners, that it is not a sharing of space, that it is not a sharing of protective laws. It is the sharing of living well for both households and families for the sake of the complete and self-sufficient (*autarchēs*) life (1280b33–35). It seems now that Aristotle has taken us away from the *politeia* as the unifying element to a more basic foundation, namely sharing the goal of a good life. The citizens are not just ordered in a certain fashion, a *taxis,* nor are they moving in unison as a chorus on the Attic stage. They share as well a goal, as do the many and differing sailors on a ship. Without that unifying goal there is no city.

The Potluck Dinner

The issue of unity and diversity is perhaps nowhere more vividly explored (though not without its own confusions) in Aristotle than in his discussion in chapter 11 of Book 3, where he pursues the claims to rule of the many against the claims of the "best." To compare the two he must bring the many together into a whole composed of parts and demonstrate their combined superiority to the individually excellent men.

This is one of many places where, as we follow Aristotle through his thinking process, we see him change his position. Eager to find the source of unity within the city, he explores the possibility that the many as one can have as good a claim to rule as the few excellent ones. The city as composed of many may be in a position to rule itself. He begins by recognizing that this is problematic (*tin' echein aporian*) (1281a41), but that it has a bit of truth as well. And so we turn to the first analogy, the potluck dinner (*ta sumphorēta deipna*), which is better than one "orchestrated" (*chorēgēthentōn*) from one expenditure (1281b2–3). Why should the former be superior to the latter? The cryptic Aristotle does not specify whether the many do in fact spend more, or that the greater variety— falafel with sushi—is better than a meal orchestrated with one theme such as Northern Italian in mind. Rather, he suggests that, among the many, "each has a part of virtue and prudence." He then adds that a multitude coming together "with its many hands and many feet (*polupoda kai polucheira*) and many senses" is similar to "a single human (*hena anthrō-pon*), with regard to character and mind (*ēthē* and *dianoian*)" (1281b5–7). A human being with many hands and feet—this sounds like a monster, not the model for a well ruled city.[9] In the previous book (as we saw in the previous chapter), Aristotle explicitly criticized Socrates for turning the city into an individual, and yet Aristotle here suggests that this artificially constructed being composed of *hoi polloi* (1281b8) will be the better judge of the productions of musicians and poets. Why this is so is not explained.

Instead of art appreciation we get art creation so that, "by bringing together that which is dispersed into one," the creator will be able to join the more beautiful parts of each. In the move from evaluation to creation, Aristotle has shifted from the many as "the city" to the statesman as founder of the city. The many as members are a chance conglomerate; the statesman, similar to the artist, can draw together the best out of many. The question at the beginning of the chapter about the legitimacy of the claim of the many has forced Aristotle away from wisdom to questions of beauty. The many as one is *not* beautiful with its monstrous collection of limbs in one body—or even worse, where does the definition of the many find its boundaries? As he tries to conceptualize the many as one, Aristotle is suddenly confronted with the problem of boundaries, and the argument falters when we realize how precisely we may have to define the multitude, for it "is clear that it is impossible about certain multitudes. For the same speech would apply for wild beasts" (1281b18–19). There is not a unity of all. We are not looking, as the pre-Socratics had, for the underlying unifying element. In fact, we discover, as we try to understand the unity of the city, that we must search for what separates the city from other wholes that exist around it.

The argument about the wisdom of the many had brought Aristotle to an impasse and left him with a many-limbed monster. Unity cannot come from simple aggregation. Rather, he finds far greater satisfaction in the model offered by practical legislators, Solon in particular. They have created the city not in which the people as one rule, but in which they share (*metechein*) in the selection and judging. This time Aristotle makes no claims for the wisdom of the many and the analogy shifts from potlucks to nourishment—contaminated food made purer by being mixed with the pure. A city requires friendships, and if many are excluded, "it is necessary that it be filled with enemies" (1281b30). The resolution appears to be

9. See also Winthrop (1978:159 n. 11).

sharing rather than unity—blending rather than the claims of the wisdom of the many. The city is not—nor should it ever strive to be—one. As he reiterates in chapter 13, within one city (*mia polis*) there are many (*pantes*): the good, the wealthy, the wellborn, the multitude (1283b1–2). No one group can claim authority because no matter what the grounds of the claim, one will be superior: one is the wealthiest, the wisest, or the bestborn.

In chapter 12 of Book 3, Aristotle gives us the object of political philosophy (*philosophian politikēn*) (1282b23). We accept that justice is the distribution of equals to equals. But Aristotle acknowledges that, of course, the difficulty is determining what criterion is to be used in our definition of equality. The difficulty, though, is greater than it may at first appear: any individual is a complex combination of a variety of elements. To which one of the characteristics do we turn to determine if an individual is equal to another? Clearly, it would be a "lie (*pseudos*)" to use color and height and excess of whatever good as the criterion for distribution of political power (1282b28–30). Flute players are not judged by whether they are born well or whether they are beautiful (or whether they are male or female). The distribution of instruments then cannot be according to birth or beauty (or gender) (1282b34–42). Similarly, the human being, like the city, cannot be understood as having only one quality. He or she is multiple with many parts and qualities, from gender to the ability to play the flute.

Thus, to which quality do we attend in the distribution of political power? If some men are slow and others fast, it is not necessary on account of this that some have more and others have less. This, we learn, is the subject of political philosophy and this is the source of debate in cities. Were the individual whole, defined by a unique quality such as gender or birth or wealth alone, the complexity of political life and political justice would disappear. Or as he tells the *politikos*, the one knowledgeable about politics, at the beginning of Book 4, the *politikos* must be able to aid those political regimes that have been established. "But this is impossible if one does not know how many forms (*eidē*) of *politeia* there are" (1289a7–8). The cause of the multiplicity of forms is the multiplicity of parts (1289b27–28). This complexity within both the individual and the city Aristotle is unwilling to yield for the sake of political or individual order and it is precisely this complexity to which he turns political philosophy; he asks not how to unify, but how to choose, in a world of multiplicity, the criteria that those sharing political power must share. Because the city is a unity of parts, we must engage in the science of politics. Were it, or could it be, one, there would be no political science and no political philosophy.

The Limits of Unity

> Though there are many types of oligarchies and democracies,
> Socrates says that each transformation (*metabolē*) is only of
> one sort.
>
> *Politics*

Back at the beginning of Book 3, Aristotle faced a problem that he chose
not to answer. The disagreement about what is a city in the first place
arises because of transformations of the city. He had asked, as have others:
If the city changes regimes, is it the same or different? Is Athens the democracy the same city as Athens the oligarchy? More particularly, if an
oligarchy that incurred debts becomes a democracy, are those debts still
owed? Though no answer is offered and we along with Aristotle are left
puzzling over this question and the nature of a city's justice, we do acknowledge that the question itself arises precisely because the city is multiple, not static, that it does change, and *staseis* (a word usually translated
as "revolutions") and *metabolai* (a word usually translated as "transformations" or "overturnings") will occur. There always will be conflicts within
the city. The issue of who is responsible for debts incurred by a city can
only mean that we do not think of the city as one, that despite all the
efforts to conceptualize a unity, to create an object of public adoration,
the artificial entity has its parts and, in particular, parts that may not always work in unison with the other parts. The unity that emerges as we
create a city through the structure of a *politeia* and through identifying
what the members of that city share is always tenuous. Not grounded in
nature, dependent on fallible human choice, buffeted by human greed, the
city exists as a temporary moment of time. The particular configuration
(without even worrying about the change in particular members) is ten-
tative. As a composite, the city can always decompose.

Socrates too had acknowledged the potential for decomposition of his
city, and Book 8 of the *Republic* traces the decline—the dividing into factions (*staseis*), as he recalls the first words of Homer's *Iliad* (545d). The
beautiful city, united and overcoming differences such as gender between
its members, decomposes since, as Socrates explains, "for everything that
has come into being there is decay" (546a). Aristotle directly attacks this
claim as simply inadequate, not worthy of the serious student of political
life. "In the *Republic*, Socrates speaks about transformations (*metabolōn*),
but he does not speak well (*kalōs*). . . . He says the cause is that nothing
remains but changes in a certain period of time, that this is the beginning
of these things" (1316a1–5). Aristotle also quotes from the *Republic*
the numerical ratios that Socrates proposes before he questions whether
"time" explains *metabolai* when not everyone is part of the city for the

same period. Like the river, the population of the city comes into being and passes on. Socrates' city, which is founded and exists across time, has difficulty handling such transformations.

Further, Socrates' presentation of the decline of regimes fails because it gives a prescribed order to that decline from Callipolis through timocracy and down to tyranny. Aristotle asks, "For what reason does the regime change (*metaballei*) from this one [Callipolis] into the Spartan one?" (1316a17–18). It could change in all sorts of directions and, recalling for us the tyranny of Sicyon, the oligarchy at Chalcis, the democracy at Syracuse, the aristocracies at Lacedaemon and at Carthage, the tyrannies at Leontini and at Gela and at Rheguim, Aristotle reminds his readers that regimes "transform" in all sorts of directions. Socrates' straight descent captures none of this potential and historical variety. Aristotle's understanding of change does not rely on a natural deterioration of all things that has the underlying premise that all change is deterioration, a decline from the perfection of an unchanging, undivided city, the polity as the Parmenidean One. Rather, Aristotle begins with a city that grows and dies from a multiplicity of causes, which can never be summarized briefly nor captured by the pessimism of a view that simply ascribes death to all that comes into being.

In the beginning chapters of the *Politics,* Aristotle had considered how the city came into being, its *genesis,* just as Socrates had considered this question in Book 2 of the *Republic.* In Book 5 of the *Politics* Aristotle, like Socrates in Book 8 of the *Republic,* considers the demise of the regime—but, unlike Socrates, he adds to his study that which can preserve a regime and forfend its transformation into something other than what it was. The regime as a *taxis* of parts enjoys no permanence and most particularly can make no claim to adhere to a natural order that preserves it. As a construction of human art devised for the ordering of a multiplicity of parts, the regime—not the transcendence of parts—faces all sorts of claims that can be made against the imposed order. The fundamental inadequacy of all claims for authority in any regime provides for the fundamental instability of all regimes. "All [claims] have a certain justice, but they err with regard to an unqualified justice" (1301a35–36). The perfection of an unqualified justice is reserved for a world where ambiguity and multiplicity are banished. Perhaps this may be Callipolis, but it is certainly not the city-state of ancient Greece. And so Aristotle explores the origins of conflict and the origins of change, and the fifth Book of the *Politics* provides us with his straightforward answer, one that has nothing to do with cycles or the claims about the deterioration of all things: "Everywhere on account of equality there is conflict (*stasis*)" (1301b26–27).

He does not ask here whether there *is* inequality, and the question is not that of an inequality that comes from nature as when we talk about the natural slave or the relation between human and inhuman. Rather, conflict comes from claims about differences among ourselves, differences that appear as the basis of claims when we focus on one or another of our traits such as free birth, gender, virtue, or wealth—or any combination of these. Because we ourselves, as a composite of a multiplicity of characteristics, vary along so many dimensions, the political regime is forced to establish boundaries and select criteria to define the order of its polity, but always those boundaries are subject to dispute and to counterclaims. Thus, change is built into regimes by their very complexity, not by their simply being.

In his earlier critique of Socrates in the *Republic*, Aristotle in Book 2 had raised questions about a unity that turned the city into an individual and whether that should ever be the statesman's goal. He also recognizes that, even should we foolishly desire such a unity, its attainment is impossible. Among human beings there will always be conflict. The city built out of parts is precarious. Unlike the house put together by the art of housebuilding with the correct proportions of stone to mortar, and unlike the body that combines hand and foot by nature, the city entails parts that will always make claims against one another. Seldom, if ever, will we find the hand at war with the foot or the mortar at war with the bricks. But we often—too often—will find citizen at war with citizen. Thus, Aristotle presents us in Book 5 with the stories of regimes confronting the fragile unity of their particular political configurations. The political world, based on choice, on chance, on natural drives, displays enormous variety such as we have seen above, but precisely because there are so many possibilities there are also alternatives that create the instability from which revolutions arise. Even in his study of decline, Socrates had proposed too much uniformity. Again, Aristotle wants to illuminate the variety we discover when we study what has been, what is, what we can see. No book of the *Politics* is more replete with historical examples, stories of betrothals gone awry, of friendships betrayed, of impieties of leaders, of sycophancy, and more. The study of the multiple causes that Socrates failed to acknowledge depends on the study of regimes that have changed.

Aristotle, with his penchant for lists and enumeration, offers seven causes for *stasis* but admits that there may be more. Some revolutions arise from characteristics of individuals, their arrogance, their desire for gain, their fears. The city composed of many men will find these men of passion clashing with one another (1302a34–b2). As Aristotle describes these conflicts, one almost thinks one is reading Hobbes's preface to his description of the natural condition of mankind. Aristotle writes of honor and dishonor, of preeminence and ostracism, of contempt, all of which set men one against another and bring conflict to the city. He also goes well beyond individual passions to structural problems and, in particular, growth that is "out of proportion" (*para to analogon*) (1302b3). At first this may be the disproportionate eminence of an individual that may lead to monarchy or tyranny. This eventuality, though, may be avoided by ostracism—as is done in Argos and Athens. More serious, though, is the disproportionate growth of a part; and, the body analogy of the first Book seems to intrude again. "Just as a body is composed of parts and it is necessary for it to increase proportionately in order for proportion to remain, and if not, it is destroyed, whenever a foot is four cubits and the rest of the body is two *spithamai*, . . . so too is a city composed of parts of which one part often escapes notice as it increases, such as the number of poor in democracies and polities" (1302b34–1303a2). Disproportionate growth of any part—a foot, for example—means death to the composite whole.

Using this organic image, Aristotle asks us to imagine a huge foot and a small body. This is no longer a human being; it is a monster, we might respond. By nature the human being displays a certain proportion; indeed, careful attention to such proportions gives us the elegance of fourth-century statuary and the strength of fifth-century works. Disproportion appears hideous in its unnaturalness. But Aristotle here is referring to bodies that come into being by nature. In the city, disproportion does *not* lead to monsters and things hideous to the sight. Disproportionate growth brings about new regimes—a change in the parts to create something new, destroy what was—but not necessarily turn it into a monstrosity. Thus, a democracy may arise when the wealthy are killed off for one reason or another, or less frequently, an oligarchy may come into being when more citizens become rich. The old proportion is disturbed and a new relationship between parts emerges. This is possible as cities change form. However, despite the organic analogy with which Aristotle introduced the discussion of disproportionate growth, what can happen in the city is impossible for the body. The city, truly composed of independent parts that may increase or decrease independently of the whole, is composed of separate parts and thus subject to transformation, *metabolai;* the body, not composed of parts that can increase or decrease independently of the whole, no longer is a body should disproportionate growth occur. The city remains a city, though the regime changes; under similar circumstances, the body dies.[10]

We can only talk of disproportionate growth if we conceptualize parts—be it of body or of city. If all were identical there would be no

10. "Or we see just the opposite when the growth is not disproportionate," but when "parts that appeared to be opposites in the city become equals to one another such as the wealthy and the poor" (1304a39–b1).

disproportion. Thus a city comprised of all poor would not suffer disproportion should the poor increase. But the city is not made up only of
the poor—nor could it be. Cities encompass all forms of destabilizing
differences. Aristotle spends considerable time describing the various cities
plagued by differences in *phulon* (race, tribe) causing factions "until [they]
might breathe together" (1303a25–26); by differences when one group
settles a place early and another later; and by differences of place where
land is not contiguous, and where there is the "town" (*astu*) and yet some
live in the port area, as is the case for the Athenians living in the Piraeus.
All such differences can lead to a diversity of attitude such that, for instance, the Athenians of the Piraeus are more "demotic" (1303b10–12)
than those in town. Aristotle uses a military analogy here: "Just as in
wars, the crossing of channels, even very small ones, separates the ranks,
so too does every difference (*diaphora*) seem to cause conflict (*diastasin*)"
(1303b12–14). Divisions that seem slight can become great as the city
tries to overcome those divisions to create a unified whole.

Any unity remains illusory, then, and ready to fracture at any moment,
and small things, just like small channels, can become the precipitating
factors for dissolution: a betrayed love affair, conflict over inheritance, a
marriage that fails to occur, disputes over care of heiresses. Since the city,
split into so many potential parts, retains such a tenuous unity, little conflicts can transform cities by drawing out the differences that inhere in all
cities. We cannot have cities without parts, and we cannot have parts without conflicts between those parts. The goal could be, as it was with previous playwrights and philosophers, to remove parts and to focus on the
identity of the units—no conflicting claims, no choices, no tragedies, and
no tranformations would then invade the city. Such a dream eludes, indeed
holds no attraction for, the Aristotle of this book.

Instead, as he finishes his discussion of what destroys and transforms
regimes, he notes that "opposites are productive of opposites and destruction is the opposite of saving" (1307b29–30). The parts, each asserting
its claims within the whole or each growing disproportionately and gain-
ing dominance with regard to the others, are destructive. Safety for the
regime entails the blending of parts and in particular preserving that
blending. As he warns at the beginning of chapter 8, one must protect
against transgression of the laws, especially small ones. A monetary
example intrudes here: frequent small expenditures exhaust all one's property. Small transgressions frequently enacted bring about complete transformations. "The whole and all things are not something small, but are
put together out of small things" (1307b38–39). As wealth entails discrete units of money or jewelry or pots, so the city entails discrete units of
law-abidingness.

Having enjoined his readership to guard against the disobedience of parts, he proceeds to explain how to maintain that obedience necessary for the preservation of the city. In particular, rulers should recognize the needs and the claims of those who are not rulers—that is, again see the city as composed of parts. Aristocracies and oligarchies, he urges, ought not to rely on those things contrived against the multitude; rather, those regimes survive when the rulers treat well those who hold office as well as those outside the regime and those in the citizen body (1308a5–7). "In democracies the demagogues err where the many have authority over the laws, for fighting with the well-off they make the city two, when it is necessary that they seem to do just the opposite, speaking on behalf of the well-to-do; and in oligarchies, the oligarchic leaders should seem to speak out on behalf of the people" (1310a3–7). Concluding this argument, he urges oligarchs to swear: "I will not do injustice to the people," and vice versa for the people in a democracy (1310a11–12). Democracies must likewise attend to the welfare of the well-off.

Chapter 8 of Book 5 is a series of recommendations for blending, but also for equalizing wealth; forgetting about the earlier demands concerning the political animal, he suggests: "The poor do not wish to rule . . . but rather to attend to their private affairs, but the wealthy rule because they have no need of those things shared. So it turns out the poor become wealthy on account of spending time on their work" (1309a4–9). He proposes that inheritance be by family and not by gift: "Thus wealth would be more equal and more of the poor would be established among the well-to-do" (1309b25–26). This is a leveling, the attempt to overcome the sharp divisions within the city.[11] In some ways it may sound like a more moderate form of transforming the females of Callipolis into men, but while Socrates imagines this unity to be fully accomplished through legislation and training, Aristotle has no illusions that the rich and the poor will dissolve into one middle class. Although such a scenario would be a prerequisite for the stability of the polity as a regime, he reaffirms that cities have two parts, human beings who are poor and human beings who are well-off. Both, he asserts, must see themselves as being saved because of the rule in the city (1315a31–34). This works in a tyrannical regime, as well as in all other regimes. No regime is uniform, no regime is a whole, undivided by conflicting claims, no regime enjoys unquestioned authority. Thus the act of politics must always entail assuaging those who are not in power—acknowledging the differences within the regime that will always have the potential to destroy the regime.

11. See also the advice given to tyrants: drawing on the story told by Herodotus, Aristotle recalls the advice Periander gave to Thasyboulos as he walked through the cornfields cutting off the tops of the tallest stalks. To rule as a tyrant one must eliminate preeminence (1311a20–22).

The city that Aristotle studies is complex in the relation of all its various parts. The statesman trying to preserve one regime or another is challenged by the need to accommodate or blend the parts, recognizing that he can never achieve an impossible unified perfection. The multiplicity of human experience and organizations that Aristotle has observed has made him recognize a stability not built on the denial of difference, but on its embrace. The science of politics as an endeavor of study and the institution of regimes as political practice organizes the diversity discovered by the senses. The *politikos* is the one who accepts and structures this diversity rather than fears it.

The study of politics, factions, and transformations in Book 5 becomes the study of different claims. Before Aristotle could study those claims, as he does, however, he had to acknowledge their legitimacy. And to do that he needed to observe cities as they functioned, as they experienced revolution. To acknowledge those claims he could not deny what he observed and discover an unseen unity. He needed to accept the diversity he observed as objects worthy of study in their complex interactions with one another. Though we may begin from what we share, we must also acknowledge what we do not share. There are no excessive dreams about the unity an art can create. Always there will be *stasis*, because always there will be differences. The political art is not the obliterating of parts, but rather the blending. While Aristotle seems almost to contradict the Aristotle of Book 2 in Books 7 and 8 by turning to plans for the "best regime," the work, to the consternation of many, trails off in midsentence. It is the core of the *Politics* with its descriptions of various regimes, its stories, its puzzles, its sense of the multiple, that continues to capture what the political scientist is all about.

Parmenides had tried to deny our senses, make us reject what we see, and turn to the unchanging "what is" that only the mind could see. Praxagora had pretended that the bodies of male and female could be interchangeable, that beauty and ugliness could be overcome by laws, that mine and thine were only conventions that could be transformed. Socrates through his poetry strove to make the gods one god and all in his city reflect that divine unity. Eteocles with his crass dismissal of the noisy women from the offices of the city had done likewise on the tragic stage, he along with Antigone and Creon and the xenophobic Athenians of *Ion*. Aristotle recognizes well the attraction of the "one," of the uniform, of the whole, but he does not allow that attraction to overwhelm his eyes. When he looks at the city he does not see a whole, unified in its movements or its wisdom or its beauty. He sees variety, a multiplicity of individuals each with a multiplicity of qualities, just as when he looks at a chorus he sees many who can act as one for brief moments in time. Observing the multiple and acknowledging it, Aristotle goes beyond the tragedy of the playwrights who gave us the unattainable visions of a world without multiplicity. He rather delights, "like women and children," in the multiplicity of colors, of regimes, of individuals. He does so, though, not in a childlike way of mere wonder. Through his study of a politics of a multiplicity of parts rather than a politics of unity, he demonstrates the skills of the first political scientist, for whom observation is as satisfying as the search to transcend the observed.

The political art is to understand the need for diversity within the city and not to fear it, to acknowledge that it is the diversity that, while building the city, can never bring about a city that has escaped the conflicts of political claims. To be human is to be a part of a city that is neither whole nor stable. The unity established in Callipolis, the unity achieved with the net of Hephaestus, may lead to a unified whole, but, as with the Parmenidean One, it is the denial of life. Aristotle celebrates life in all its many confusions and debates. In accepting the "city of parts" and demanding that we see its parts, as well as recognize their centrifugal force, he gives birth to political science and opens the door for a diversity that so many of his predecessors seemed to fear. Diversity previously had meant the need for suppression or destruction, epistemological and political. For Aristotle it means life, epistemologically and politically.

Epilogue

The pre-Socratic philosophers self-consciously questioned how we know. Not satisfied with a dependence on the eyes that saw only multitudes and differences, they turned away from the fallible, unreliable senses. Dismissing what we see and turning to what we know through the faculties of intellection, they sought a unity where previously they had seen only diversity. That epistemology, asking us to rise above our fallible senses, enables us to transcend the transitory world and become almost divine in our comprehension of the whole rather than the parts. This epistemological vision finds a home in the political vision of the polis, where the city unites by rising above the multiple particularities that the senses experience. The democratic city of Athens, in particular, dismisses that which is other, builds a political structure through collective speech and abstraction from familial bonds, and overcomes the transitory mortal nature of human bodies.

The paradigm of such a city finds expression in the Funeral Oration of Pericles. There immortality depends not on bodily reproduction, but rather on a collective memory that unites all into the concept of the city while ignoring particularity and the family. The pre-Socratic philosophers and the spokesmen for the city tried to ignore the body, the particular, and the senses that perceive the body. Thucydides, however, with his sickeningly vivid description of decaying bodies as the plague spreads through Athens, reminds his readers of the hubris and thus of the limits of the Periclean vision of the city of Athens where death is "unfelt" (2.43). The playwrights and the philosophers discussed in this volume offer the same warning about an arrogance that suggests that we can rise above our differences, our bodily separateness, as we reach for a unifying net of Hephaestus with our minds. Bodies, families, and the particular will always intrude.

While the writings of Aristotle that we have studied alert us most vividly to the diversity at the core of the city, I have also tried to illustrate that the playwrights and even Plato (contrary to many of the popular and scholarly views of him) do so as well. The playwrights, by portraying on the Athenian stage characters such as Eteocles, Creon, Antigone, the more comic Praxagora, and the Tutor of *Ion*, offer powerful portraits of the political fear of diversity, the belief that the city constructed of those who are similar cannot endure the intrusion of those perceived as other, those who might shatter the uniformity of the whole. But the playwrights are not the characters in their plays any more than Plato is the Socrates of the dialogues. The characters who long for unity, simplicity, and the beauty in that which is one must suffer as they learn the costs of trying to dismiss a dependence on body and on family. They and the audiences who watch the failure of their efforts must learn that the political drive to reenact the pre-Socratic epistemology on the level of the city brings destruction to the self and to those about whom one cares.

Plato, who may or may not have been the idealist philosopher, heir to Parmenides, with his forms and ascension from the uncertain world of the senses, warns as well about the political consequences of translating this epistemology to the city. My chapters on Plato's dialogues have pointed to that questioning, whether in the portrayal of the foolish Euthyphro, whose acceptance of a simple principle of piety ignores the multiplicity of ties one may have because one is body, that is, he has a father; or the depiction of the Laws of Athens in the *Crito*, who pretend that speech can give birth to citizens; or the picture of the Socrates who founds Callipolis on principles that exclude him and the very dialogue in which the city is founded. Plato, no doubt, recognizes the epistemological tug of Diotima's Beautiful and the Socratic Good of the *Republic*, but he does not unambiguously present that as the model for our political life. Our individual and bodily particularity precludes that. Plato throughout forces us to acknowledge what must be lost for the sake of political unity. The tragic heroes of the plays, motivated by principles grounded in their abstraction from the particular, learn only too late about the costs.

Aristotle, less dramatic than the tragedians or Plato, confronts the issue directly by puzzling though the problem of an epistemology and a politics that demands both an acknowledgment of the diversity of the world around us and a perception of an insensible unity without which we cannot know or act as political beings. Aristotle goes beyond the others who warned of the dangers and the tragedy of the excessive pursuit of unity. He embraces diversity as the others had not. The city is made up of parts, and the one interested in politics must not simply accept those parts; he or she must study, analyze, incorporate those parts. We need not lament the lost beauty of a unifying vision, the lost speech that could bind and make whole. Aristotle shows us instead the potential perversities of such a vision: many-limbed monsters or the impieties of incestuous sexual relations. According to Aristotle, the senses must not be banned; they will reveal the many who may share, who may be structured by a *politeia*, who may even move together as does a chorus, but who never shed that which is particular and that which separates. This embracing of the multiple will mean conflict, disagreement about the good and the bad, the just and the unjust. It will mean conflict between owners, between families, and between lovers, but in the cities that Aristotle studies, unlike the imagined Thebes of Creon or the Callipolis of Socrates or even the Athens of the *Crito*'s Laws, there are owners, there are families, and there are lovers. The study of politics becomes, under Aristotle's guidance, the study of particulars, of what we see with our eyes. He battles the exclusive victory of the mind that had characterized the thought of the pre-Socratics, and he brings back the senses.

While Aristotle openly reasserts our reliance on the senses and with them the multiple, he does not simply describe particulars, the cities he has studied, or the political conflicts he has observed. He begins his inquiry into the political world asking that we observe, but we cannot simply observe. Like the pre-Socratics, we must use the mind to go behind the multiplicity of our observations. The typologies that fill almost every page of Aristotle's *Politics* show him uniting and separating, finding the underlying unity and significant differences. In asking the question that begins Book 3 of the *Politics*, "What in the world is the polis?" he too is urging us to go beyond our senses, to acknowledge that we talk about that which we cannot see, that we create institutions that come into being simply through speech. Clearly, Aristotelian political science cannot come from the dismissal of the mind any more than the nature philosophies of the pre-Socratics can dismiss the senses. Rather, Aristotelian moderation comes from engaging both, neither fearing diversity nor being childishly enamored of the multicolored. The two perspectives play against each other, and Aristotle gives birth to political science by granting the senses and their appreciation of the particular an epistemological and political stature others had questioned.

From the playwrights reacting to the excessive love of unity and the fear of diversity on the part of their characters, we learned that such a love can destroy the city. At the same time, though, the characters pursuing such a unified vision were heroes, worthy of admiration for their aspirations and worthy of pity when they fell. They sought divinity by rising above a dependence on the senses; they sought beauty outside the divisions of human experience. The playwrights leave us distressed, however, torn apart by the recognition of the beauty of political unity, of the simplicity of the sphere, and yet recognizing the dangers of such a vision when translated to our existence as humans living in cities. Callipolis is the beautiful city, in its perfection satisfying our demand for intellectual and political order rather than chaos. It is on the level of the mind, a city to dream about and pray for, but it can also hide the greatest impieties, the greatest imperfections, the greatest contradictions once the body is acknowledged. We lament the deterioration described in Book 8 of the *Republic,* but we also recognize its inevitability in a world of particular bodies and bodily needs. Aristotle insists that we look at the particular, but he also knows that viewing the particular can teach us little about the science of politics unless we are also able to go beyond the senses and our experience of the many to ask, What is the polis, who is the citizen, what transforms a collection of people into the unity of the political community? Political science cannot be born without the attention to the particular and the senses that Aristotle elevates against his pre-Socratic predecessors and the Socrates of the *Republic,* but Aristotle also draws from those predecessors the capacity to go behind the senses, to see, for example, varieties of democracies and to call them all democratic.

In the discussion of Plato's *Symposium,* we saw that it was the ugly Hephaestus who recognized that Aphrodite and Ares would not want to be eternally bound by the net Hephaestus had fashioned. The handsome and swift Hermes would have welcomed it. The net, binding what is multiple into one, is alluring and promises beauty unalloyed, but the lame smith had warned of its destructive force. Socrates, Alcibiades in the *Symposium* warns us, with his flute-like voice and his Siren-like song, likewise draws us towards a similar destruction, holding before us a beauty inaccessible to the senses and unalloyed by the messiness of human bodies. Aristotle's political science offers no such beauty, no such unity, no such allure. His study is filled with classifications that move us briefly beyond the senses to the mind, but he, like the lame smith and the drunken Alcibiades, warns about the seductive beauty of excessive unity. He recognizes the dangers of reaching too quickly for the net of Hephaestus.

Bibliography

Adkins, A. W. H. 1972. *Moral Values and Political Behavior in Ancient Greece: From Homer to the End of the Fifth Century*. New York: Norton.

Allen, R. E. 1970. *Plato's "Euthyphro" and the Earlier Theory of Forms*. London: Routledge and Kegan Paul.

———, trans. 1984. *The Dialogues of Plato*, vol. 1. New Haven: Yale University Press.

Arthur, Marylin B. 1973. Early Greece: The Origins of the Western Attitude toward Women. *Arethusa* 6:7–58.

Austin, Scott. 1986. *Parmenides: Being, Bounds, and Logic*. New Haven: Yale University Press.

Bacon, Helen H. 1964. The Shield of Eteocles. *Arion* 3, no. 3:27–38.

Barker, Ernest, ed. and trans. 1946. *The Politics of Aristotle*. Oxford: Clarendon Press.

Barnes, Jonathan. 1984. *The Complete Works of Aristotle*. 2 vols. Princeton: Princeton University Press.

Benardete, Seth. 1967. Two Notes on Aeschylus' *Septem. Weiner Studien* 80:22–30.

———. 1973. Eidos and Diaeresis in Plato's *Statesman. Philologus* 107:193–226.

———. 1974–1975. A Reading of Sophocles' *Antigone. Interpretation* 4:148–96; 5:1–55, 148–84.

———, trans. 1984. *The Being of the Beautiful: Plato's Theaetetus, Sophist, and Statesman*. Chicago: University of Chicago Press.

———. 1989. *Socrates' Second Sailing*. Chicago: University of Chicago Press.

Blitz, Jan. 1980. The Holy and the Human: An Interpretation of Plato's *Euthyphro. Apeiron* 14:19–40.

Bloom, Alan, trans. 1968. *The Republic of Plato*. New York: Basic Books.

———. 1977. Response to Hall. *Political Theory* 5:315–30.

Bonner, Robert J., and Gertrude Smith. 1938. *The Administration of Justice from Homer to Aristotle*, vol. 2. Chicago: University of Chicago Press.

Brann, Eva. 1978. The Offense of Socrates: A Re-reading of Plato's *Apology. Interpretation* 7:1–21.

Brown, Wendy. 1988a. Supposing Truth Were a Woman: Plato's Subversion of Masculine Discourse. *Political Theory* 16:594–616.

————. 1988b. *Manhood and Politics: A Feminist Reading in Political Theory.* Totowa, N.J.: Rowman and Littlefield.

Burian, Peter. Forthcoming. Introduction to *Euripides' "Ion,"* trans. W. S. di Pieso.

Burnett, Anne Pippin. 1962. Human Resistance and Divine Persuasion in Euripides' *Ion. Classical Philology* 57:89–103.

Caldwell, Richard, 1973. The Misogyny of Eteocles. *Arethusa* 6:197–231.

Cherniss, Harold F. 1935. *Aristotle's Criticism of Presocratic Philosophy.* Baltimore: Johns Hopkins University Press.

Clavaud, Robert. 1980. *Le Menèxene de Platon et la rhétorique de son temps.* Paris: Société d'édition "Les Belles Lettres."

Clay, Diskin. 1983. The Tragic and Comic Poet of the *Symposium.* In *Essays in Ancient Greek Philosophy,* vol. 2, ed. J. P. Anton and A. Preus. Albany: State University of New York Press.

————. 1988. Reading the Republic. In *Platonic Writings/Platonic Readings,* ed. Charles L. Griswold, Jr. London: Routledge and Kegan Paul.

Conacher, D. J. 1967. *Euripidean Drama: Myth, Theme and Structure.* Toronto: University of Toronto Press.

Coxon, A. H. 1968. The Text of Parmenides: fr. 1.3. *Classical Quarterly,* n.s. 18:69.

————. 1986. *The Fragments of Parmenides: A Critical Text with Introduction, Translation, the Ancient Testimonia and a Commentary.* Assen/Maastrict, The Netherlands: Van Gorcum.

Diels, Hermann, and Walther Kranz. 1961. *Die Fragmente der Vorsokratiker.* 6th ed. Berlin: Weidmann.

Diogenes Laertius. 1950. *Lives of Eminent Philosophers,* with an English translation by R. D. Hicks. Cambridge, Mass.: Harvard University Press.

Dobbs, Darrell. 1985. Aristotle's Anticommunism. *American Journal of Political Science* 29:29–46.

Dover, Kenneth J. 1978. *Greek Homosexuality.* Cambridge, Mass: Harvard University Press.

duBois, Page. 1982. *Centaurs and Amazons: Women and the Pre-History of the Great Chain of Being.* Ann Arbor: University of Michigan Press.

————. 1988. *Sowing the Body: Psychoanalysis and Ancient Representations of Women.* Chicago: University of Chicago Press.

Eco, Umberto. 1983. *The Name of the Rose.* New York: Harcourt Brace Jovanovich.

Edelstein, Ludwig. 1945. The Role of Eryximachus in Plato's *Symposium. Transactions of the American Philological Association* 76:85–103.

Ehrenberg, Victor. [1960] 1964. *The Greek State.* New York: W. W. Norton.

Euben, J. Peter. 1986. Introduction. In *Greek Tragedy and Political Theory,* ed. J. Peter Euben. Berkeley: University of California Press.

————. 1990. *The Tragedy of Political Theory: The Road Not Taken.* Princeton: Princeton University Press.

Finley, M. I. 1981. Between Slavery and Freedom. In *Economy and Society in Ancient Greece,* ed. M. I. Finley. London: Chatto and Windus.

Foley, Helene P. 1981. The Conception of Women in Athenian Drama. In *Reflections of Women in Antiquity,* ed. Helene P. Foley. New York: Gordon and Breach Science Publishers.

————. 1982. The "Female Intruder" Reconsidered: Women in Aristophanes' *Lysistrata* and *Ecclesiazusae*. *Classical Philology* 77:1–21.

Fraenkel, Hermann. [1955] 1974. Xenophanes' Empiricism and His Critique of Knowledge. In *The Pre-Socratics: A Collection of Critical Essays*, ed. Alexander P. D. Mourelatos. Garden City, N.Y.: Anchor Books.

————. 1975. Studies in Parmenides. In *Studies in Presocratic Philosophy*, vol. 2, ed. R. E. Allen and David J. Furley. London: Routledge and Kegan Paul.

Freeman, Kathleen. 1953. *The Pre-Socratic Philosophers: A Companion to Diels, Fragmente der Vorsokratiker*. 3d ed. Oxford: Basil Blackwell.

Furley, David. 1987. *The Greek Cosmologists*. Vol. 1: *The Formation of the Atomic Theory and Its Earliest Critics*. Cambridge: Cambridge University Press.

Fustel de Coulanges, Numa Denis. [1864] 1980. *The Ancient City: A Study of the Religion, Laws, and Institutions of Greece and Rome*. Baltimore: Johns Hopkins University Press.

Gadamer, Hans-Georg. 1980. *Dialogue and Dialectic: Eight Hermeneutical Studies on Plato*. Trans. P. Christopher Smith. New Haven: Yale University Press.

Gagarin, Michael. 1979. The Prosecution of Homicide in Athens. *Greek, Roman and Byzantine Studies* 20:301–323.

————. 1981. *Drakon and Early Athenian Homicide Law*. New Haven: Yale University Press.

Gellrich, Michelle. 1988. *Tragedy and Theory: The Problem of Conflict since Aristotle*. Princeton: Princeton University Press.

Glotz, Gustave. [1929] 1969. *The Greek City and Its Institutions*. Trans. N. Mallinson. London: Routledge and Kegan Paul.

Gomme, A. W. 1937. The Position of Women in Athens in the Fifth and Fourth Centuries B.C. In *Essays in Greek History and Literature*, ed. A. W. Gomme. Oxford: Basil Blackwell.

Gregoire, Henri. 1923. "Euripide, *Ion*, text établi et traduit," In *Euripide*, vol. 3. Paris: Société d'Édition "Les Belles Lettres."

Grote, George. 1851–56. *History of Greece*. 3d ed. London: J. Murray.

Hansen, Mogens Herman. 1981. The Prosecution of Homicide in Athens: A Reply. *Greek, Roman and Byzantine Studies* 22:11–30.

Harrison, A. R. W. 1968. *The Law of Athens*. vol. 1: *The Family and Property*. Oxford: Clarendon Press.

Hartsock, Nancy C. M. 1985. *Money, Sex, and Power: Toward a Feminist Historical Materialism*. Boston: Northeastern University Press.

Hawking, Stephen W. 1988. *A Brief History of Time: From the Big Bang to the Black Hole*. New York: Bantam Books.

Hecht, A., and Helen H. Bacon. 1973. *Aeschylus: Seven against Thebes*. New York: Oxford University Press.

Heidegger, Martin. 1984. *Early Greek Thinking*. Trans. David Krelland and Frank Capuzzi. New York: Harper and Row.

Heidegger, Martin, and Eugen Fink. 1979. *Heraclitus Seminar 1966/67*. Trans. Charles H. Seibert. Tuscaloosa: University of Alabama Press.

Henderson, Jeffrey. 1975. *The Maculate Muse: Obscene Language in Attic Comedy*. New Haven and London: Yale University Press.

Humphreys, Sally. 1983. *The Family, Women and Death: Comparative Studies*. London: Routledge and Kegan Paul.

Hutchinson, G. O., ed. 1985. *Aeschylus "Septem Contra Thebas"*. Oxford: Clarendon Press.

Irwin, Eleanor. 1974. *Colour Terms in Greek Poetry*. Toronto: Hakkert.

Jowett, Benjamin. 1885. *The Politics of Aristotle*. Oxford: Clarendon Press.

Kahn, Charles H. 1960. *Anaximander and the Origins of Greek Cosmology*. New York: Columbia University Press.

———. 1963. Plato's Funeral Oration: The Motive of the *Menexenus*. *Classical Philology* 58 : 220–34.

———. 1979. *The Art and Thought of Heraclitus: An Edition of the Fragments with Translation and Commentary*. Cambridge: Cambridge University Press.

Kirk, G. S., ed. 1954. *Heraclitus: The Cosmic Fragments*. Cambridge: Cambridge University Press.

Kirk, G. S., J. E. Raven, and M. Schofield. 1983. *The Presocratic Philosophers: A Critical History with a Selection of Texts*. 2d ed. Cambridge: Cambridge University Press.

Kitto, H. D. F. 1951. *The Greeks*. Baltimore: Penguin Books.

Klein, Jacob. 1977. *Plato's Trilogy*. Chicago: University of Chicago Press.

Knox, Bernard. 1964. *The Heroic Temper: Studies in Sophoclean Tragedy*. Berkeley: University of California Press.

———. 1979. *Word and Action: Essays on the Ancient Theater*. Baltimore: Johns Hopkins University Press.

Kovacs, David. 1979. Four Passages from Euripides' *Ion*. *Transactions of the American Philological Association*. 109 : 111–24.

Lane, Warren J., and Ann M. Lane. 1986. The Politics of *Antigone*. In *Greek Tragedy and Political Theory*, ed. J. Peter Euben. Berkeley: University of California Press.

Lattimore, Richmond. 1951. *The Iliad*. Chicago: Chicago University Press.

———. 1967. *The Odyssey of Homer*. New York: Harper and Row.

Lee, Edward N. 1989. Plato's Theory of Social Justice in *Republic* II–IV. In *Essays in Ancient Greek Philosophy*, vol. 3, *Plato*, ed. J. P. Anton and A. Preus. Albany: State University of New York Press.

Lefkowitz, Mary R. 1986. *Women in Greek Myth*. Baltimore: Johns Hopkins University Press.

Levi-Strauss, Claude. 1967. *Structural Anthropology*. Garden City, N.Y.: Doubleday.

Lewis, Marlo. 1984. An Interpretation of Plato's *Euthyphro* (Intro.; pt. 1, secs. 1–3), *Interpretation*. 12 : 225–59.

Liddell, Henry George, and Robert Scott, 1968. *A Greek-English Lexicon*. Rev. and augmented by Henry Stuart Jones. Oxford: Clarendon Press.

Lloyd, G. E. R. 1966. *Polarity and Analogy: Two Types of Argumentation in Early Greek Thought*. Cambridge: Cambridge University Press.

Loraux, Nicole. 1979. L'autochthonie: une topic athènienne, le myth dans l'espace civique. *Annales, économies, socials, culturals* 1 : 3–26.

————. 1981. *Les enfants d'athèna: idées athèniennes sur la citoyennete et la division des sexes.* Paris: Francois Maspero.

————. 1986. *The Invention of Athens: The Funeral Oration in the Classical City.* Trans. Alan Sheridan. Cambridge, Mass.: Harvard University Press.

Lord, Carnes. 1978. Politics and Philosophy in Aristotle's *Politics. Hermes* 106, no. 2:336–57.

————, trans. 1984. *Aristotle, the Politics.* Chicago: University of Chicago Press.

MacDowell, Douglas M. 1963. *Athenian Homicide Law in the Age of the Orators.* Manchester, England: Manchester University Press.

————. 1978. *The Law in Classical Athens.* Ithaca: Cornell University Press.

MacIntyre, Alisdair. 1981. *After Virtue: A Study in Moral Theory.* Notre Dame: Notre Dame University Press.

Maletz, Donald Joseph. 1976. Plato's *Menexenos* and the Funeral Oration of Pericles. Ann Arbor, Mich.: University Microfilms.

Mansfeld, Jaap. 1985. Aristotle and Others on Thales, or the Beginnings of Natural Philosophy. *Mnemosyne.* 38:109–29.

Miller, Mitchell H., Jr. 1980. *The Philosopher in Plato's "Statesman".* The Hague: Martinus Nijhoff Publishers.

Modrak, Deborah K. W. 1987. *Aristotle: The Power of Perception.* Chicago: University of Chicago Press.

Montaigne, Michel de. [1588] 1965. *The Complete Essays of Montaigne.* Trans. Donald M. Frame. Stanford: Stanford University Press.

Mourelatos, Alexander P. D. 1965. The Real, Appearances and Human Error in Early Greek Philosophy. *Review of Metaphysics.* 19:346–65.

————. 1970. *The Route of Parmenides: A Study of Word, Image, and Argument in the Fragments.* New Haven: Yale University Press.

Mulgan, Richard. 1990. Aristotle and the Value of Political Participation. *Political Theory* 18:195–215.

Neumann, Harry. 1966a. The Problem of Piety in Plato's *Euthyphro. The Modern Schoolman* 43:266–77.

————. 1966b. On the Comedy of Plato's Aristophanes. *American Journal of Philology.* 87:420–26.

Newman, W. R. 1887. *The Politics of Aristotle.* 4 vols. Oxford: Clarendon Press.

Nichols, Mary P. 1983. The Good Life, Slavery and Acquisition: Aristotle's Introduction to Politics. *Interpretation* 11:171–83.

————. 1984. The *Republic's* Two Alternatives: Philosopher-King and Socrates. *Political Theory* 12:252–74.

————. 1987. *Socrates and the Political Community: An Ancient Debate.* Albany: State University of New York Press.

Nilsson, Martin P. 1951. *Cults, Myths, Oracles, and Politics in Ancient Greece.* Lund, Sweden: G. W. K. Gleerup.

Nussbaum, Martha C. 1972. *Psuche* in Heraclitus, I and II. *Phronesis* 17:1–16, 153–70.

————. 1978. *Aristotle's De Motu Animalium: Text with Translation, Commentary and Interpretive Essays.* Princeton: Princeton University Press.

———. 1979a. The Speech of Alcibiades: A Reading of Plato's *Symposium*. *I hilosophy and Literature* 3:131–72.

———. 1979b. Eleatic Conventionalism and Philolaus on the Conditions of Thought. *Harvard Studies in Classical Philology* 83:63–108.

———. 1981. Shame, Separateness and Political Unity: Aristotle's Criticism of Plato. In *Essays on Aristotle's Ethics*, ed. Amelie Oksenberg Rorty. Berkeley: University of California Press.

———. 1986. *The Fragility of Goodness: Luck and Ethics in Greek Tragedy and Philosophy*. Cambridge: Cambridge University Press.

O'Brien, Mary. 1981. *The Politics of Reproduction*. Boston: Routledge and Kegan Paul.

Okin, Susan Moller. 1979. *Women in Western Political Thought*. Princeton: Princeton University Press.

Orwin, Clifford. 1980. Feminine Justice: The End of the *Seven against Thebes*. *Classical Philology* 75:187–96.

Osborne, Catherine. 1987. *Rethinking Early Greek Philosophy: Hippolytus of Rome and the Presocratics*. London: Gerald Duckworth and Company.

Osborne, Robin. 1985. *Demos: The Discovery of Classical Attika*. Cambridge: Cambridge University Press.

Ostwald, Martin. 1986. *From Popular Sovereignty to the Sovereignty of Law: Law, Society, and Politics in Fifth-Century Athens*. Berkeley: University of California Press.

Owen, A. S., ed. 1939. *Euripides' Ion*. Oxford: Clarendon Press.

Owen, G. E. L. 1974. Plato and Parmenides on the Timeless Present. In *The Presocratics: A Collection of Critical Essays*, ed. Alexander P. D. Mourelatos. Garden City, N.Y.: Anchor Books.

———. 1975. Zeno and the Mathematicians. In *Studies in Presocratic Philosophy*, vol. 2, ed. R. E. Allen and David J. Furley. London: Routledge and Kegan Paul.

Peck, A. L. 1953. *Aristotle, Generation of Animals*. Loeb ed. With an English translation. Cambridge, Mass.: Harvard University Press.

Perodotto, John. 1977. Oedipus and Erichthonius: Some Observations on Paradigmatic and Syntagmatic Order. *Arethusa* 10:85–101.

Pomeroy, Sarah B. 1975. *Goddesses, Whores, Wives, and Slaves: Women in Classical Antiquity*. New York: Schocken Books.

Price, A. W. 1989. *Love and Friendship in Plato and Aristotle*. Oxford: Clarendon Press.

Rosen, Stanley. 1987. *Plato's Symposium*. 2d ed. New Haven: Yale University Press.

———. 1988. *The Quarrel between Philosophy and Poetry: Studies in Ancient Thought*. New York: Routledge and Kegan Paul.

Rosenmeyer, Thomas G. 1963. *The Masks of Tragedy: Essays on Six Greek Dramas*. Austin: University of Texas Press.

Salkever, Stephen G. 1990. *Finding the Mean: Theory and Practice in Aristotelian Political Philosophy*. Princeton: Princeton University Press.

Saxonhouse, Arlene W. 1976. The Philosopher and the Female in the Political Thought of Plato. *Political Theory* 4:195–212.

————. 1980. Men, Women, War and Politics: Family and Polis in Aristophanes and Euripides. *Political Theory* 8:65–81.

————. 1982. Family, Polity and Unity: Aristotle on Socrates' Community of Wives, *Polity*, 15:202–19.

————. 1983a. An Unspoken Theme in Plato's *Gorgias:* War. *Interpretation* 11:139–69.

————. 1983b. Classical Conceptions of Public and Private. In *Conceptions of Public and Private in Social Life*, ed. S. I. Benn and Gerald Gauss. London: Croom-Helm; New York: St. Martin's Press.

————. 1984a. Aeschylus' *Oresteia:* Misogyny, Philogyny and Justice. *Women and Politics* 4:11–32.

————. 1984b. Eros and the Female in Greek Political Thought: An Interpretation of Plato's *Symposium*. *Political Theory* 12:5–27.

————. 1985a. The Net of Hephaestos: Aristophanes' Speech in Plato's *Symposium*. *Interpretation* 13:15–23.

————. 1985b. *Women in the History of Political Thought: Ancient Greece to Machiavelli*. New York: Praeger.

————. 1986a. Reflections on the Theme of Autochthony in Euripides' *Ion*. In *Greek Tragedy and Political Theory*, ed. J. Peter Euben. Berkeley: University of California Press.

————. 1986b. From Hierarchy to Tragedy and Back Again: Women in Greek Political Thought. *American Political Science Review* 82:403–18.

————. 1988a. The Tyranny of Reason in the World of the Polis. *American Political Science Review* 82:1261–75.

————. 1988b. *Thymos*, Justice and the Moderation of Anger in the Story of Achilles. In *Understanding the Political Spirit: Philosophical Investigations from Socrates to Nietzsche*, ed. Catherine Zuckert. New Haven: Yale University Press.

————. 1988c. The Philosophy of the Particular and the Universality of the City: Socrates' Education of Euthyphro. *Political Theory* 16:281–99.

————. 1989. Political Theory through the Gender Lens. *Review of Politics* 51:292–94.

Schama, Simon. 1988. *The Embarrassment of Riches: An Interpretation of Dutch Culture in the Golden Age*. Berkeley: University of California Press.

Schaps, David M. 1979. *The Economic Rights of Women in Ancient Greece*. Edinburgh: Edinburgh University Press.

Schochet, Gordon. 1975. *Patriarchalism in Political Thought*. Oxford: Basil Blackwell.

Scodel, Harvey Ronald. 1986. *Diaeresis and Myth in Plato's Statesman*. Gottingen: Vandenhoeck & Ruprecht.

Segal, Charles. 1964. Sophocles' Praise of Man and the Conflicts of the *Antigone*. *Arion* 3:46–66.

————. 1978. The Menace of Dionysus: Sex Roles and Reversals in Euripides' *Bacchae. Arethusa* 11:185–201.

————. 1981. *Tragedy and Civilization: An Interpretation of Sophocles*. Cambridge, Mass.: Harvard University Press.

Seligman, Paul. 1962. *The "Apeiron" of Anaximander: A Study in the Origin and Function of Metaphysical Ideas.* London: Athlone Press.

Seltman, Charles. 1956. *Women in Antiquity.* London: Thames and Hudson.

Shaw, Michael. 1975. The Female Intruder: Women in Fifth Century Drama. *Classical Philology* 70:255–66.

Shorey, Paul. 1933. *What Plato Said.* Chicago: University of Chicago Press.

Sinclair, R. K. 1988. *Democracy and Participation in Athens.* Cambridge: Cambridge University Press.

Sinclair, T. A. 1981. *Aristotle: The Politics.* Trans. and rev. Trevor J. Saunders. Harmondsworth, Middlesex, England: Penguin Books.

Slatkin, Laura. 1986. *Oedipus at Colonus:* Exile and Integration. In *Greek Tragedy and Political Theory,* ed. J. Peter Euben. Berkeley: University of California Press.

Sophocles. 1960. Antigone. In *Greek Tragedies,* vol. 1, trans. Elizabeth Wyckoff; ed. David Grene and Richmond Lattimore. Chicago: University of Chicago Press.

Sorum, Christina Elliot. 1982. The Family in Sophocles' *Antigone* and *Electra. The Classical World* 75:201–11.

Stokes, Michael C. 1971. *One and Many in Presocratic Philosophy.* Cambridge, Mass: Harvard University Press.

Strauss, Leo. 1953. *Natural Right and History.* Chicago: University of Chicago Press.

———. 1964. *The City and Man.* Chicago: University of Chicago Press.

———. 1980. *Socrates and Aristophanes.* Midway Reprint. Chicago: University of Chicago Press.

Taylor, A. E. 1956. *Plato: The Man and His Work.* New York: Meridian Books.

Thalmann, William G. 1978. *Dramatic Art in Aeschylus' "Seven against Thebes."* Yale Classical Monographs. New Haven: Yale University Press.

Ussher, R. G., ed. 1973. *Aristophanes' "Ecclesiazusae".* Oxford: Clarendon Press.

Vernant, Jean-Pierre. 1982. *The Origins of Greek Thought.* Trans. Ithaca: Cornell University Press.

———. 1988a. Oedipus without the Complex. In *Myth and Tragedy in Ancient Greece,* ed. Jean-Pierre Vernant and Pierre Vidal-Naquet; trans. Janet Lloyd. New York: Zone Books.

———. 1988b. Tensions and Ambiguity in Greek Tragedy. In *Myth and Tragedy in Ancient Greece. See* Vernant 1988a.

———. 1988c. Ambiguity and Reversal: On the Enigmatic Structure of *Oedipus Rex.* In *Myth and Tragedy in Ancient Greece. See* Vernant 1988a.

Vidal-Naquet, Pierre. 1986. *The Black Hunter: Forms of Thought and Forms of Society in the Greek World.* Trans. Andrew Szegedy-Maszak. Baltimore: Johns Hopkins University Press.

———. 1988. The Shields of the Heroes: Essay on the Central Scene of the *Seven against Thebes.* In *Myth and Tragedy in Ancient Greece. See* Vernant 1988a.

Vlastos, Gregory. 1947. Equality and Justice in Early Greek Cosmologies. *Classical Philology* 42:156–78.

———. 1955. On Heraclitus. *American Journal of Philology.* 76:337–68.

———. 1981. The Individual as an Object of Love in Plato. In *Platonic Studies*. 2d ed. Princeton: Princeton University Press.

Walsh, George B. 1978. The Rhetoric of Birthright and Race in Euripides' *Ion*. *Hermes* 106:301–15.

Whitman, Cedric H. 1964. *Aristophanes and the Comic Hero*. Cambridge, Mass.: Harvard University Press.

———. 1974. *Euripides and the Full Circle of Myth*. Cambridge, Mass.: Harvard University Press.

Winnington-Ingram, R. P. 1980. *Sophocles: An Interpretation*. Cambridge: Cambridge University Press.

———. 1983. *Studies in Aeschylus*. Cambridge: Cambridge University Press.

Winthrop, Delba. 1975. Aristotle and Political Responsibility. *Political Theory* 3:406–22.

———. 1978. Aristotle on Participatory Democracy. *Polity* 11:151–71.

Woolf, Virginia. 1931. *The Waves*. London: Harcourt Brace Jovanovich.

Yack, Bernard. 1985. Community and Conflict in Aristotle's Political Philosophy. *The Review of Politics* 47:92–112.

Zeitlin, Froma I. 1978. The Dynamics of Misogyny: Myth and Mythmaking in the *Oresteia. Arethusa* 11:149–84.

———. 1982. *Under the Sign of the Shield: Semiotics and Aeschylus' "Seven against Thebes."* Rome: Edizioni del'Ateneo.

Zuckert, Catherine. 1983. Aristotle on the Limits and Satisfactions of Political Life. *Interpretation* 11:185–206.

Index

Achilles, x, 141, 145; in purged poetry of *Republic*, 137–40

Adeimantus, 132, 134–35, 144, 146–48, 155

Aeschylus, 54–64, 87, 165. Works: *Oresteia*, 83, 95–96; *Prometheus Bound*, 165; *Seven against Thebes*, 53, 54–64, 65, 76, 89

Agamemnon, 141

Agathon (character in *Symposium*), 158, 163, 174

Age of Cronos (in *Statesman*), 125–30

Age of Zeus (in *Statesman*), 126–30

Alcibiades, 109, 159–60; attempted seduction of Socrates, 181; revenge on Socrates, 182–83; speech in *Symposium*, 179–84

Anaxagoras, 106

Anaximander, 26–28

Andromache, 140

Antigone, 52, 64–76, 89

Antigone, 64–76, 145, 231; attachment to family, 64, 72; attachment to nature, 66; on death, 70, 73; denial of creativity, 69, 72–73; denial of efficacy of speech, 67–68; denial of *erōs*, 71; meaning of name, 69–70; in *Seven against Thebes*, 54, 62–63

Apathy, in Callipolis, 201–2

Apeiron (the boundless), in Anaximander, 27–28

Aphrodite, 71, 167, 236; born from Uranus's castration, 136–37; caught in the net of Hephaestus, 162, 169

Apollo: and the flaying of Marsyas, 180; and the lyre, 109; and the rape of Creusa (*Ion*), 78, 81–82; speech in the *Oresteia*, 83, 96; in speeches in *Symposium*, 168, 171, 180; unsavory role in *Ion*, 77–87

Apollodorus (character in *Symposium*), 164, 179–80

Apology of Socrates, 104–7, 108–9

Archē (as primary substance), 25, 26–27

Archon basileus, 93–95, 101

Ares, 51, 236; chained by Ephialtes and Otus, 167; caught in the net of Hephaestus, 162, 169

Aristodemus (character in *Symposium*), 164, 179–80, 183

Aristophanes: as character in *Symposium*, 158–59; poet of the body, 160, 163, 165; hiccups of, 164–65, 169; impiety of, 168, 172–73; speech in *Symposium*, 160–73, 178, 202. Works: *Birds*, 2; *Clouds*, 97; *Ecclesiazusae*, x, 1–19, 51; *Lysistrata*, 2, 5

Aristotle, 21, 25, 37, 185–232, 234–36; analogies in, 192, 204, 215–24; on Aristophanes speech in *Symposium*, 160–61, 163–64, 169, 172, 202; on the Athenian Constitution, 94; on blending, 229–31; on bodies, 196; on conflict, 203, 226–30; criticism of Callipolis, 153, 161, 185, 195–208, 227; criticizes Socrates on the decline of regimes, 225–26; dependence on observation, 187, 191, 214, 231; on hierarchy by nature, 191–94, 216; on the majority (*hoi polloi*), 185–86, 223; on multiplicity, 206, 234–35; observer of nature, 193; organic images